THE FIRST FRONTIER:
LIFE IN COLONIAL AMERICA
recreates the everyday experiences of the
earliest generations of Americans. Told
through the skillful use of original letters,
public documents, diary entries and the
comments of perceptive travelers—all
interspersed with a lively running text by
the author—the volume provides a remarkable
insight into the joys and sorrows, the
tranquilities and the dangers, the discontents
and aspirations, the pieties and pretensions
of a polyglot people. Here are the English,
Dutch, Germans, Swedes, and French.
Here are the first Americans.

John C. Miller, graduated from Harvard in
1930, received his M.A. degree in 1932
and his Ph.D. degree in 1939 from that
university. Formerly on the faculty at Bryn
Mawr, he has been Robinson Professor of
American History at Stanford University
since 1950. He is the author of *Origins
of the American Revolution* and *Triumph
of Freedom, 1775–1783*.

THE FIRST FRONTIER:
LIFE IN COLONIAL
AMERICA

JOHN C. MILLER

Copyright © 1966 by

John C. Miller

University Press of America,® Inc.

4720 Boston Way
Lanham, MD 20706

This edition published in 1986 by
University Press of America, Inc.
by arrangement with Dell Publishing Company, Inc.

Library of Congress Cataloging in Publication Data

Miller, John Chester, 1907-
    The first frontier.

    Reprint. Originally published: New York : Dell
Pub. Co., c1966.
    Includes bibliographical references.
    1. United States—Civilization—To 1783.   I. Title.
E162.M63   1986   973.02   86-1572
ISBN 0-8191-4977-2 (pbk. : alk. paper)

All University Press of America books are produced on acid-free
paper which exceeds the minimum standards set by the National
Historical Publications and Records Commission.

ACC LIBRARY SERVICES AUSTIN, TX

CONTENTS

Preface   9

Life in the First Settlements   15

The Puritan Way   50

The Quaker Way   73

Sports and Recreations   84

Life on a Southern Plantation   94

Social Rank and Dress   108

Life in the Colonial Cities   122

Life on the Frontier   135

Black and White Labor in Colonial America   143

Ways of Making a Living   163

Housing   173

Food and Drink   182

Courtship   189

Marriage   200

Children   209

Education   221

The Practice of Medicine   237

Crime and Punishment   253

The Religious Scene   266

Conclusion   280

Acknowledgments: Excerpts from the following works are reproduced by permission of the author or publisher:

AUTOBIOGRAPHY OF DEVEREAUX JARRETT, *William and Mary Quarterly* (3rd Series, IV), 1952. By permission of Douglass Adair.

JOHN WINTHROP'S JOURNAL, Volume 2. NARRATIVES OF EARLY VIRGINIA edited by Leon Tyler. By permission of Barnes & Noble, Inc.

GOTTLIEB MITTELBERGER: JOURNEY TO PENNSYLVANIA edited by Oscar Handlin and John Cave. By permission of The Belknap Press of Harvard University.

SOCIAL HISTORY OF THE AMERICAN FAMILY by Arthur W. Calhoun. Reprinted by permission of the publishers, The Arthur H. Clark Company.

THE JOURNAL AND LETTERS OF PHILIP VICKERS FITHIAN edited by H. D. Farish. By permission of Colonial Williamsburg Press.

ENGLISH HISTORICAL DOCUMENTS, Vol. 9: AMERICAN COLONIAL DOCUMENTS, Oxford University Press, Pages 544-545. By permission of The Connecticut Historical Society.

OUR REVOLUTIONARY FOREFATHERS: LETTERS OF FRANÇOIS, MARQUIS DE BARBE-MARBOIS. By permission of Dodd, Mead & Company.

LETTERS FROM AN AMERICAN FARMER by J. Hector St. John de Crèvecoeur, Dutton Paperback Series. By permission of E. P. Dutton & Co., Inc. and J. M. Dent & Sons, Ltd.

REMINISCENCES OF AN AMERICAN LOYALIST by Jonathan Boucher. By permission of Houghton Mifflin Company.

OF PLYMOUTH PLANTATION edited by Samuel Eliot Morison. By permission of Alfred A. Knopf, Inc.

ENGLISH HISTORICAL DOCUMENTS, Vol. 9: AMERICAN COLONIAL DOCUMENTS edited by Merrill Jensen. Oxford University Press, Inc., 1955. Reprinted by permission of the publisher and by Eyre & Spottiswoode.

PATRICIAN AND PLEBEIAN IN VIRGINIA by Thomas J. Wertenbaker. Russell & Russell, Inc., 1958. Reprinted by permission.

CAROLINA CHRONICLES OF DR. FRANCIS LE JAU by Frank J. Kingsblood. By permission of University of California Press.

THE CAROLINA BACK COUNTRY edited by Richard J. Hooker. THE HISTORY AND PRESENT STATE OF VIRGINIA by Robert Beverly, edited by Louis B. Wright. By permission of University of North Carolina Press.

WILLIAM BYRD OF WESTOVER, 1709-1712 edited by Louis B. Wright and Marian Tinling, The Dietz Press, Inc. By permission of Louis B. Wright.

A JOURNEY TO THE LAND OF EDEN AND OTHER PAPERS by William Byrd. SAMUEL SEWALL'S DIARY edited by Mark Van Doren. By permission of Vanguard Press, Inc.

SKETCHES OF EIGHTEENTH CENTURY AMERICA by J. Hector St. John de Crèvecoeur. JOURNAL OF A LADY OF QUALITY edited by Evangeline W. and Charles McL. Andrews. By permission of Yale University Press.

IT WOULD be a task worthy a speculative genius, to enter intimately into the situation and characters of the people, from Nova Scotia to West Florida; and surely history cannot possibly present any subject more pleasing to behold. . . . Numberless settlements, each distinguished by some peculiarities, present themselves on every side; all seem to realize the most sanguine wishes that a good man could form for the happiness of his race. Here they live by fishing on the most plentiful coasts in the world; there they fell trees, by the side of large rivers, for masts and lumber; here others convert innumerable logs into the best boards; here again others cultivate the land, rear cattle and clear large fields. . . .

By the literal account hereunto annexed, you will easily be made acquainted with the happy effects which constantly flow, in this country, from sobriety and industry, when united with good land and freedom. [J. Hector St. John de Crèvecoeur, *Letters from an American Farmer*]

PREFACE

BEGINNING in the early seventeenth century as a few, isolated settlements clinging precariously to the eastern seaboard of the North American continent, the British colonies, by the time they declared their independence of Great Britain, had spread over the coastal area from Maine to Georgia and were beginning to penetrate the region beyond the Appalachian Mountains. During this long period—the 170 years it covered is almost equal to the present duration of the United States as an independent nation—the American people attained the highest standard of living of any people, sovereign or colonial, in the world. The two million white inhabitants of the thirteen continental British colonies were better clad and housed and had food in greater abundance than even the common people of England, who spoke with all the pride of sovereignty of "our colonies" and "our subjects in the plantations."

Barbé-Marbois, the French chargé d'affaires who resided in the United States during the War of Independence, reported that

Prosperity and abundance reign in all the dwellings. From Boston here [Pennsylvania], we have not seen a single pauper, we have not met a peasant who was not well dressed and who did not have a good wagon or at least a good horse. The best of our kings was satisfied to wish that each peasant might have every Sunday a hen in his pot. Here, we have not entered a single dwelling in the morning without finding there a kettle in which was cooking a good fowl, or a piece of beef, or mutton with a piece of bacon; and a great abundance of vegetables;

bread, cider, things from the dairy, and a profusion of firewood; clean furniture, a good bed, and often a newspaper.[1]

The material well-being enjoyed by Americans as British subjects was used by Loyalists as an argument against independence. Jonathan Boucher, a Maryland clergyman and Loyalist, said that if his fellow Americans would compare their situation with that of nine-tenths of the people of the world, they would discover that "the general diffusion of the necessaries, the conveniences, and pleasures of life, among all orders of people here; the innumerable avenues to wealth . . . and the entire security of their fortunes, liberty, and lives" made them the most fortunate of mankind. In that event, he was persuaded that they would lay down their muskets and devote themselves exclusively to counting their blessings and accumulating more wealth.

But, eager as were Americans to get on with the business of producing and consuming, the flourishing state of the colonies tended to work against submission to the mother country. Prosperity engendered a sense of self-sufficiency, a feeling of pride of achievement and a demand for equality of rights within the British Empire that, in the end, defeated every attempt to abridge American liberties. "I think, considering our age, the great toils we have undergone, the roughness of some parts of the country, and our original poverty," said an American shortly before the Revolution, "that we have done the most in the least time of any people on earth. Call it industry or what you will." [2]

In colonial America, there was no single, pervasive, uniform way of life. Instead, geography, religion and occupation tended to create markedly different kinds of society. The mode of life of a frontiersman, for example, bore little resemblance to that of a wealthy merchant or planter of the eastern seaboard; few New England Pur-

[1] F. Barbé-Marbois. *Our Revolutionary Forefathers. The Letters of François, Marquis de Barbé-Marbois* (New York: Duffield & Co., 1929), p. 126.

[2] J. Hector St. John de Crèvecoeur, *Sketches of Eighteenth Century America* (New Haven: Yale University Press, 1925), p. 141.

itans felt at home among the Southern planters; and the early Quakers set themselves apart from the rest of the community, especially from the New England Puritans, at whose hands they had suffered many years of persecution. Nowhere was religious and cultural heterogeneity more apparent than in Pennsylvania, the focal point of British and European immigration during the eighteenth century. Economically and socially, North Carolina had little in common with South Carolina, and Georgia represented a unique experiment in social and economic planning. Even Puritan New England, the most homogeneous area in British North America, had at its doorstep Rhode Island, a colony described by the Reverend Cotton Mather as "the common receptacle of the convicts of Jerusalem and the outcasts of the Land." He could imagine no greater contrast with Boston.

Despite the unifying effects of a common language, common political institutions and ideas, the growing intimacy between the people of the various colonies and the increasing opposition to a governing authority three thousand miles away, Americans began their struggle for independence without benefit of a strong feeling of common identity that overrode all provincial attachments. In 1774, John Adams observed that in the Continental Congress, the members of which were drawn from all the colonies, there was "a diversity of religions, educations, manners, interests, such as it would seem almost impossible to unite in any one plan of conduct." As a result, when the American union was formed in 1777 and rendered more perfect in 1789, it was based upon a respect for diversity. The absence of uniformity was one of the facts of life in the United States that the architects of union could not fail to take into account.

Michel Guillaume Jean de Crèvecoeur, a Frenchman who, in 1769, settled down as an American farmer in Orange County, New York, and took the name of John Hector St. John, attributed the religious liberty enjoyed by Americans to the diversity of their creeds. "It has been demonstrably proved," he said, "that variety, nay, a discord of religious opinions is the true principle on which the harmony of society is established." Crèvecoeur believed that from the complex of religions, and peoples of different national origins that he observed in Orange County was being evolved what he called "The New Man," The American, set apart from the rest of mankind by his industry, self-reliance, versatility, mechanical ingenuity and tolerance of religious and political differences.

To Crèvecoeur, the true American epic was "the progressive steps of a poor man, advancing from indigence to ease; from oppression to freedom; from obscurity and contumely to some degree of consequence—not by virtue of any freak fortune, but by the gradual operation of sobriety, honesty and emigration." Crèvecoeur did not celebrate the grandeur of empire nor even the accumulation of great wealth by individuals: in his view, the metamorphosis of the European peasant into a free American citizen was one of the most important events in history. He held up to Americans a mirror of their felicity: the abundance of land, sufficient for the most distant generation; equal laws; mild, stable government; the right to retain the rewards of industry; the opportunity to provide for one's children; and the absence of a titled and oppressive aristocracy.

The American farmer, as depicted by Crèvecoeur, resembles man before the Fall: simple, virtuous and inoffensive. He asked nothing of government except that it keep order, dispense justice and provide education for his children. This New Man not only had attained happiness but, what is more remarkable, knew it. "I envy no man's prosperity, and wish no other portion of happiness than that I may live to teach the same philosophy to my children," said Crèvecoeur; "and give each of them a farm, show them how to cultivate it, and be like their father, good substantial independent American farmers." In short, he was content with a competence and did not confuse the pursuit of happiness with the accumulation of worldly goods. In this respect, Crèvecoeur's American bore a closer resemblance to Crèvecoeur himself than to any large number of his fellow citizens. More typically, the American was a hard-driving, ambitious individualist who, far from being satisfied with what he had, was forever imagining a future state of bliss in which he had more and contrasting his own share of the wealth with the vast potential store that lay around him or, more usually, a little farther West. "The desire of finding better embitters the enjoyment even of the inhabitants of Connecticut," said Brissot de Warville, a French traveler who supposed that the Land of Steady Habits possessed all the ingredients necessary for perfect happiness. Americans were not a nation of philosophers but of doers who were engaged in conquering a wilderness—and from this work they did not learn moderation in all things. Small farmers aspired to become big farmers and shopkeepers hoped to see the day when they would be rich merchants. In New England, for example, the more enterprising farmers were constantly adding to their acreage and operating taverns, grist mills, tanneries and blacksmith shops for extra profit. Americans, in short, gave free rein to their acquisitive instincts and he who accumulated the most property was esteemed the most successful and the most happy.

America always put a high premium upon success. If a man could not succeed in America, where everything worked in his favor, where could he hope to succeed? The cardinal sin was to neglect one's opportunities of getting ahead in the world; if nothing succeeded like success, nothing failed like failure. Those who fell by the way in the triumphant march to affluence were usually regarded as the victims of their own improvidence, laziness and incompetence. "Whence do all our miseries proceed, but from lack of industry!" exclaimed Parson Weems, the biographer of George Washington. "In a land like this, which Heaven has blessed above all lands . . . a land where the poorest Lazarus may get his fifty cents a day for the commonest labour—and buy the daintiest bread of corn flour for a cent a pound; why is any man hungry, or thirsty or naked, or in prison? why but through his unpardonable sloth?" Weems attributed Washington's success to his unremitting diligence: "Since the day that God created man on the earth, none ever displayed the power of industry more significantly than did George Washington."

This, then, was the pattern of life in America. Long before Benjamin Franklin laid down the rules in *The Way to Wealth,* it was recognized that industry, thrift and sobriety—as much work and as little play as possible—was the key to success. In America, the whole environment conspired to accentuate the Puritan ethic of hard work and frugality: a virgin continent awaited occupation and exploitation by adventurous Europeans. Here, Crèvecoeur told prospective immigrants, "Thou may go to toil and exert the whole energy and circle of thy industry and try the activity of human nature in all situations." If it was, as the publicists claimed, "a poor man's country" and "the general asylum of mankind," it was not a place where the poor and downtrodden could lay their burdens down and find peace and contentment; rather, it was a country where one took up new burdens and got on with the job. In consequence, contrary to Crèvecoeur, the American's lot was not wholly a happy one: he worked not to enjoy but to accumulate the things he might enjoy if he ever stopped working long enough.

LIFE IN THE
FIRST SETTLEMENTS

I. VIRGINIA

THE comparative affluence enjoyed by most white Americans of the colonial period was dearly bought by those Englishmen and Englishwomen who first attempted to establish lodgements upon an unknown and hostile continent. They experienced hunger, privation and sickness to the limits of human endurance. The 100 men and 17 women who were put ashore on Roanoke Island in 1587 disappeared without leaving a trace. Among them was Virginia Dare, the first child born of English parents within the present boundaries of the United States. Between 1607 and 1624, four-fifths of the settlers at Jamestown died of disease, starvation and Indian attacks. The winning of a beachhead in Virginia cost far more casualties, in proportion to numbers engaged, than did the conquest of any of the Japanese-held islands in World War II.

Those who fell in this unequal struggle had been sent to the New World by the Virginia Company, a trading and colonizing company. By a charter granted in 1606 it was given exclusive rights of colonization and jurisdiction over an area comprising about half of the United States. As William Byrd remarked in the eighteenth century, most of the British colonies in North America were carved out of Virginia.

The Virginia Company was financed by private capital, most of which was derived from English raids upon Spanish treasure fleets and from the newly opened trade with the Levant and the East Indies. Over 100,000 pounds—roughly the equivalent in purchasing power of seven million of today's dollars—was expended by the Virginia Company. From the point of view of the investors, it was money thrown away: the Company paid no dividends and its stock became worthless paper. Both those who ventured their capital and their lives in the effort to colonize North America fared badly.

Because the ships carrying the first group of settlers to Virginia made a long detour to the West Indies, the voyage consumed four months. Even so, despite the head winds encountered in the English Channel in December, 1606, the crossing was comparatively easy. Except for the signs of dissension among the leaders of the expedition, the voyage afforded no inkling to the settlers of the ordeal that lay ahead. However, within a few days of their arrival in the Chesapeake they were made to feel the hostility of the Indians. It was an ominous prelude to the great Massacre of 1622, when the Indians took the Virginians by surprise and almost succeeded in wiping out the colony.

On the 19 of December, 1606, we set sail, but by unprosperous winds, were kept six weeks in the sight of England; all which time Mr. Hunt, our Preacher, was so weak and sick that few expected his recovery. Yet although he were but 10 or 12 miles from his habitation (the time we were in the Downs) and notwithstanding the stormy weather, nor the scandalous imputations (of some few, little better than Atheists, of the greatest rank amongst us) suggested against him, all this could ever force from him so much as a seeming desire to leave the business, but preferred the service of God, in so good a voyage, before any affection to contest with his godless foes, whose disastrous designs (could they have prevailed) had even then overthrown the business, so many discontents did then arise, had he not, with the water of patience, and his godly exhortations (but chiefly by his true devoted examples) quenched those flames of envy and dissension.

We watered at the Canaries, we traded with the Savages at Dominica; three weeks we spent in refreshing ourselves amongst these west-India Isles. . . . Gone from thence in search of Virginia, the company was not a little discomforted, seeing the Mariners had three days passed their reckoning and found no land, so that Captain Ratcliffe (Captain of the Pinnace) rather desired to bear up the helm to return for England than make further search. But God, the guider of all good actions, forcing them by an extreme storm to haul all night, did drive them by his providence to their desired port, beyond all their expectations, for never any of them had seen that coast. The first land they made they called Cape Henry; where anchoring, Mr. Wingfield, Gosnold and Newport, with 30 others, recreating themselves on shore, were assaulted by 5 Savages, who hurt 2 of the English very dangerously. That night (April 26, 1607) was the box opened and the orders read, in which Bartholomew Gosnold, Edward Wingfield, Christopher Newport, John Smith, John Ratcliffe, John Martin and George Kendall, were named to be the Council and to choose a President among them for a year, who, with the Council, should govern. Matters of moment were to be examined by a Jury, but determined by the major part of the Council in which the President had 2 voices. Until the 13 of May, they sought a place to plant in, then the Council was sworn, Mr. Wingfield was chosen President and an oration made, while Captain Smith was not admitted to the Council as were the rest.

Now falleth every man to work, the Council contrived the Fort, the rest cut down trees to make place to pitch their Tents; some to provide clapboard to reload the ships, some make gardens, some nets, &c. The Savages often visited us kindly. The President's overweening jealousy would admit no exercise at arms, or fortification but the boughs of trees cast together in the form of a half moon by the extraordinary pains and diligence of Captain Kendall. Newport, with Smith and 20 others, were sent to discover the head of the river. By divers small habitations they passed and in 6 days they arrived at a town called Powhatan, consisting of some 12 houses pleasantly seated on a hill; before it, 3 fertile Isles, about it many of their cornfields. The place is very pleasant, and strong by nature. Of this place the Prince is called Powhatan, and his people Powhatans. To this place, the river is navigable, but higher within a mile by reason of the Rocks and Isles, there is not passage for a small Boat: this they call the Falls. The people in all parts kindly treated them, till being returned within 20 miles of Jamestown, they gave cause of jealousy. But had God not blessed the discoverers otherwise than those at the fort, there had then been an end of that plantation. For at the fort, when they arrived the next day, they found 17 men hurt, and a boy slain by the Savages. And had it not chanced a cross bar shot from the ships struck down a bough from a tree amongst them, that caused them to retire, our men had all been slain, being securely all at work and their arms [weapons] in dry fats.

Hereupon the President was contented the Fort should be pallisadoed, the ordnance mounted, his men armed and exercised, for many were the assaults and Ambuscadoes of the Savages, and our men by their disorderly straggling were often hurt, when the Savages by the nimbleness of their heels well escaped. What toil we had, with so small a power to guard our workmen by day, watch all night, resist our enemies and effect our business, to reload the ships, cut down trees and prepare the ground to plant our corn &c. I refer to the reader's consideration.[1]

Bent upon showing a quick profit, the Virginia Company ordered one-third of the colonists to concentrate their efforts upon a search for gold and silver mines and a passage to the South Sea, which at this time was thought to lie within easy sail of the Chesapeake. Since the large number of gentlemen who accompanied the expedition were debarred by their social status from performing manual labor, they devoted themselves almost wholly to these enterprises. As a result, during the first few months, the effort to plan an English colony in the New World resembled a rush to the gold fields. Neither the stockholders of the Virginia Company nor the settlers themselves were content to establish a mere agricultural colony; after it was discovered that the "gold" of Virginia was merely iron pyrites, the hope persisted that the settlement would prove to be a way station on the road to the riches of Cathay.

Jamestown, because it was built upon a peninsula defensible against the Indians and Spaniards, struck John Smith as "a verie fit place for the erecting of a great cittie." This advantage was outweighed by the fact that its situation was unhealthy—so unhealthy, indeed, that instead of

[1] Edward Arber (ed.), *The Works of Captain John Smith* (The English Scholar's Library, 2 vols., Birmingham, 1884), Vol. I, pp. 90–93.

becoming a great city it became the grave of hundreds of Englishmen.

Sir Thomas Gates described Jamestown in 1610:

True it is, I may not excuse this our Fort, or James Town, as yet seated in somewhat an unwholesome and sickly air, by reason it is in a marish ground, low, flat to the River, and hath no fresh water Springs serving the Town, but what we draw from a Well six or seven fathom deep, fed by the brackish River oozing into it, from whence I verily believe, the chief causes have proceeded of many diseases and sicknesses which have happened to our people, who are indeed strangely afflicted with Fluxes and Agues. . . . all which (if it had been our fortunes, to have seated upon some hill, accommodated with fresh Springs and clear air, as do the Natives of the Country) we might have, I believe, well escaped. And some experience we have to persuade ourselves that it may be so, for of our hundred and odd· men, which were seated at the Falls, the last year when the Fleet came in with fresh and young able spirits, under the government of Captain Francis West, and of one hundred to the Seawards (on the South side of our River) in the Country of the Nansamundes, under the charge of Captain John Martin, there did not so much as one man miscarry, and but very few or one fall sicke, whereas at Jamestown, the same time, and the same months, one hundred sickened and half the number died. Howbeit, as we condemn not Kent in England, for a small Town called Plumsted, continually assaulting the dwellers there (especially new comers) with Agues and Fevers; no more let us lay scandal, and imputation upon the Country of Virginia, because the little Quarter wherein we are set down (unadvisedly so chosed) appears to be unwholesome, and subject to many ill airs, which accompany the like marish places.[2]

Baron de la Warr, governor of Virginia from 1610 to 1611, enumerated the multitude of ailments by which he was beset:

Presently after my arrival in Jamestown, I was welcomed by a hot and violent Ague, which held me a time, till by the advice of my Physician, Doctour Lawrence Bohun (by blood

[2] Samuel Purchas, *Hakluytus Postumus; or Purchas his Pilgrimes* (20 vols., Glasgow: J. MacLehose and Sons, 1905–07), Vol. 19, pp. 58–59.

letting) I was recovered. . . . That Disease had not long left me, till (within three weeks after I had gotten a little strength) I began to be distempered with other grievous sicknesses, which successively and severally assailed me. For besides a relapse into the former Disease, which with much more violence held me more than a month, and brought me to great weakness, the Flux surprized me, and kept me many days; then the Cramp assaulted my weak body, with strong pains; and afterwards the Gout (with which I had heretofore been sometimes troubled) afflicted me in such sort, that making my body through weakness unable to stir, or to use any manner of exercise, drew upon me the Disease called the Scurvy; which though in others it be a sickness of slothfulness, yet was in me an effect of weakness, which never left me, till I was upon the point to leafe the World. . . .

In these extremities I resolved to consult my friends, Who finding Nature spent in me, and my body almost consumed, my pains likewise daily increasing, gave me advise to prefer a hopeful recovery, before an assured ruin, which must necessarily have ensued, had I lived but twenty days longer in Virginia: wanting at that instant, both food and Physick, fit to remedy such extraordinary Diseases, and restore that strength so desperately decayed.[3]

Baron de la Warr was fortunate to escape from Virginia with his life, but most of the ordinary people had no alternative but to remain in Jamestown to the end—which, mercifully, was swift in coming. By the autumn of 1607, half the company was dead and the survivors were hardly more than shadows of the lusty, devil-may-care adventurers who had set foot upon the New World barely six months before.

George Percy, one of the settlers, described the sufferings of the colonists in 1607–08:

Our men were destroyed with cruel diseases, as Swellings, Fluxes, Burning Fevers, and by wars. Some departed suddenly, but for the most part they died of meer famine. There were never Englishmen left in a foreign Country in such misery as we were in this new discovered Virginia. We watched every three nights, lying on the bare cold ground, what weather so-

[3] *Ibid.*, Vol. 19, pp. 86–87.

ever came, and warded all the next day which brought our men to be most feeble wretches. Our food was but a small Can of Barley sod in water, to five men a day, our drink cold water taken out of the River, which was at a flood very salt, at low tide full of slime and filth, which was the destruction of many of our men. Thus we lived for the space of five months in this miserable distress, not having five able men to man our Bulwarks upon any occasion. If it had not pleased God to have put a terror in the Savages' hearts, we had all perished by those wild and cruel Pagans, being that weak state as we were, our men night and day groaning in every corner of the Fort most pitiful to hear. If there were any conscience in men, it would make their hearts to bleed to hear the pitiful murmurings and outcries of our sick men without relief, every night and day, for the space of six weeks, some departing out of the World, many times three or four in a night; in the morning, their bodies trailed out of their Cabins like Dogs to be buried. In this sort did I see the mortality of divers of our people.

It pleased God, after a while, to send those people which were our mortal enemies to relieve us with victuals, as Bread, Corn, Fish and Flesh in great plenty, which was the setting up of our feeble men, otherwise we had all perished. Also we were frequented by divers Kings in the Country, bringing us store of provision to our great comfort.[4]

While death stalked the settlement and relief ships from England failed to arrive, the leaders quarreled among themselves and their animosities infected the rank and file. Edward Maria Wingfield, the President of the Council, was accused of raiding the hen roost and drinking more than his share of the brandy, a charge he indignantly denied. The hen roost, he pointed out, had long since been depleted and the larder contained only a few squirrels. As for the brandy, he insisted that he was holding it in reserve for the communion table against the wishes of the members of the Council who "longed to sup up that little remnant for they had now emptied all their own bottles."

In 1608, hastened by quarreling, disease and Indian attacks, the process of elimination brought Captain John

[4] Lyon Tyler (ed.), *Narratives of Early Virginia, 1606–1625* (New York: Barnes and Noble, 1946), pp. 21–22.

Smith to power as President of the Council. Although Smith was able to restore order and procure supplies from the Indians—sometimes at the pistol point—his high-handed ways aroused the resentment of many of the settlers. In September, 1609, charged with various crimes—including a plot to marry Pocahontas and make himself Emperor of Virginia—Smith was sent back to England for trial.

But getting rid of Smith merely meant that matters in Virginia went from bad to worse. Though the designation of "Starving Time" hardly distinguishes it from other periods in the early history of Virginia, the seven months from October, 1609, to April, 1610, bear this name. "Doggs, catts, ratts, and mice" were esteemed delicacies and boiled shoes became a regular article of diet. Death—in the form of starvation, sickness and Indian arrows—had a field day at the expense of the settlers. Of the 500 men and women living in Jamestown in October, 1609, only 60 were alive in April, 1610. The Englishmen who had come to Virginia to emulate the exploits of Cortez and Pizarro were reduced to living on the uncertain charity of the Indians.

Now we all found the loss of Captain Smith, yea his greatest maligners could now curse his loss. As for corn provision and contribution from the Savages, we had nothing but mortal wounds, with clubs and arrows; as for our Hogs, Hens, Goats, Sheep, Horse, or what lived, our commanders, officers and Savages daily consumed them. Some small portions sometimes we tasted, till all was devoured; then swords, arms, pieces, or any thing, we traded with the Savages, whose cruel fingers were so oft imbrewed in our blood, that what by their cruelty, our Governors' indiscretion, and the loss of our ships, of five hundred within six month's after Captain Smith's departure [October, 1609 to March, 1610] there remained not past sixty men, women and children, most miserable and poor creatures. And they were preserved for the most part, by roots, herbs, acorns, walnuts, berries, now and then a little fish; they that had starch in these extremities, made no small use of it; yea, even the very skins of our horses.

Nay, so great was our famine, that a Savage we slew and

buried, the poorer sort took him up again and eat him; and so did divers one another boiled and stewed with roots and herbs. And one amongst the rest did kill his wife, powdered [salted] her, and had eaten part of her before it was known; for which he was executed, as he well deserved: now whether she was better roasted, boiled or carbonado'd, I know not; but of such a dish as powdered wife I never heard of.[5]

To silence these tales of mass starvation and cannibalism, the Virginia Company published Sir Thomas Gates's version of events in Virginia. According to Sir Thomas, the "tragical story" of The Man Who Ate His Wife had been fabricated by some renegades who stole a ship in Virginia and, after their arrival in England, attempted to pass themselves off as heroes. The truth was, said Sir Thomas, that

There was one of the Company who mortally hated his Wife, and therefore secretly killed her, then cut her in pieces and hid her in divers parts of his House. When the woman was missing, the man suspected, his House searched, and parts of her mangled body were discovered. To excuse himself he said that his Wife died, that he hid her to satisfy his hunger, and that he fed daily upon her. Upon this, his House was again searched, where they found a good quantity of Meal, Oat-meal, Beans and Peas. He thereupon was arraigned, confessed the Murder, and was burned for his horrible villainy.[6]

Despite the best efforts of the publicists—many of whom were clergymen—hired by the Virginia Company to create the image of a public-spirited corporation dedicated to expanding the religion, power and glory of England, the news from Virginia was so dismal that, in 1610, the Company seriously considered calling the colonists home. As for the settlers themselves, when the question was put to a vote in September, 1610, only one man voted in favor of remaining in Jamestown. Before leaving the settlement on the James River, they wished to burn the hated place to the ground, but Sir Thomas Gates refused to permit such wanton destruction of the property of the Virginia Company. Only the timely arrival of a relief expedition under

[5] Edward Arber (ed.), op. cit., Vol. I, pp. 170–71.

[6] Samuel Purchas, op. cit., Vol. 19, pp. 68–69.

Baron de la Warr saved Virginia from being returned to the wilderness and the Indians.

For the next five years, Virginians lived under the "Laws Divine, Morall, and Martiall," usually called "Dale's Laws." Promulgated in 1611 by Governor Gates and his successor, Sir Thomas Dale, these laws were the most Draconic ever imposed upon an English colony. Dale was a Puritan army officer who had been furloughed from the Dutch army, then engaged in fighting the Spaniards in the Netherlands. Like the zealous Puritan he was, Dale attempted to establish in Virginia a "heavenly Jerusalem" along the lines later followed in New England. But it required English soldiers to compel Virginians to work, pray and conduct themselves in the way Dale demanded. Moreover, the punishments meted out by Dale made John Smith's "dictatorship" seem benign by comparison. Whereas Smith punished blasphemers by pouring a can of cold water down their sleeves, Dale ordered incorrigible offenders to be put to death.

Governor Dale's admirers rejoiced that at last "God's Church" had been erected in Virginia:

Every Sunday we have sermons twice a day, and every Thursday a Sermon, having true preachers, which take their weekly turns, and every morning at the ringing of a Bell, about ten of the clocke, each man addresseth himself to prayers, and so at four of the clock before Supper. Every Sunday, when the Lord Governor, and Captain General goeth to Church, he is accompanied with all the Counselors, Captains, other Officers, and all the Gentlemen, and with a Guard of Halberdiers in his Lordship's Livery, fair red cloaks, to the number of fifty, both on each side, and behind him: and being in the Church, his Lordship hath his seat in the Choir, in a green Velvet Chair, with a Cloth, with a Velvet Cushion spread on a Table before him, on which he kneeleth, and on each side sit the Council, Captains, and Officers, each in their place, and when he returneth home again, he is waited on to his house in the same manner.[7]

It was of no avail for the settlers to appeal to the royal charter granted the Virginia Company by which they and

[7] *Ibid.*, pp. 56–57.

their descendants were promised full enjoyment of "all the rights and liberties of Englishmen." Legal or constitutional rights simply did not exist in Virginia: the governor's will was law and anyone who questioned it was likely to pay dearly for his temerity. All told, during Dale's governorship, eight men were put to death for various offenses, some of which would not have been considered capital crimes in England.

Besides dragooning the settlers into the semblance of God-fearing Puritans, Dale tried to convert and pacify the Indians who, having neglected their opportunity to wipe out the defenceless settlement, seemed increasingly disposed to atone for that oversight. In the case of Pocahontas, Dale met with notable success. The Indian princess, a frequent visitor at Jamestown, where, naked, she did cartwheels in the streets, was in 1612 kidnapped by Captain Samuel Argall and held for ransom—a ransom that the English progressively raised whenever Powhatan offered to meet their terms. Dale saw to it that Pocahontas was instructed in the Christian religion and he finally enjoyed the gratification of witnessing her marriage, as a communicant of the Church of England, to John Rolfe. "Were it but the gaining this one soule," Dale declared, "I will thinke my time, toile and present well spent." To follow up this good work, Governor Dale, even though he had a wife in England, asked Powhatan's consent to take his youngest daughter, Pocahontas's sister, for "his nearest companion, wife and bedfellow"—thereby, as he said, consummating the union of Indians and English as "one people in the bond of love." But Powhatan had already sold the girl to an Indian brave for two baskets of beads. When Dale suggested that Powhatan return the beads and call off the deal, the old sachem inquired if white men always treated their promises so lightly.

John Rolfe's services to the colony did not end with his marriage to Pocahontas: in 1614, after several years of experimentation, he succeeded in growing in Virginia a variety of sweet-scented West Indian tobacco. Thenceforth, nothing—not even King James's *Counterblast to To-*

bacco and the acreage restrictions upon the growing of tobacco imposed by the Company itself—could prevent Virginians from devoting almost all their energies to the cultivation of the weed. In these early years, tobacco was almost worth its weight in silver and it was actually used as a currency. The onetime gold prospectors were now reported to be "rooting in the ground about tobacco like slaves"; every clearing and even the streets of Jamestown were planted in tobacco.

It was during Dale's rule that Virginia began to assume the appearance of a settled agricultural colony. Until 1614, the settlers had been hired employees of the Virginia Company. They lived in Company towns, bought supplies at a Company store, and cultivated Company ground with Company tools. Dale allowed each settler three acres of land upon which to grow his own crops and reduce the work load exacted by the Company to one month in the year provided that the settler paid a tax of two and a half barrels of corn annually.

In the meantime, Virginia had acquired the reputation in England of "a misery, a death, a hell." Few Englishmen were willing to risk their lives in the inferno on the James River and, since the settlers died faster than they could be replaced, the colony was threatened with extinction. Governor Dale proposed to replenish the population of Virginia by emptying the jails of England. With a few thousand convicts at his command, he told the Virginia Company, he could do wonders. Certainly, he added, they would be no more unmanageable than the "abandoned wretches" he already had on his hands. Desperate for fresh recruits, the Virginia Company appealed to King James I for a supply of felons. The King graciously gave his consent: the Company was permitted to select 100 of the likeliest-looking rogues with whom to plant Western civilization in the New World. In 1615, the King issued a proclamation ordering the transportation to Virginia of convicted felons, except those guilty of rape, murder, burglary or witchcraft.

Besides convicts and "sturdy beggars," in which England then abounded, the Virginia Company sent 100 homeless children rounded up from the streets of London to serve as apprentices in the colony. "Some of the ill-disposed children," reported Edwin Sandys, treasurer of the Virginia Company, "who, under severe masters in Virginia, may be brought to goodness, and of whom the city is specially desirous to be disburdened" astonished the city fathers by refusing to go to Virginia. It proved necessary to put the children forcibly aboard ship.

But what Virginia needed more than down-at-heels Englishmen, convicts and slum children was women. Except for the wives of the officials and a few settlers, the colony was composed wholly of males, most of them in the prime of life. Repelled by the pungent odor of bear's grease with which Indian women anointed themselves, few Englishmen were inclined to follow John Rolfe's example. Besides, there were not nearly enough princesses to go round, and the English Court had made plain in the case of John Rolfe and Pocahontas that it disapproved of commoners' marrying royalty.

Deprived of women, the settlers became unruly, quarrelsome, morose and eager to return to England. Realizing that the colony would not be secure until Englishmen were anchored in Virginia by wives and children and all the responsibilities that went with them, a group of stockholders of the Virginia Company formed a subsidiary company whose purpose was to supply the planters with wives. In 1620, ninety young women, certified as "pure and spotless," were put up at auction for 120 pounds of tobacco a head. It was stipulated in their contracts that they were not to be married to servants but to independent landowners of good reputation.

These lusty bachelors, it was reported, did "willinglie and lovinglie receive the new comers" and engage in spirited bidding for their persons. In 1621, when 38 additional women arrived, the price was raised to 150 pounds of tobacco per head. All told, 140 marriageable women

were sent to Virginia and none lacked for husbands. Supplying women to the colonists was the only financially rewarding enterprise undertaken during the existence of the Virginia Company. It was so profitable that the happy stockholders petitioned for a grant of land where they proposed to build a town called "Maydes Towne."
1621.

We send you in this shipp one widdow and eleven maids for wives for the people in Virginia. There hath been especiall care had in the choise of them for there hath not any one of them beene received but uppon good commendations. . . . There are neare fiftie more which are shortly to come, we sent by our most honorable Lord William the Earle of Southampton [Treasurer of the Virginia Company] and certain worthy gentlemen who taking into their consideration, that the Plantation can never flourish till families be planted and the respect of wives and children fix the people in the soyle, therefore have given this faire beginninge for the reimbursinge of whose charges, it is ordered that every man that marries them give 120 lb waight of best leafe Tobacco for each of them, and in case any of them dye that proportion must be advanced to make it upp to uppon those that survive. . . . And though we are desirous that marriadge be free according to the law of nature, yett under vow not have those maids deterred and married to servants but only to such fremen or tenants as have meanes to maintaine them: we pray you therefore to be fathers to them in this bussiness not enforcing them to marrie against their wills; neither send we them to be servants but in case of extremitie, for we would have their condition so much better as multitudes may be allured thereby to come unto you; and you may assure such men as marry those women that the first servants sent over by the Company shall be consigned to them, it being our intent to preserve families and proper married men before single persons.[8]

The arrival of the "maids" occasioned greater excitement and did more to raise morale in the colony than did the summoning in 1619 of the House of Burgesses—the

[8] Edward Neill, *History of the Virginia Company of London* (Albany, New York, 1869), pp. 234–35.

first popularly elected legislative body in the New World. Virginians had no way of knowing that they were witnessing the laying of the foundations of self-government in America, but they did have a very good idea, even though they were sadly out of practice, of the way of a man with a maid.

By 1620, Virginians had secured the right to own land; they had won a voice in the management of the colony's affairs; they had developed a profitable staple for export; they had wives and were in the process of producing families; and the Indians, after alternating between friendship and hostility, seemed to have become "generally very loving." The results of these changes were evident on every hand: men who would not bestir themselves to labor for the Virginia Company now worked long hours for their own profit in the tobacco fields, striving to accumulate enough land to qualify as bidders for wives and to win election to the House of Burgesses, a high social as well as political honor.

No longer was it necessary for the Virginia Company to scour the streets and invade the jails to people the colony. Sir Edwin Sandys, whose ambition it was to send "multitudes" of men and women to Virginia, succeeded so well that they starved to death by the hundreds: the Company failed to supply the food necessary for the subsistence of the people it transported to Jamestown, and the mortality rate from disease remained appallingly high. Moreover, the Indians were far from pacified: in 1622, they struck almost without warning and 350 whites lost their lives in the Massacre. The census of 1624 disclosed that Virginia had a population of only 1,275. Of the 140 maids who became wives of the planters, only 35 were alive in 1624.

Yet the beachhead had been established and the process of consolidation had begun. When the English Crown took over the colony from the bankrupt and dissension-torn Virginia Company in 1624, one thing was certain: there would always be a Virginia.

II. PLYMOUTH

Although the founding of Virginia was proclaimed to be a "Holy Business" in which spreading the Gospel took precedence over all other concerns, few Englishmen came to Virginia in search of religious liberty. The first to embark upon such a mission were the Pilgrims, a small group of extreme Puritans who had separated themselves from the Church of England and, in some instances even from the realm of England itself by migrating to Holland in search of religious freedom. When, in 1620, they set out for America from Holland and England they hoped to establish a Wilderness Zion very different from the Established Church and State they had known in England.

The *Mayflower,* a former wine carrier, brought the Pilgrims safely across the Atlantic—the *Speedwell,* their other ship, sprang a leak and had to turn back—but it landed them in New England late in the year and over a hundred miles from their destination. The Pilgrims had hoped to reach the New World in the late summer and they intended to settle near the Hudson River in the northern part of the Virginia Company's grant. As a result of these miscalculations the Pilgrims had to do some quick improvising: they were in a strange land, winter had already set in and they were out of reach of succor from Jamestown.

William Bradford, Governor of Plymouth Plantation, described the sensations of the Pilgrims when they arrived in the New World:

Being thus passed the vast ocean, and a sea of troubles before in their preparation . . . they had now no friends to welcome them nor inns to entertain or refresh their weatherbeaten bodies; no houses or much less towns to repair to, to seek for succour. It is recorded in Scripture as a mercy to the Apostle and his shiprecked company, that the barbarians showed them no small kindness in refreshing them, but these savage barbarians, when they met with them (as after will appear) were readier to fill their sides full of arrows than otherwise. And for the season it was winter, and they that know the winters of that country know them to be sharp and violent, and subject to cruel and fierce storms, dangerous to travel to known places, much more to search an unknown coast. Besides, what could they see but a hideous and desolate wilderness, full of wild beasts and wild men—and what multitudes there might be of them they knew not. Neither could they, as it were, go up to the top of Pisgah to view from this wilderness a more goodly country to feed their hopes; for which way soever they turned their eyes (save upward to the heavens) they could have little solace or content in respect of any outward objects. For summer being done, all things stand upon them with a weather beaten face, and the whole country, full of woods and thickets, represented a wild and savage hue. If they looked behind them, there was the mighty ocean which they had passed and was now as a main bar and gulf to separate them from all the civil parts of the world. If it be said they had a ship to succour them it is true; but what heard they daily from the master and company? But that with speed they should look out a place (with their shallop) where they would be, at some near distance; for the season was such as he would not stir from thence till a safe harbor was discovered by them, where they would be, and he might go without danger; and that victuals consumed apace but he must and would keep sufficient for themselves and their return. Yea, it was muttered by some that if they got not a place in time, they would turn them and their goods ashore and leave them. Let it also be considered what weak hopes of supply and succour they left behind them, that might bear up their minds in this sad condition and trials they were under; and they could not but be very small. . . .

What could now sustain them but the Spirit of God and his grace? May not and ought not the children of these fathers rightly say: "Our fathers were Englishmen which came over this great ocean, and were ready to perish in this wilderness; but they cried unto the Lord, and He heard their voice and looked on their adversity," etc. "Let them therefore praise the Lord, because He is good; and His mercies endure forever." "Yea, let them which have been redeemed of the Lord, shew how He hath delivered them from the hand of the oppressor. When they wandered in the desert wilderness out of the way, and found no city to dwell in, both hungry and thirsty, their soul was overwhelmed in them. Let them confess before the Lord His lovingkindness and His wonderful works before the sons of men." [9]

In these respects, at least, the Pilgrims were well qualified for the work in hand: they were not drawn to the New World by the hope of pecuniary gain and there was among them only one gentleman, Edward Winslow, and he did not disdain manual labor. The Pilgrims were farmers, artisans and small shopkeepers. Nevertheless, hardly more than the Virginians were they prepared to cope with the American environment. But they did have what Governor Thomas Dale tried to inculcate in the Virginians: a high sense of religious purpose, a determination to endure hardships for the sake of an ideal and a closely knit community life. As the Pilgrims said of themselves: "It was not with them as with other men, whom small things oould discourage, or small discontents cause to wish themselves home again."

The Pilgrims expected to engage in fishing, fur trading and farming in the New World. But their fishing equipment was useless; they knew nothing of fur trading; and they had no experience in growing Indian corn. During the first month in Plymouth the Pilgrims caught only one cod, although the sea was filled with them. Their first fish was a live herring that had washed up on shore. At this point, the Pilgrims seemed likely to go down in history not as Founding Fathers but as the world's worst fishermen. Early in January, 1621, however, their hunger was temporarily assuaged when three seal and one cod were caught in the Bay. Miles Standish contributed an eagle to the larder; the hungry Pilgrims pronounced the meat to be as tasty as mutton. Even so, they could not have survived without shellfish they dug on the beaches and groundnuts they found in the forest.

Governor William Bradford described the Starving Time in Plymouth:

[9] William Bradford, *Of Plymouth Plantation, 1620–1647*, edited by S. E. Morison (New York: Alfred A. Knopf, Inc., 1959), pp. 61–63.

(The Starving Time)

But that which was most sad and lamentable was, that in two or three months' time half of their company died, especially in January and February, being the depth of winter, and wanting houses and other comforts; being infected with the scurvy and [55] other diseases which this long voyage and their inaccommodate condition had brought upon them. So as there died some times two or three of a day in the foresaid time, that of 100 and odd persons, scarce fifty remained. And of these, in the time of most distress, there was but six or seven sound persons who to their great commendations, be it spoken, spared no pains night nor day, but with abundance of toil and hazard of their own health, fetched them wood, made them fires, dressed them meat, made their beds, washed their loathsome clothes, clothed and unclothed them. In a word, did all the homely and necessary offices for them which dainty and queasy stomachs cannot endure to hear named; and all this willingly and cheerfully, without any grudging in the least, showing herein their true love unto their friends and brethren; a rare example and worthy to be remembered. Two of these seven were Mr. William Brewster, their reverend Elder, and Myles Standish, their Captain and military commander, unto whom myself and many others were much beholden in our low and sick condition. And yet the Lord so upheld these persons as in this general calamity they were not at all infected either with sickness or lameness. And what I have said of these I may say of many others who died in this general visitation, and others yet living; that whilst they had health, yea, or any strength continuing, they were not wanting to any that had need of them. And I doubt not but their recompense is with the Lord.

But I may not here pass by another remarkable passage not to be forgotten. As this calamity fell among the passengers that were to be left here to plant, and were hasted ashore and made to drink water that the seamen might have more beer, and one in his sickness desiring but a small can of beer, it was answered that if he were their own father he should have none. The disease began to fall amongst them also, so as almost half of their company died before they went away, and many of their officers and lustiest men, as the boatswain, gunner, three quartermasters, the cook and others. At which the Master was something strucken and sent to the sick ashore and told the

Governor he should send for beer for them that had need of it, though he drunk water homeward bound.

But now amongst his company there was far another kind of carriage in this misery than amongst the passengers. For they that before had been boon companions and drinking and jollity in the time of their health and welfare, began now to desert one another in this calamity, saying they would not hazard their lives for them, they should be infected by coming to help them in their cabins; and so, after they come to lie by it, would do little or nothing for them but, "if they died, let them die." But such of the passengers as were yet aboard showed them what mercy they could, which made some of their hearts relent, as the boatswain (and some others) who was a proud young man and would often curse and scoff at the passengers. But when he grew weak, they had compassion on him and helped him; then he confessed he did not deserve it at their hands, he had abused them in word and deed. "Oh!" (saith he) "you, I now see, show your love like Christians indeed one to another, but we let one another lie and die like dogs." Another lay cursing his wife, saying if it had not been for her he had never come this unlucky voyage, and anon cursing his fellows, saying he had one this and that for some of them; he had spent so much and so much amongst them, and they were now weary of him and did not help him, having need. Another gave his companion all he had, if he died, to help him in his weakness; he went and got a little spice and made him a mess of meat once or twice. And because he died not so soon as he expected, he went amongst his fellows and swore the rogue would cozen him, he would see him choked before he made him any more meat; and yet the poor fellow died before morning.[10]

Despite the Pilgrims' apprehensions, the Indians helped the colony through its first trying years. Instead of filling the Pilgrims' sides with arrows, as Bradford had feared, the natives helped to fill the Pilgrims' sides with fish, corn and venison.

Four years before the Pilgrims arrived, the tribes living in this part of New England had been almost completely exterminated by a smallpox epidemic. An explorer reported that "the bones and skulls upon the severall places of their habitations, made such a spectacle after my coming into

[10] *Ibid.*, pp. 77–79.

those partes, that as I travailed in that Forrest, nere the Massachusetts, it seemed to mee a new found Golgatha." Like religious-minded people of all denominations—whether Lutherans, German Pietists, or Episcopalians—the Pilgrims regarded epidemics among the Indians as proof of the Almighty's intention of clearing the land of heathens in order to make way for the advent of white Christians.

Among the advantages of this plague for the whites was that the Pilgrims were able to move immediately into abandoned Indian dwellings at Plymouth. While they occasionally caught glimpses of Indians in the woods and saw their fires at night, the Pilgrims did not meet up with the redskins until March, 1621, when Samoset boldly walked into the settlement and introduced himself. Samoset, an Algonquin Indian from Maine, had picked up a few words of English from the English fishermen who frequented that coast. The Pilgrims knew that Samoset was civilized by his first request: he asked for a drink of beer. Being short of beer, the Pilgrims gave him instead "strong water and biscuit, and butter, and cheese, and pudding, a piece of mallard; all which he liked well." Little as the half-famished Pilgrims could afford to regale a visiting Indian with such delicacies, they were eager to establish good relations with the natives and they hoped to use Samoset to open up diplomatic channels.

Later Samoset returned with his friend Squanto, a Patuxent Indian who had been shanghaied by English fishermen and brought to England. When he returned to New England he jumped ship and escaped to the woods, only to find himself the sole survivor of his tribe. It was Squanto who saved the day for the Pilgrims. He taught them how to fish, hunt and plant Indian corn, squash and beans, served as interpreter and acted as peacemaker between the Pilgrims and the decimated tribes living in the vicinity of Plymouth. Governor William Bradford pronounced this invaluable Indian to be "a special instrument sent of God for their good beyond their expectation."

Even so, the wary Pilgrims made it a point to keep

their powder dry. In November, 1621, when the Narragansett Indians sent to Plymouth a bundle of arrows tied together with a snakeskin—the symbolic gage of battle—Governor William Bradford bluntly told the savages that the Pilgrims were ready for them: "That if they loved war rather than peace, they might begin when they would, they had done them no wrong, neither did they fear them, or should they finde them unprovided." The Indians called off the war.

In general, the Pilgrims treated the Indians with Christian charity and forebearance. When they landed at Plymouth they fell upon their knees but it is not true that they also fell upon the Indians. Instead, they scrupulously paid for the supplies furnished by the natives and extinguished Indian land titles by purchase. No white was permitted to sell or give liquor or firearms to the tribesmen. "Praying Indians" (those converted to Christianity) sometimes served on juries in cases involving members of their own race. The leaders of the Pilgrim community carried their sense of justice even to the length of trying and executing several Englishmen for the murder of an Indian despite the fact that "some of the rude and ignorant sort murmured that any English should be put to death for an Indian."

By the autumn of 1621, the Pilgrims were living comparatively high. Although their pea crop was a failure, they harvested twenty acres of corn, planted Indian-fashion in hillocks fertilized with fish. Moreover, they were by now such good shots that, when Governor Bradford sent four men on a fowling expedition, they returned with enough game to serve the entire company of about fifty people for a week. Finally, a ship arrived with a cargo of provisions. To celebrate these auspicious events, the Pilgrims invited Massasoit, the Indian chief who had entered into a covenant of peace with the Pilgrims, and 90 of his braves to a feast. The Indians, whom the Pilgrims discovered to be "very loving and ready to pleasure us," contributed five deer for the occasion. Surrounded by this unaccustomed abundance, Pilgrims and Indians sat down to the first Thanksgiving. Everyone agreed that it was such a success that it ought to be done again—provided, of course, that the Pilgrims had something to be thankful for.

But the tribulations of the Pilgrims were by no means over. Because of a drought, their corn withered on the stalks (despite their prayers, fasts and days of humiliation, when the rains came they were too late to save the crop) and the supply ships from England failed to arrive on time. As a result, bereft of corn and wheat, they went back to their diet of fish, clams and groundnuts. The summer of 1622, in particular, was a period of hunger and privation; and in 1623, when two ships carrying additional colonists arrived in Plymouth, the best dish that the "Old Comers" could set before the "New Comers" was a lobster, a piece of fish and a cup of "fair spring water."

Like the early Virginians, the Pilgrims were simply hired laborers of a commercial company based in England. True, they were stockholders of the company— their wages were to be paid in stock—but they could not expect to benefit from this arrangement until the final settlement was made, assuming that they held out that long. To pay their debt to the capitalists in England who had financed the voyage of *Mayflower* and other ships, they were required to send beaver and fish to England, paying an interest rate as high as 45 per cent on the capital they had borrowed. It was not until 1643 that they finally freed themselves of the financial burden they had assumed to make the passage to the New World. Thus, in effect, the Pilgrims were 23 years working their way across the Atlantic.

Long before this, they had abandoned community ownership of land and goods in favor of private property and individual enterprise. In 1620–21, heads of families in Plymouth were given a town lot and required to build their own houses as well as to work on community buildings. In 1624, each person in the colony was given an acre of land for subsistence farming. It was observed that this incentive "made all hands very industrious."

Thus the beginnings of Plymouth Plantation, like those

of Virginia, were "raw, small and difficult." Unlike Virginia, however, Plymouth never developed a lucrative cash crop for export nor did it become a large commercial center like several other New England seaports. As a result, the Pilgrim settlement never became very large or prosperous and, since most of the people remained farmers or fishermen, it was distinguished by a degree of economic and social equality greater than that which prevailed in any other English colony in North America. There were no heated debates upon abstruse points of theology, and politics scarcely ruffled the placid surface of life in Plymouth. From 1621 to 1656, William Bradford was elected governor 30 times; his total period of service was 33 years. Except for a quickly contained "crime wave" in 1644, there was no serious disciplinary problem: for many years scarcely any legislation existed on the statute books of the colony.

Plymouth survived its early trials largely because of the Pilgrims' courage in the face of adversity and their conviction that they had been designated by God to accomplish His purposes. The "Saints" at Plymouth were "knit together as a body in a most strict and sacred bond and covenant of the Lord" by virtue whereof each individual held himself "straightly tied to all care of each other's goods and of the whole, by every one and so mutually." A mere community of rugged individualists, each going his own way, indifferent to the welfare of his fellows, would not have endured at Plymouth. In fact, Thomas Weston, an English merchant who helped finance the Pilgrims in 1620, attempted to establish at Weymouth, near Plymouth, a fishing and trading settlement. Weston's employees had no religious purpose and little sense of responsibility to the community. They quarreled over the division of the profits and, by their sharp dealing, alienated the Indians. Only timely action on the part of the Pilgrims saved Weston's men from being massacred by the Indians. The discouraged survivors packed up for home. In 1622, by contrast, when a ship arrived in Plymouth and offered to take passengers back to England, not a single Pilgrim took advantage of the opportunity.

III. MASSACHUSETTS BAY

The settlement of Massachusetts Bay was part of the "Great Migration" that, from 1628 to 1640, brought almost 50,000 Englishmen to the New World. Of this number, about 21,000 came to New England. These were the Puritans, distinguished from the Pilgrims chiefly by the fact that they were not originally disposed to separate themselves from the Church of England. A reformest element within the Established Church, the Puritans were resolved to establish a truly "apostolic" church in the New World, thereby bringing the Church of England to change its "popish" ways and return to the primitive simplicity the Puritans identified with true Christianity.

The 17 vessels that set sail from England in 1630, carrying over 1,500 settlers to Massachusetts Bay, was one of the best organized expeditions sent out during the colonial period for the purpose of founding an English colony. It was also one of the most expensive, requiring the outlay of almost 200,000 pounds. During the next ten years, 298 ships transported people from Old to New England. Of these vessels, only one miscarried—the *Gabriel* was lost at Pemaquid, Maine, in 1635.

In general, the people who boarded ship for New England during this period were more affluent, better educated and of a higher social class than any other large group of colonists who came to America. Many brought with them their household furniture and servants, and they paid the entire cost of the voyage by selling or mortgaging their property in England. Unlike the Pilgrims and early Virginians, they were not the employees of a London-based corporation; except for the servants among them, they came as their own masters and took up land as independent proprietors. Every £50 invested in the stock of the Massachusetts Bay Company entitled the purchaser to 200 acres of land; each settler was given 50 acres; and every person who paid the six pounds required to transport a servant to New England was given a bonus of 50 acres of land.

Profiting from the experience of their predecessors at Jamestown and Plymouth, the Puritans took precautions against a repetition of the mass starvation that had given those places a grisly eminence. Puritanical as they were, they had no desire to mortify the flesh to that extent! Accordingly, in 1628–29, an advance party of over 200 servants was sent to Salem to build houses and plant corn in preparation for the coming of the Puritan colonists. The passengers who crossed the Atlantic in 1630 on the *Arabella* and other ships brought with them large quantities of food, nails, glass, iron, guns and ammunition, swine, goats, sheep and cows.

Despite the elaborateness of this inventory, it was impossible to provide against all the contingencies involved in effecting a settlement upon the coast of New England. In a letter to the Countess of Lincoln, whom he had served in the capacity of steward, Thomas Dudley recounted some of the unanticipated hardships experienced by the Puritans during their first winter in Massachusetts Bay:

Touching the plantation which we here have begun, it fell out thus about the year 1627 some friends being together in Lincolnshire, fell into some discourse about New England and the planting of the gospel there; and after some deliberation, we imparted our reasons by letters & messages to some in London and the west country where it was likewise deliberately thought upon, and at length with often negotiation so ripened that in the year 1628, we procured a patent from his Majesty for our planting between the Massachusetts Bay and Charles river on the South; and the River of Merrimack on the North and 3 miles on either side of those Rivers & Bay, as also for the government of those who did or should inhabit within that compass. And the same year we sent Mr. John Endecott & some with him to begin a plantation & to strengthen such as he should find there which we sent thither from Dorchester & some places adjoining; from whom the same year receiving hopeful news. The next year, 1629, we sent diverse ships over with about 300 people, and some cows, goats & horses many of which arrived safely. These by their too large commendations of the country, and the commodities thereof, invited us so strongly to go on that Mr. Winthrop of Suffolk (who was well known in his own country and well approved here for his piety, liberality, wisdom & gravity) coming in to us, we come to such resolution that in April 1630, we set sail from Old England with 4 good ships. And in May following, 8 more followed, 2 having gone before in February and March, and 2 more following in June and August, besides another set out by a private merchant. These 17 Ships arrived all safe in New England, for the increase of the plantation here this year 1630 but made a long, a troublesome, and a costly voyage being all wind bound long in England, and hindered with contrary winds after they set sail and so scattered with mists and tempests that few of them arrived together. Our 4 ships which set out in April arrived here in June and July, where we found the colony in a sad and unexpected condition above 80 of them being dead the winter before and many of those alive weak and sick: all the corn and bread amongst them all hardly sufficient to feed them a fortnight, insomuch that the remainder of 180 servants we had the 2 years before sent over, coming to us for victuals to sustain them we found ourselves wholly unable to feed them by reason that the provisions shipped for them were taken out of the ship they were put in, and they who were trusted to ship them in another failed us, and left them behind; whereupon necessity enforced us to our extreme loss to give them all liberty; who had cost us about 16 or 20 pounds a person furnishing and sending over. But bearing these things as we might, we began to consult of the place of our sitting down: for Salem where we landed, pleased us not. And to that purpose some were sent to the Bay to search up the rivers for a convenient place. . . . But there receiving advertisements by some of the late arrived ships from London and Amsterdam of some French preparations against us (many of our people brought with us being sick of feavers and the scurvy and were thereby unable to carry up our ordnance and baggage so far) we were forced to change counsel and for our present shelter to plant dispersedly. . . . This dispersion troubled some of us, but help it we could not, wanting ability to remove to any place fit to build a Town upon, and the time too short to deliberate any longer lest the winter should surprise us before we had builded our houses. The best counsel we could find out was to build a fort to retire to, in some convenient place if any enemy pressed thereunto, after we should have fortified ourselves against the injuries of wet and cold. So ceasing to consult further for that time they who had health to labour fell to building wherein many were interrupted with sickness and many died weekly, yea almost daily. Amongst whom were Mrs. Pinchon, Mrs. Coddington, Mrs. Phillips and Mrs. Alcock a sister of Mr. Hookers. Insomuch that the ships being now upon their return, some for England, some for Ireland, there was, as I take it, not much less than an hundred (some think many more) partly out of dislike of our government which restrained and punished their excesses, and partly through fear of famine not seeing other means than by their labour to feed themselves) which returned back again. And glad we were so to be rid of them. Others also afterwards hearing of men of their own disposition, which were planted at Piscataway went from us to them, whereby though our numbers were lessened yet we accounted ourselves nothing weakened by their removal.

Before the departure of the ship we contacted with Mr. Peirce Master of the Lyon of Bristol to return to us with all speed with fresh supplies of victuals & gave him directions accordingly. . . . The ships being gone, victuals wasting & mortality increasing, we held diverse fasts in our several congregations, but the Lord would yet be deprecated; for about the beginning of September, died Mr. Gager, a right godly man, a skillful surgeon and one of the deacons of our congregation. And Mr. Higginson, one of the ministers of Salem, a zealous & profitable preacher; this of a consumption, that of a feaver; & on the 30th September died Mr. Johnson, another of the 5 undertakers (the lady Arabella his wife being dead a month before). This gentleman as a prime amongst us, having the best estate of any, zealous for religion and the greatest furtherer of this plantation. He made a most godly end, dying willingly, professing his life better spent in promoting this plantation than it would have been in any other way. He left to us a loss greater than the most conceived. . . . And of the people who came over with us from the time of their setting sail from England in April, 1630, until December following there died by estimation about 200 at the least. So low hath the Lord brought us! Well, yet they who survived were not discouraged but bearing God's corrections with humility and trusting in his mercies, and considering how after a greater ebb he had raised up our neighbors at Plymouth we began again in December to consult about a fit place to build a Town upon.

I should also have remembered how the half of our cows and almost all our mares and goats sent us out of England, died at sea in their passage hither, and that those intended to be sent us out of Ireland were not sent at all; all which together with the loss of our six months building, occasioned by our intended removal to a town to be fortified, weakened our estates, especially the estates of the undertakers. . . . Yet many of us laboured to bear it as comfortably as we could, remembering the end of our coming hither & knowing the power of God who can support and raise us again, and useth to bring his servants low, that the meek may be made glorious by deliverance, Psal. 112. . . .

Touching the discouragement which the sickness and mortality which every first year hath seized upon us, and those of Plymouth, as appeareth before, may give to such who have cast any thoughts this way (of which mortality it may be said of us almost as of the Egyptians, that there is not an house where there is not one dead, and in some houses many) the natural causes seem to be in the want of warm lodging, and good diet to which Englishmen are habituated at home; and in the sudden increase of heat which they endure that are landed here in summer, the salt meats at sea having prepared their bodies thereto, for those only these 2 last years died of fevers who landed in June and July; as those of Plymouth who landed in winter died of the Scurvey, as did our poorer sort whose houses and bedding kept them not sufficiently warm, nor their diet sufficiently in heart.[11]

Instead of wasting time looking for nonexistent gold or a passage to the South Sea, the Puritans immediately got down to the business of clearing land, building houses and planting crops. Nor did John Winthrop and other Puritan leaders, even though they possessed the rank of "gentlemen," disdain to work with their hands:

. . . Now so soone as Mr. Winthrop was landed, perceiving what misery was like to ensewe through theire Idlenes, he pres-

[11] Merrill Jensen (ed.), *American Colonial Documents to 1776* (Vol. 9 of *English Historical Documents*, New York: Oxford University Press, 1955), pp. 143–47.

ently fell to worke with his owne hands, & thereby soe encouradged the rest that there was not an Idle person then to be found in the whole Plantation & whereas the Indians said they would shortly retorne as fast as they came, now they admired to see in what short time they had all housed themselves & planted Corne sufficient for theire subsistance.[12]

While the mortality rate was far lower in New England than in Jamestown, the work was equally hard and exhausting. In 1631, discouraged by the privatións they had suffered in New England, about 100 Puritans returned to England. To one young man, home never seemed sweeter than after he had experienced the hardships of life in a new country:

Letter to William Pond

Most Loving and Kind Father and Mother:
My humble duty remembered unto you, trusting in God you are in good health. And I pray remember my love unto my brother Joseph and thank him for his kindness that I found at his hand at London, which was not the value of a farthing. I know, loving father, and do confess that I was an undutiful child unto you when I lived with you and by you, for which I am much sorrowful and grieved for it, trusting in God that he will guide me that I will never offend you so any more and I trust in God that you will forgive me for it. My writing unto you is to let you understand what a country this New England is where we live. Here are but few Indians, a great part of them died this winter, it was thought it was of the plague. They are a crafty people and they will cozen and cheat, and they are a subtle people, and whereas we did expect great store of beaver here is little or none to be had. . . . They [the Indians] are proper men and cleanjointed men and many of them go naked with a skin about their loins, but now some of them get Englishmens' apparell. The country is very rocky and hilly and some champaign ground and the soil is very thin and here is some good ground and marsh ground but here is no Michaelmas daisy. Cows thrive well here, but they give small store of

[12] "A Relation Concerning some occurrences in New England" (Captain Israel Stoughton to Dr. Stoughton, his brother) (*Proceedings of the Massachusetts Historical Society, 1860–62*, Boston, 1862), pp. 130–31.

milk. . . . Here is timber in good store, acornes in good store, and here is good store of fish if we had boats to go for and lines to serve to fish. Here are good store of wild fowl, but they are hard to come by. It is harder to get a shot than it is in Old England and people here are subject to disease, for here have died of the scurvy and of the burning fever nigh two hundred and odd; besides as many layeth lame and all Sudbury men are dead but three, and three women and some children, and provisions are here at a wonderful rate . . . and all kind of spices very dear and almost none to be got. If this ship had not come when it did we had been put to a wonderful straight, but thanks be to God for sending of it in. I received from the ship a hogshead of meal, and the Governor telleth me of a hundred weight of cheese the which I have received part of it. I humbly thank you for it. I did expect two cows, the which I had none, nor do I earnestly desire that you should send me any, because the country is not as we did expect it. Therefore, loving father, I would intreat you that you would send me a firkin of butter and a hogshead of malt unground, for we drink nothing but water, and a coarse cloth of four pound price so it be thick. For the freight, if you of your love will send them I will pay the freight, for here is nothing to be got without we had commodities to go up to the Eastern parts amongst the Indians to traffic, for here where we live is no beaver. Here is no cloth to be had to make apparell, and shoes are at 5 shilings a pair for me, and that cloth that is worth 2 shillings 8 pence a yard is worth here 5 shillings. So I pray, father, send me four or five yards of cloth to make us some apparell, and loving father, though I be far distant from you yet I pray you remember me as your child, and we do not know how long we may subsist, for we can not live here without provisions from Old England. Therefore, I pray do not put away your shop stuff, for I think that in the end, if I live, it must be my living, for we do not know how long this plantation will stand, for some of the magnates that did uphold it have turned off their men and given it over. Besides, God hath taken away the chief sun in the land, Mr. Johnson and Lady Arabella his wife, which was the chief man of estate in the land and one that would have done most good.

Here came over twenty five passengers and there came back again four score and more persons, and as many more would have come if they had the wherewithal to bring them home, for here are many that come over the last year which was worth two hundred pounds before they came out of Old England that between this and Michaelmas will be hardly worth thirty pounds. So here we may live if we have supplies every year from Old England, otherwise we cannot subsist. I may, as I will, work hard, set an acre of Eindey wheat, and if we do not set with fish and that will cost twenty shillings, if we set it without fish they shall have but a poor crop. So father, I pray, consider of my cause, for here will be but a very poor being, no being without, loving father, your help with provisions from Old England. I had thought to come home in this ship, for my provisions were almost all spent, but that I humbly thank you for your great love and kindness in sending me some provisions, or else I should and mine been half famished, but now I will, if it please God that I have my health, I will plant what corn I can, and if provisions be not cheaper between this and Michaelmas and that I do not hear from you what I was best to do, I purpose to come at Michaelmas.

My wife remembers her humble duty unto you and to my mother, and my love to my brother Joseph and to Sarey Myler. Thus I leave you to the protection of Almighty God.

From Watertown in New England, the 15th of March, 1631.

[No signature]

We were wonderful sick as we came at sea, with the smallpox. No man thought that I and my little child would have lived. My boy is lame and my girl too, and there died in the ship that I came in fourteen persons.[18]

But hard work and thrift, without which New Englanders could not have survived the rigors of the wilderness, soon brought the Puritans a measure of comfort and security. By 1638, so rapid was the growth of population, some parts of the country bore almost as settled and prosperous an appearance as the mother country itself.

IV. MARYLAND

As more colonies were established, the work of founding new settlements became progressively easier. Winning the

[18] Merrill Jensen (ed.), *op. cit.*, pp. 148–49.

first foothold was the hardest part of the task: the early Virginians bore the brunt of the hardships, partly because there was no other English community on the continent to lend them aid. By 1621, however, Virginia was in a position to send much-needed supplies of food to Plymouth, and in May, 1632, a Dutch ship arrived in Boston carrying 2,000 bushels of corn from Virginia. Similarly, Plymouth served as a source of supply, particularly of corn and cattle, for the Puritans in nearby Massachusetts Bay.

All these colonies, especially Virginia, lent aid to the 17 Roman Catholic "gentlemen," the two Jesuit priests and the 280 farmers and laborers, most of whom were Protestants, who arrived in Maryland in 1634. Thanks to the corn, hogs, goats, cows and chickens furnished by Virginia and New England, the Marylanders escaped the worst of the ordeal of planting a new colony. Moreover, the settlers immediately set to work planting peas, corn, beans, apples and sugar cane. Father White, one of the Jesuit priests, reported that in ten days beans grew 14 inches high, that the apricots were so abundant that it was necessary to feed them to hogs, and that the fowling and hunting were unsurpassed. "And to say truth," another Marylander observed, "there wanteth nothing for the perfecting of this hopeful plantation but greater numbers of our countrymen to enjoy it."

To complete this felicity, the Indians seemed to delight in rendering hospitality to the newcomers. An Indian hut did service as the first church in the colony and the whites made themselves at home in an Indian village, where they held open house for the tribesmen. One settler said:

Daily the poor souls are here in our houses and take content to be with us, bringing sometimes turkeys, sometimes squirrels as big as English rabbits, but much more dainty; at other times fine white cakes, partridges, oysters, ready boiled and stewed; and do run unto us with smiling countenance when they see us, and will fish and hunt for us, if we will; and all this with an intercourse of very few words, but we have hitherto gathered their meaning by signs.

True, it took a little time to become accustomed to the unprepossessing appearance of these benevolent savages. It was observed:

As for their faces, they have other colours at times, as blue from the nose upward, and red downward, and sometimes contrariwise in great variety and in very ghastly manner; sometimes have no beards till they come to be very old, and therefore draw from each side of their mouths lines to their very ears, to represent a beard; and this sometimes of one colour and sometimes of another[14].

Thus, by 1634, the most arduous part of the task of securing a footing upon the littoral of North America was over. Ahead lay the slow and laborious work of conquering and peopling the interior of the continent.

[14] Clayton Colman Hall (ed.), *Narratives of Early Maryland* (New York: Charles Schribner's Sons, 1910), pp. 29–43; 70–90.

Bibliography

Adams, James Truslow. *The Founding of New England*. Boston: Little, Brown and Co., 1927.

Andrews, Matthew Page. *The Soul of a Nation*. New York: Charles Scribner's Sons, 1943.

Bakeless, John. *The Eyes of Discovery*. Philadelphia: J. B. Lippincott Co., 1950.

Burrage, Henry S. *Early English and French Voyages 1534–1608. (Original Narratives of Early American History)* New York: Barnes and Noble, Inc., 1906.

Craven, Frank Wesley. *The Southern Colonies in the Seventeenth Century*. Baton Rouge: Louisiana State University Press, 1949.

Dorson, Richard M., editor. *America Begins*. New York: Pantheon Books, Inc., 1950.

Fleming, Thomas J. *One Small Candle*. New York: W. W. Norton, 1964.

Hatch, Charles E., Jr. *The First Seventeen Years*. Williamsburg: Colonial Williamsburg Press, 1957.

Marlowe, John. *The Puritan Tradition in English Life*. London: The Cresset Press, 1956.

Morgan, Edmund S. *The Founding of Massachusetts*. Indianapolis: Bobbs-Merrill Co., Inc., 1964.

Morison, Samuel Eliot. *The Story of the "Old Colony" of New Plymouth*. New York: Alfred Knopf, Inc., 1960.

Notestein. *The English People on the Eve of Colonization.* New York: Harper and Brothers, 1954.

Parry, J. H. *The Age of Reconnaissance: Discovery, Exploration, and Settlement 1450–1650.* Cleveland: World Publishing Co., 1963.

Smith, Bradford. *Captain John Smith.* Philadelphia: J. B. Lippincott Co., 1953.

Stannard, Mary Newton. *The Story of Virginia's First Century.* Philadelphia: J. B. Lippincott Co., 1928.

Strachey, William. *The Historie of Travell into Virginia Britania.* London: Hakluyt Society, 1953.

Willison, George F. *Saints and Strangers.* New York: Reynal and Hitchcock, 1945.

Young, Alexander. *Chronicles of the First Planters of the Colony of Massachusetts Bay.* Boston: Little, Brown and Co., 1846.

THE PURITAN WAY

THE Puritans exposed themselves to the casualties of the sea and to "famine and nakedness, . . . sore sickness and grievous diseases" in order to establish the kind of churches, government and social order that they believed God had ordained in the Bible. Their goal was absolute purity; to live without sin in a sinful world was to them the supreme challenge of life. They were derisively called "Puritans" because they sought to purify the Church of England of "the popish and antichristian stuff" with which they believed the simplicity of the primitive Christian church had been encrusted. But fleeing from the corruptions of the Old World was the least important part of their quest for righteousness: of far more consequence was the task they set themselves of erecting in the New World a "City Upon a Hill" that would serve as a model of the true church for all Christendom.

Thus, in the eyes of the Puritan leaders, the settlement of New England appeared to be the most significant act of human history since Christ bade farewell to His disciples. The City of God was about to be built upon earth and the Puritans intended to take up residence on the ground floor. An entire community living as God had directed men to live—this was the vision that impelled thousands of people to cross the Atlantic. It has fallen to the lot of few men to engage themselves in an enterprise where the stakes were so high and the reward so glorious.

To facilitate the accomplishment of this holy work, God had laid down in the Bible, the Puritans believed, full and explicit directions. The Puritans, it has been said, substituted an infallible book for an infallible pope; certainly they looked to the Bible for guidance in every phase of belief and conduct. Their Heavenly City was built according to the specifications they found in Holy Writ; they not only believed in the Bible, they believed in nothing but the Bible.

While Puritans internalized the struggle between good and evil—every man was a battleground between God and the Devil—Puritanism was also a way of life. To the question Why was man created?, the Puritans had a ready answer: man's only purpose was to glorify God on earth and, if he were especially fortunate, to continue the good work in Heaven.

For the Puritans, glorifying God meant concentrating one's whole being upon God, working diligently in one's "calling," and living by the strict moral code enjoined by the Bible. Life could not be separated into religious and secular activities: every act and thought was a glorification of God—or its opposite. Thus, working hard in one's "calling," as well as prayer, fasting, churchgoing and Bible-reading, was a form of homage to the Almighty. The important thing was to be mindful of God at all times: pride, complacency or mere gratification of the senses must not be permitted to usurp the place that belonged rightfully to the Almighty. When one enjoyed a pot of beer, a pipe of tobacco or took pretty Priscilla upon one's knee, it was essential to keep one's thoughts upon holy things.

So, when the Puritan shied from the delights of the senses, it was because he feared that they would divert his attention from the main business of life. Mere pleasure, including sport and recreation, tended to be regarded as snares of Satan. Nevertheless, the Puritans did not come to New England to mortify the flesh—in that respect, they received more than they had bargained for—for Puritanism was not a religion of asceticism. Austere by comparison with the roistering, sport-loving, hard-drinking Englishmen of this time, the Puritans aspired to live as well in other respects as did other middle-class Englishmen.

They did not necessarily identify Sin with the Flesh. Eating and drinking well, sexual indulgence within the bounds of matrimony, and enjoying the comforts of life were not proscribed in New England.

In actuality, the Puritans were waging war upon certain human propensities that they regarded as evils: covetousness, materialism, the love of ostentation, and concern with the externals of religion rather than with the things of the spirit. As a result, no Puritan could have conceived of the phrase "the pursuit of happiness." Theirs was the pursuit of godliness: the question they put to themselves was: "What can I do for God this day?" When they felt that they had fallen short of the standards set for them by the Almighty, they flagellated themselves remorselessly with introspective cross-examinations that usually took the form of "thoughts of eternal reprobation and torment." Engaged as they were in a struggle with Original Sin, Puritans could not afford to let down their guard for an instant.

A true Puritan was equipped with a built-in clock that insistently reminded him of the passage of time and the necessity of spending it profitably. Idleness was deemed a trap laid by the Old Deluder, but no Puritan worth his salt was taken in by that threadbare trick. The rule of life in New England was work and pray, and then work and pray some more. As the Reverend Cotton Mather said: "I tell you, with *Diligence,* a man may do marvellous things. Let your *Business* engross the most of your time."

In Puritan thinking, getting on in the world and getting to Heaven were not wholly dissimilar pursuits. Prospering in one's "calling" was accounted presumptive, but not conclusive, evidence of God's favor; in the Puritan scheme of things, property was distributed not by economic laws but by Divine Decree, and it was usually granted to those whose conduct was pleasing to Jehovah. Particularly if wealth were acquired through the exercise of hard work, thrift and sobriety, there was a strong presumption that the Almighty had a hand in it; but monopolizing, squeezing the poor, forestalling and extortion were condemned by the Puritan clergy. Moreover, a great deal depended upon what one did with one's money: if a rich man squandered his substance upon luxuries, frivolity and other forms of self-indulgence, he was, according to Puritan doctrine, courting God's displeasure. If, on the other hand, he lived frugally, opened his purse to the church and supported good works, his chances of being counted among the elect were excellent.

But the Puritans did not base their hopes of salvation upon material success. Particularly during the early period, they attached much more significance to the spiritual and intellectual qualities of man. John Winthrop died in the odor of sanctity that, to the Puritans, was far more important than the smell of money. The Puritan ideal was an enterprise where religion and profit went hand in hand. Until materialism gained the upper hand, the Puritans believed that the settlement of New England epitomized this happy conjunction of spiritual and material betterment.

In founding New England, the Puritans flattered themselves that God had sifted a whole nation in order to plant the choice seed in the wilderness. As John Winthrop said, the holy work in Massachusetts Bay required very different people from the kind that had settled Virginia: "unfitt instruments—a multitude of rude and misgoverned persons, the very scumm of the people." But, admittedly, the separation of the wheat from the chaff had not been so thorough as many Puritans desired. Some "profane and debauched persons" unaccountably filtered through the sieve. In 1635, the Reverend Nathaniel Ward said that "our thoughts and fears grow very sad to see such multitudes of idle and profane young men, servants and others, with whom we must leave our children, for whose sake and safety we came over." Some discouraged Puritans even contemplated leaving these unregenerates to their wicked ways in New England and seeking another refuge in the hope that a second winnowing would eliminate all undesirables.

Because the Calvinistic theology to which the Puritans

adhered emphasized the total depravity of man and his utter loathsomeness in the eyes of God, they did not suppose that every man was capable of rising to the level of thought and conduct demanded by the Almighty. In their opinion, only a minority of mankind was destined to be redeemed by Christ's sacrifice. Accordingly, they confined church membership and voting privileges—to the precious remnant of "visible Saints," "the Elect of God," who had received unequivocal assurances of salvation by means of a sanctifying spiritual rebirth. True, the bleak Calvinistic doctrine of predestination was softened by the Puritan belief in a covenant—the so-called Covenant of Grace—whereby each individual who executed his part of the bargain could claim salvation from God. But, in practice, comparatively few were able to give convincing evidence of their right to demand fulfillment of the terms of the contract. As a result, they were debarred from membership in the Congregational churches and, presumably, from Heaven. In 1641, the Reverend Thomas Shepard said that "the devil hath his drove and swarms to go to hell as fast as bees to their hives; Christ hath his flock, and that is but a little flock." In this competition, the Devil seemed to have much the better of it. Two-thirds of the population failed to qualify as church members.

In consequence, in the "City on a Hill" built by the New England Puritans, the mansions of the blessed where the "sons of God, of the blood royal," resided were in close proximity to a large spiritual slum where dwelt the majority of the people. These were the damned, living in a state of total depravity and consigned to everlasting torment by an incensed but just God. Nevertheless, they were not excused for that reason from living godly lives. Non-church members were required to conform in every particular to the moral code prescribed for the "Saints"; they, too, were obliged to glorify God even though their chances of meeting Him in the hereafter were very small. Accordingly, attendance at church was made compulsory for all. Regenerates and unregenerates sat together in the same meetinghouse, but the latter were not permitted to partake of the Communion nor to have their children baptized. In effect, therefore, the Massachusetts Puritans created two churches, one for the elect, the other for those outside the pale of salvation.

Besides listening to interminable sermons, the non-church members were subjected to the full force of the discipline administered by the clergy and the magistrates. This discipline took the form of "good and wholesome laws" rigorously executed. Puritan lawmakers compiled seemingly exhaustive lists of prohibited "carnall delights," such as attending plays, dancing round a Maypole, bowling on the green, playing at shuffleboard, quoits, dice and cards. The Selectmen of Boston refused to permit an exhibition of tight-rope walking "lest the said divertisement may tend to promote idleness in the town and great mispense of time, and, in 1681, a French dancing master was ordered out of town lest "profane and Promiscuous Dancing" corrupt the morals of the citizens. Acting upon the principle that "an hour's idleness is as bad as an hour's drunkenness," the Massachusetts General Court enacted laws against beachcombing and rebuked "unprofitable fowlers"—i.e., bad shots who wasted their time and powder on the birds. Even though fowling was his favorite recreation, Governor John Winthrop gave it up. But Winthrop was an uncommonly poor marksman and, being a good Puritan, he suffered a twinge of conscience whenever he missed the bird.

For a time, even tobacco was put under the ban. In early Massachusetts Bay, indulgence in the weed was restricted to a pipe after dinner; and in New Haven the authorities offered informers part of the fine assessed upon violators of the law:

It is ordered that no tobacco shall be taken in the streets, yards, or about the houses in any plantation or farm in this jurisdiction, or without doors near or about the town, or in the meeting-house, or body of the train soldiers, or any other places where they may do mischief thereby, under the penalty of six pence a pipe or a time, which is to go to him that informs and prosecutes; which, if refused, is to be recovered by distress; in which case, if there be difference, it may be issued without a court by any magistrate, or where there is no magistrate by any deputy or constable; but if he be a poor servant and hath not to pay, and his master will not pay for him, he shall then be punished by sitting in the stocks one hour.[1]

To the Puritans' way of thinking, there was a close connection between hair and holiness. The wearing by men of long hair ("long" was defined as covering the ears) was enough to bring an offender under suspicion of being a subversive. As evidence of God's displeasure with the custom, fashionable among dapper young Puritans, the Biblical passage was quoted: "God shall wound the hairy scalp of such a one as goes on still in his wickedness." In Boston, frequent visits to the barber were regarded as a form of insurance against Divine wrath.

Certainly there seemed to be no end of ways in which a Puritan could sin: swearing, Sabbath-breaking, sleeping during sermons, drinking in the taverns, sexual laxity, health-drinking, overdressing, etc. Wherever the Puritan turned, a sin was lying in wait for him—and someone was ready to nab him if he yielded to temptation. Even the amount of liquor consumed in a tavern was strictly regulated. In 1637, Boston had two taverns, a traveler reported,

into which, if a stranger went, he was presently followed by one appointed to that Office, who would thrust himself into his Company uninvited, and if he called for more drink than the Officer thought in his judgment he could soberly bear away, he would presently countermand it, and appoint the proportion, beyond which he could not get one drop.[2]

Even so, some of these sumptuary laws were repealed after a few years' trial or observed only in the breach. The Bible, for example, could not be cited authoritatively against the use of tobacco and even some of the clergy were

[1] J. Hammond Trumbull, *The True-Blue Laws of Connecticut and New Haven* (Hartford: American Publishing Company, 1876), p. 251.
[2] John Josselyn, *An Account of Two Voyages to New England* (Boston: William Veazie, 1915), pp. 132–33.

soon finding consolation in their pipes. Health-drinking was too deeply rooted in English custom to be exorcised by a law. As for gay apparel, John Winthrop noted that since "divers of the elders' wives being in some measure partners in this disorder," the law tended to become a dead letter—killed by the very people who were supposed to set an example to the less godly citizens.

Many of the acts punishable in New England as sinful, "carnall," and a waste of precious time were expressly permitted in England. The *Book of Sports,* issued by James I and reissued by Charles I, enumerated among the rights of Englishmen most of the recreations, with the exception of bear-baiting, condemned by the Puritans. Thus, in crossing the Atlantic, an Englishman forfeited, among other things, the freedom to spend his leisure as he pleased. On the other hand, he gained, according to the Puritans, the inestimable advantage of enjoying the company of the pure in spirit and of living according to God's Holy Ordinances.

These ordinances applied to the most minute details of daily life. The unrelenting scrutiny maintained by the civil and ecclesiastical authorities in Puritan New England made the controls imposed by Archbishop Laud—who figures in Puritan annals as a cruel and tyrannous prelate—seem mild by comparison. Moreover, the official inspection in New England was supplemented by the practice of neighbor's spying upon neighbor in order to ferret sin out of its most secret hiding places.

A Puritan could not be content with personal holiness; to feel secure, he had to enjoy the assurance that the whole community was as free of sin as he could make it. His ideal was a Bible Commonwealth "wherein the least known evils are not to be tolerated" and where not even a sinful thought could find lodgement. It was therefore incumbent upon every individual who walked with God to make sure that none of his neighbors got out of line. The consequence of neglecting this duty promised to be catastrophic: the transgressions of one individual, it was believed, endangered the success of the entire Puritan experiment. For not only were the sins of one generation visited upon the next generation, but the sin of one individual might be the cause of the downfall of the entire community. Provoked by the delinquency of one reprobate, the Almighty was believed to vent His wrath upon whole cities, nations, and even upon the world itself.

Since every disaster that befell New England was traced to some private or community dereliction, the Puritan scrutinized his own conscience and that of the members of his social group with almost equal anxiety. In Boston, there was no such thing as "snooping": it came under the heading of "doing the Lord's work." Every Puritan had been commissioned by God to be his brother's keeper, and his own salvation might depend upon how thoroughly he did the job.

This work of keeping conduct under the close surveillance of clergy, magistrates and self-righteous individuals was greatly facilitated by the New England town system. The Puritan leaders built their Wilderness Zion upon a foundation of compact settlements in which everyone lived within convenient reach of the church and the school. To the town system, therefore, was owing a large measure of the social and religious solidarity that distinguished colonial New England. Like-mindedness was the goal of the Founding Fathers of Puritanism, and they attained it not so much by persecution and repression as by the town system.

This system ensured that domestic privacy was almost unknown in seventeenth-century New England. The passion for running other peoples' lives was given free rein. Certain musical instruments were forbidden and even diet was regulated by law—and offenders transgressed at the peril of being reported by observant neighbors. Young unmarried men and women were not permitted to live alone or in pairs. Sixteen young men were arraigned before the selectmen of the town of Dorchester on the charge of not living with families; in 1652, the town of Windsor, Connecticut, gave permission to two young men to keep house together provided that they lived soberly and did not "entertain idle persons to the evil expense of time by day or night." Harboring strangers or even relatives was sometimes construed into a serious offense: single women, or wives whose husbands were away, could not entertain lodgers or overnight guests lest they give the "appearance of sin."

In New England towns, groups of ten families were put under the charge of a tithing man, who checked on how people were spending their time and made sure that everyone who could walk got to church on the Sabbath. When not engaged in these labors, he inspected taverns, alerted the selectmen to any disorderly conduct and warned undesirables to leave town. His duties did not end here: inside the meetinghouse he kept order by throwing out stray dogs, waking those who dozed during the sermon and rapping the knuckles of unruly children.

Under these circumstances, no New Englander could boast that his house was his castle. If he tried to stand on *that* principle he was certain to find himself in serious trouble with the authorities of both church and state.

No part of domestic life was excluded from the probing eye of the authorities of church and state. Quarreling or separated couples were brought into court where the marriage counseling usually took the form of a court order to stop bickering and live together in Christian charity —or take a turn in the stocks or pillory, or, in particularly stubborn cases, to suffer a sound whipping. If this method did not promote love between ill-assorted spouses, it at least kept the family intact, which to the Puritan leaders was the cardinal objective.

Much of the freedom and individualism traditionally associated with American life was conspicuously absent in Puritan New England. Highly individualistic in their approach to God, in their insistence upon private judgment and in their method of establishing churches by means of covenants subscribed to by the congregation, the Puritans nevertheless emphasized discipline, conformity and collective action in their daily lives. They were firm believers in group activity: they mobilized the whole community against sin and they sought to create a new Jerusalem by organized effort. The individual was subordinated to the group and to the cause; righteousness must prevail no matter how ruthlessly the individual was coerced.

Inevitably, from the point of view of some of those who stood outside the pale of church membership, the Puritan Establishment appeared in the guise of a repressive police state. Everyone was obliged to conform to a creed and obey a moral code; deviationists were classed as subversives and banished to the wilderness; and the powers of church and state were exercised by a minority that claimed the right to rule by virtue of superior godliness. The people were told that all this was in exact conformity to the will of God. Only the continued acceptance by the majority of the people of this assurance that they were indeed living in the City of God and that the rules laid down by the clergy and magistrates had the prior approval of Heaven sustained the Puritan church and state.

In the Puritan colonies and, indeed, everywhere in British America, the family was regarded as the cornerstone of the social order. Society was envisaged as an association of families rather than of individuals, and it was assumed that, unless these component parts were sound, the whole social structure would assuredly collapse. The Puritans acted upon the principle that religion, morality, deference to authority, and good conduct began in the home. In Puritan New England, the family was an instrument of church and state to aid in the promotion of piety, good order and orthodoxy in the community.

Accordingly, the government spared no effort to ensure that the family remained united and harmonious. To that end, the authority of the father was made well-nigh absolute. For the ideal was a patriarchy: as a husband and father, the American male never had it so good. Everyone knew that behind the figure of the father loomed the even more awesome presence of the magistrates and clergy, ready at all times to back up the exercise of his disciplinary powers. In consequence, the Puritan family was a model of piety and filial respect: every child and adult was exposed to family prayers at morning and night, family religious services and family reading of the Bible. Unremitting togetherness was an essential part of a Puritan upbringing.

Servants and apprentices were considered members of the family but black slaves were outside the pale. Besides children, the family often included grandparents and grandchildren, all living more or less cozily under the same roof. Immemorial custom decreed that grown sons and daughters should be responsible for the physical comfort of their aged or incapacitated parents—which meant, in most cases, that the old folks moved in with their children and spent their declining years in a household overflowing with their descendants. In such a family, the oldest male usually enjoyed patriarchal honors and authority. Even the most domineering females stood in awe of the old gentleman who ruled his domain from the chimney corner and who had only to call in the clergy and magistrates to put any and all of that sex, including mothers-in-law, in their place.

Family discipline was rigid and the father himself nipped in the bud all signs of incipient insubordination or delinquency. If he neglected to perform his parental duties, the town selectmen were ready to step in. If that occurred, the children were usually removed from their own home and placed in a household where no unruliness was permitted; often they were apprenticed to learn a useful trade in the home of some craftsman. In colonial New England, no child was permitted to grow up outside a God-fearing family that had been duly certified as pure and wholesome by the authorities of church and state.

I. THE CONNECTICUT VALLEY

The prevalence of orthodoxy in Massachusetts Bay was in part owing to the fact that neighboring colonies provided an outlet for discontent and potential opposition to the ruling powers. Those who found fault with Massachusetts Bay—some regarded it as too liberal while others complained of its repressive conservatism—could always try Rhode Island, New Hampshire, Maine, the Connecticut Valley, New Haven, Long Island and points south. Some of these places afforded better land and more religious freedom than did Massachusetts Bay, but the Connecticut Valley and New Haven offered a refuge not only to land-seekers but to straitlaced Puritans who found Boston and its environs too lax in their ways.

The Connecticut Valley, the first offspring of Massachusetts, was settled in 1636 by a group of Puritans led by the Reverend Thomas Hooker. While more fertile land was the principal magnet that drew these settlers to the Connecticut Valley—Hooker and his flock complained that Massachusetts was already overcrowded and that the best land had been preempted—there were also religious reasons behind this exodus. Hooker was alarmed by the religious discord he found in the Bay Colony and he resented the preeminence enjoyed by the Reverend John Cotton of Boston. Moreover, the Puritan urge for perfection compelled new experiments in godly living: never satisfied with what he had wrought, the Puritan always sought the absolute perfection that seemed to lie within the reach of those who followed God's Word implicitly.

Certainly the Reverend Thomas Hooker intended Connecticut to be an improvement upon Massachusetts Bay. The Fundamental Orders of Connecticut, a covenant agreed to in 1639 by the people of the towns of Windsor, Hartford and Wethersfield, created a system of church and state that bore a closer resemblance, in Hooker's eyes, to the wishes of the Almighty than anything yet attained in Boston. One of the principal differences between these two Bible Commonwealths was that, in Connecticut, all freemen, regardless of whether they were church members, were admitted to the suffrage. Yet only the most orthodox were made welcome in Connecticut. By exacting an oath of fealty from each citizen and requiring a certificate of good behavior and the approval of three magistrates from every prospective resident, the colony was in effect closed to all who questioned the superior wisdom of the ruling elders, magistrates and ministers. "The choice of public magistrates belongs unto the people," Hooker said. "But," he added, "this privilege of election must not be exercised according to their humours but according to the blessed will and law of God." During the colonial period, that will and law were generally interpreted by the Congregational clergy to whom the magistrates looked for counsel and guidance.

After the first rush of settlers in the 1630's and '40's, comparatively few newcomers entered the colony. Nevertheless, so rapid was the increase in population that the Connecticut Valley settlements soon began to expand southward and, before the middle of the seventeenth century, had begun to undermine the position of the Dutch in New Netherlands. Wall Street was built by the Dutch to protect themselves against the Indians and New Englanders, but when the English fleet compelled the surrender of New Netherlands in 1664, the defenses of the colony had already been seriously undermined by the presence of thousands of New England Puritans.

Without a sizable seaport and therefore without much contact with the outside world, Connecticut became one of the most insular and decentralized of the American colonies—a land of steady habits, orthodox religion and traditional ways of voting, where unsettling ideas rarely disturbed the placidity of life. The people lived largely unto themselves and submitted willingly to the rule of their pastors and magistrates. Governors were elected annually, but once installed in office they served until senility or death put a period to their careers. In Connecticut people not only acted alike—they thought alike. Conformity was one of the distinguishing characteristics of the Connecticut Yankee: much as he liked to tinker and experiment with gadgets, he was content to leave church and state alone. For the man who wanted a quiet life, a modest competence, the feeling of belonging to a close-knit society, and who did not miss the kind of intellectual stimulation that comes from the expression of differences of opinion, Connecticut was a bit of heaven upon earth.

II. NEW HAVEN

To an even greater degree than did the Connecticut Valley towns, New Haven represented an effort to achieve a higher degree of purity of life and worship than prevailed in Boston. After spending a year in the Puritan metropolis, the Reverend John Davenport concluded that it was a City of the Plain, a scene of laxity, corruption and dissension. In 1638, bent upon establishing a truly apostolic church and society, Davenport and his congregation left Boston for New Haven. Here Davenport proposed to reveal the inadequacies of Boston by requiring a "full and exact conformity to heavenly rules and patternes." It was not the last time that New Haven undertook to point out the road to godliness to Boston: Yale College was founded to show the way to Harvard.

To Davenport's way of thinking, the pattern laid up in Heaven for earthly government was a theocracy: the rule of the Elect of God, acting under Divine authority. "The word of God," said Davenport, "shall be the onely rule to be attended into in ordering affayres of government in this plantation." Accordingly, he insisted that magistrates should be godlike men dedicated to the service of Christ and versed in the "heavenly rules," and prepared in all doubtful cases to seek the advice of the clergy. Then would be established the Ordinances of God in their utmost purity and men would have the ineffable satisfaction of knowing that they were being ruled "according to His owne minde, in all things."

The attainment of this earthly paradise required, among other things, the restriction of church membership (and voting privileges) to an even narrower and more select group and the exercise of greater power over the civil government by the clergy than the Massachusetts way ordained. In New Haven, the lines between elect and unregenerate were so sharply drawn that the possibility that the latter were in league with the Devil could not wholly be dismissed. Likewise, the zeal and efficiency exhibited by the New Haven theocracy in ferreting out heretics set an edifying example to all Puritan communities. When the first schoolmaster at New Haven had the temerity to disagree with Davenport, he was called before the congregation, censured, and "cast out of the body, till the proud flesh be destroyed and he be brought into a more memberlike frame." Those found guilty of traducing the ministers were whipped, branded, fined and banished. To hinder the reprobate from writing, he was branded upon his right hand. The first to win their letter at New Haven were those who were branded with the letter "H" for "heretic."

New Haven was the only Puritan colony to abolish trial by jury. This departure from the practice the settlers had brought with them from England was necessitated by the shortage of church members, the only citizens qualified for jury service. In many of the settlements that clustered around the town of New Haven there were not enough church members from which to impanel a jury.

Under the Reverend John Davenport, the Puritan ideal of a Bible Commonwealth reached its apogee. All Puritans agreed that the Scriptures contained a perfect rule for the ordering of all the affairs of church and state, family and individual alike, but no Puritan community applied this principle as literally as did the New Haven theocrats. Insofar as possible, the laws of New Haven were derived directly from the Bible.

Such a system of law was already at hand. In 1636, the Reverend John Cotton, a man of such consummate erudition that it was said that God would not permit him to be wrong, had drawn up a code of laws for Massachusetts. The provisions of this code regarding crimes and inheritances were biblical in origin and each law was annotated with marginal references to the Scriptures to prove that it was in harmony with the Word of God. Cotton's handiwork—usually known as "Moses his Judicialls" —was not adopted by Massachusetts but in 1639 the New Haven settlers appropriated the Cotton Code in its entirety and it served as the fundamental law of that colony until it was merged with Connecticut.

The so-called Connecticut Blue Laws, an elaboration of "Moses his Judicialls," were enacted by the Saints of New Haven in 1656. The Blue Laws prescribed the death penalty for blasphemy, idolatry, witchcraft, murder, false worship, incest, adultery, sodomy, bestiality, man stealing, giving false witness, reviling the magistrates, and the cursing or smiting of parents by children over sixteen years of age. Bibliolatry could scarcely be carried further: even the standard measurements for beer casks was determined by reference to Deuteronomy.

The law decreeing death for "a stubborn and rebellious son" was designed not only to punish the offender but that "others may hear and fear." In New Jersey, where Puritan influence was strong, a similar law was enacted. The Scotch Presbyterians, even more thorough-going in their Calvinism than the New England Puritans, went beyond them by providing, in 1661 that any

sonne or *daughter* above and of sixteen years not being distrated [demented] who shall beate or curse their father or mother shall be put to death without mercy.

These laws have helped fix the image of the Puritan as a blue-nosed, nasty-minded hypocrite and they give credence to the story that as soon as a New England child was able to master words of five syllables he or she was taught to spell "for-ni-ca-ti-on." Granted the Puritans' obsessive concern with sin, the Blue Laws do not prove that the New Havenites were particularly bloodthirsty. In England, during the reign of James I, 31 offenses were punishable by death whereas New Haven had only 14 capital crimes. Even so, those who did not walk the straight and narrow way were well advised to give New Haven a wide berth.

III. RHODE ISLAND

To the Puritan mind, the two most important things about religion were "the purity and the unity thereof." They did not traverse the Atlantic to establish the principle of religious freedom: they sought freedom only for themselves. In their Zion there was no place for a Tower of Babel where all creeds and opinions might be heard. Among a group as deeply committed as were the Puritans to a Heaven-directed mission to the wilderness, rampant individualism could not be tolerated. Moreover, frontier conditions always put a high premium upon social solidarity and group effort.

In theory, New England Puritanism was a monolithic creed that admitted of no dissent. Based upon immutable truths derived from the Word of God, the Puritan church-state and communal way of life were regarded as the ultimate in holiness. The Reverend John Cotton declared that Jesus Christ would approve of all the arrangements in Boston, and John Winthrop, surveying the wonders wrought by the Almighty in New England, exclaimed that he desired no more till he arrived in Heaven.

Imbued with the conviction that there was One Truth just as there was One God, the Puritans pursued unremittingly their ideal of uniformity of thought and conduct. In Connecticut, Massachusetts Bay and New Haven they achieved a large measure of success. Rhode Island, however, went its own way—and in almost every respect its direction was opposite to that followed by the rest of New England.

And yet, Rhode Island was founded by a Puritan. Roger Williams exemplified the aspects of Puritanism that were suppressed elsewhere in New England: extreme individualism, democracy, the complete separation of church and state, and the endless splintering process that always threatened to convert the Puritan movement into a chaos of competing sects. Like Governor John Winthrop and the Reverend John Cotton, his principal adversaries, Roger Williams resolved all questions by reference to the Bible, he was orthodox in his conception of the Trinity, and he accepted the doctrines of predestination, the depravity of man, and infant damnation. He believed that all his acts were approved by "the greatest and wisest politician that ever was, the Lord Jesus Christ," and he regarded the establishment of the Kingdom of God on earth as the main purpose of human existence. In Providence, Rhode Island, he tried to establish a community dedicated, like that of Massachusetts Bay, to fostering the community of the Saints. His methods, not his objectives, differed from those who condemned him to exile.

Williams's insistence upon religious freedom—the point wherein he departed most radically from the practice of Massachusetts Bay—proceeded originally from his conviction that the Visible Saints, whom he regarded as the happy few of the community, must be preserved from the contamination of the unregenerate majority. To his way of thinking, this end could be achieved only by keeping the civil government wholly out of the affairs of the church and by rigorously segregating the elect from the unregenerate mass of the people. By compelling church attendance and outward religious uniformity, the state, in Williams's opinion, produced a "racking and tormenting of souls" and filled the Church with hypocrites. The Massachusetts Bay Puritans, on the other hand, assumed that the regenerate minority could be preserved from pollution only by forcing church attendance and taxation for religious purposes upon every member of the community and by using the power of the civil government to punish heresy.

After his banishment to Rhode Island in 1636, Williams underwent a complete change of mind upon several of the issues that had brought him into trouble in the Bay Colony. Whereas in his earlier quest for purity he had separated himself from his congregation and, for a time, even from his wife, and had restricted church members to a handful of Visible Saints, he now threw open the doors to all Christians. In Rhode Island, he preached to and prayed with everyone who came to him. From the most rigidly exclusive of the New England Puritans, he became the most liberal and inclusive. He decided that there were many paths to Heaven and that every man must be free to choose his own way. Until such time as truth should be made manifest by further revelations, he demanded "a Liberty of searching after God's most holy mind and pleasure." At one time, he declared himself to be a Baptist but no organized church could long contain his Heaven-oriented spirit. Eventually he dissociated himself from all churches and became a "Seeker."

To one principle, however, he consistently adhered: church and state must be wholly separate and the state must not be permitted to exercise any kind of spiritual authority over the individual. In Rhode Island, as long as Roger Williams's influence endured, the power of magistrates was limited to matters concerning "the Bodies and Goods and outward state of men." The doctrine of the separation of church and state owes more to Roger Williams than to the Massachusetts Bay Puritans.

Despite his uncomfortable proximity to Boston, Roger Williams made Rhode Island a bastion of religious freedom. Jews, Roman Catholics and Turks, he declared, were welcome in Providence. Nor did he draw the line at Indians: "Nature knows no difference," he said, "God having of one blood made all mankind." He was equally liberal as regards the suffrage. Although he did not value political liberty as an end in itself, he advocated democracy for the same reason that he became a Seeker—because only in a free society could men truly seek God. To this end, he

established manhood suffrage and made office-holding the
prerogative of all citizens. In 1647, the Rhode Island Assembly declared:

The form of government established in Providence Plantations is Democratical, that is to say, a government held by the
free and voluntary consent of all, or the greater part of the free
inhabitants.

Rhode Island became the most democratic of all English
colonies founded in the seventeenth century; indeed, in the
nineteenth century some American states were less democratic than Rhode Island had been under Roger Williams.

Williams supposed that religious and political freedom,
restrained by the sober good sense of the people, would
produce an orderly society. But Rhode Island attracted
religious eccentrics in whom sober good sense and love of
order were conspicuously absent. Dreamers of Utopia
and founders of new religions abounded and few of the
prophets and prophetesses lacked for converts. Samuel
Gorton, for example, preached a doctrine of mystical
union between Christ and the regenerate soul, and he
stoutly maintained that his opinions were not his own but
came directly from the Holy Ghost. Unfortunately, the
message was too garbled to get through to any but Gorton
and his disciples; as one of them said, the master's books
were "written in Heaven, and no one could read and understand them unless he was in Heaven."

In contrast to the uniformity that prevailed in Massachusetts Bay, Connecticut and New Haven, the colony
founded by Roger Williams resembled a crazy quilt of
strange sects, many of which were persecuted everywhere
except in Rhode Island. Some of the local Messiahs made
Roger Williams appear orthodox and old-fashioned by
comparison. In the end, the anarchy that made Rhode Island a byword in other colonies proved too much for
Williams himself. Like many other revolutionaries, he was
dismayed by what he had wrought. "We have long drunk
of the cup of great liberties," he said in 1653, "as any
people that we can hear of under the whole heaven" but

experience had taught him that "these freedoms have made men wanton and forgetful, and it may be that though we enjoy liberties of soul and body, it is license we desire." In 1669, 14 years before his death, he remarked that his brain was "worn and withered" as a result of 30 years of struggling with a stubborn and misguided people.

After Roger Williams's death, Rhode Island settled down to more orderly—and less democratic—ways. Property qualifications for voting and office-holding were gradually increased. The Quakers, Jews and Baptists who had found refuge in Rhode Island imposed their own brand of uniformity upon their communicants. Protestantism, the dominant faith, took advantage of its position in the Rhode Island Assembly to disfranchise Roman Catholics and debar Jews from holding public office. As Williams had feared, the trinity of "Profit, Preferment, Pleasure" established its dominion, and land became an object of veneration. And, during the eighteenth century, Rhode Island merchants became deeply involved in the slave trade while domestic slavery provided the labor force for the cattle, dairying and horse-raising industries of the Narragansett planters.

Even so, the diversity of religions that characterized Rhode Island—some even arrived at the ultimate terminus of individualism, a church of one member—ensured the perpetuation of religious freedom. With the colony divided into a multitude of sects, it was impossible for any one denomination to gain unquestioned dominance. Rhode Island was one of the last places on the American continent where the ideal of religious uniformity could gain lodgement.

Throughout the colonial period, Rhode Island remained decentralized, hostile to a state-supported church, and jealous of local rights. Until 1647, each town went its own way, and even after a central government had been established, the exercise of its authority depended upon the cooperation of the towns. Long after the American Revolution, Rhode Islanders preserved the suspicion of outside authority derived from their early experience as an "outcast people" constantly threatened with invasion by their powerful neighbors.

Bibliography

Benton, Josiah H. *Warning Out in New England.* Boston: W. B. Clarke Co., 1911.

Greene, Evarts B. *Religion and the State.* New York: New York University Press, 1941.

Miller, Perry. *Errand into the Wilderness.* New York: Harper Torchbooks, 1964.

———. *Orthodoxy in Massachusetts.* Cambridge, Mass.: Harvard University Press, 1933.

———. *Roger Williams: His Contribution to the American Tradition.* New York: Atheneum Press, 1962.

Morgan, Edmund S. *The Puritan Dilemma.* Boston: Little, Brown & Co., 1958.

———. *The Puritan Family.* Boston: Trustees of the Public Library, 1941.

Morison, Samuel Eliot. *The Intellectual Life of Colonial New England.* New York: New York University Press, 1956.

Paige, L. R. *History of Cambridge, Massachusetts, 1630–1877.* Boston: H. O. Houghton & Co., 1877.

Powell, Sumner Chilton. *Puritan Village; the Formation of a New England Town.* New York: Doubleday & Co., 1965.

Simpson, Alan. *Puritanism in Old and New England.* Chicago: University of Chicago Press, 1955.

Wertenbaker, T. J. *The First Americans.* New York: Macmillan Co., 1927.

Winslow, D. Kenelm. *Mayflower Heritage.* London, 1957.

THE QUAKER WAY

THE ideal of returning to the pristine purity of apostolic Christianity—one of the strongest incentives for the proliferation of new sects in the seventeenth century—played an important part in the founding of eight English colonies in North America: Plymouth, Massachusetts Bay, Connecticut, New Haven, Rhode Island, New Jersey, Delaware, and Pennsylvania. In this effort, Puritans took the lead, but the Quakers (more properly, the Society of Friends), even though they started later, succeeded in establishing three colonies and extending their influence over several others, particularly Rhode Island, where, in the 1670's, a Quaker was elected governor. By the Friends' reckoning, true primitive Christianity was to be found in New Jersey, Delaware, Pennsylvania, Rhode Island and nowhere else—certainly not in Massachusetts Bay or any other Puritan stronghold.

Quakerism was one of the 175 or more sects that emerged from the underworld of Christianity—the region of the poor and disinherited—during the period of the Civil War in England. Most of these sects vanished without leaving a trace, but Quakerism, owing mainly to the proselytizing fervor of its founder, George Fox, who proclaimed "a golden age at hand, under the name of Christ and the saints," survived as a small, downtrodden religious society composed chiefly of craftsmen, cobblers, weavers and tenant farmers "impoverished by long troubles."

In 1646, after having experienced a personal revelation, George Fox began to preach a mystical form of Puritanism. He taught that revelation was a continuing process and that God still spoke to men as He had spoken to the prophets of old. In every man and woman, Fox asserted, gleamed an "inner light"—a spark of divinity that irradiated the soul and made possible direct contact with the Almighty without the necessity of the mediation of priest, clergyman or sacrament. Fox believed that this indwelling spirit of God was present in all human beings, including heathens. "God," he said, "through Christ, hath placed a principle in every man to inform him of his duty, and to enable him to do it." Here was the priesthood of all believers that the Puritans, together with other Protestant sects, had preached but had stopped short of applying in actual practice.

Whereas the New England Puritans usually conceived of the "new birth" as a slow, harrowing process requiring ceaseless self-scrutiny, intensive study of the Bible and striving for righteousness, George Fox and his followers waited in simplicity and purity of heart for a sudden flash that signalized the presence of the Holy Spirit. Fox assumed that the existence of God must be experienced before He could be known and that religion was wholly a thing of the heart rather than of the mind. The intellectual kind of religion favored by the Puritans seemed to Fox to lead away from God. Even so, he did not break with the authority of the Bible: in his special revelations Fox did not claim that the Holy Spirit had disclosed anything to him that could not be found in the Bible but he did insist that many things contained in the Bible had been revealed to him independently. Finally, while the Puritans doted on the Old Testament and the Jehovah who had ruled over Israel, Fox gave more emphasis to the New Testament and the example and teachings of Jesus Christ.

The first generation of Quakers were not simply inoffensive, pacifically inclined Christians who used "thee" and "thou" and asked nothing more than to be permitted to worship God in their own way. While demanding tolerance for themselves, they refused to admit the legitimacy of any established church. Against such an institution, the Quakers exhibited a fervor worthy of the early martyrs: they testified against its authority by ceaseless agitation, by holding its clergy up to scorn, by practicing civil disobedience, and by asserting their claim to be guided by the Holy Spirit. Relying upon the "inner light," they decried education, a learned ministry, tithes, and the observance of Christian holidays.

Toward the civil authorities they were equally uncompromising: they refused to observe the conventional marks of respect for rank, such as removing their hats and using titles; and they would not pay taxes for purposes they considered un-Christian or take oaths required by the state.

As a result, the Quakers were treated as lower-class revolutionaries bent upon overturning church and state. When their meetinghouses were closed by the authorities and they were proscribed by Parliament as "a dangerous and mischievous people," they refused to go underground; instead, they met in private houses or openly in the fields, even though they thereby made themselves liable to arrest. Once in the hands of the law, because they refused to pay fines or to violate their creed of nonresistance, they rarely escaped imprisonment. Not surprisingly, therefore, Quakers constituted a considerable part of the prison population of Great Britain. George Fox was jailed on eight different occasions and spent a total of six years behind bars. William Penn was confined in Newgate for more than two years. Between 1660 and 1685 over 8,000 Friends were held in prison on various charges, principally unlawful assembly. Of this number, at least 400 died in durance that might, without exaggeration, be called "vile."

Before the founding of New Jersey (originally called West and East Jersey) and Pennsylvania, the Quakers found every continental English colony except Rhode Island closed to them and almost every man's hand raised against them. Although Virginia did not put any Quakers to death, the laws against them were severe and rigorously enforced. In 1660, for example, two Quakers were pilloried, given 32 lashes with a corded whip, and expelled; and any shipmaster bringing Quakers into the colony was fined 100 pounds. It was not until 1699 that Quaker meetings were permitted in the Old Dominion.

Virginia was spared more serious trouble from Quakers

because they did not feel nearly so strong a compulsion to "testify" against sin and iniquity in Virginia as in Puritan New England. Boston became the main target of their missionary zeal, largely because the Puritans' claim to superior sanctity as "God's People" conflicted with the Quakers' conviction that *they* alone, as "children of light" and "friends of truth," occupied that exalted place.

As a result, in Puritan New England, two religious faiths, each claiming to be the emblem of true apostolic Christianity and each imbued with the belief that it enjoyed special standing in Heaven, came into conflict. The resulting concussion was that of one infallible revelation meeting another infallible revelation. Actually, the Puritans and the Quakers had more in common than either side cared to admit, but their similarities merely exacerbated the conflict.

The New England Puritans asked only to be left alone in their Wilderness Zion. They posted "No Trespassing" signs for the benefit of every dissenting religious denomination, and they whipped, scourged and banished all intruders, particularly Baptists. But the more uncomfortable New England became for non-Puritans, the more attractive it appeared to Quakers in search of martyrdom. From staging areas in Barbadoes and Rhode Island they descended upon the New Jerusalem prepared to do or die for the Lord.

For the Quakers, testifying against sin in New England took the form of bursting into meetinghouses and denouncing the minister, breaking empty bottles in church to symbolize the lack of spiritual content in the sermon and, it was alleged, stirring up discontent among the servants and other disfranchised groups. Several Quaker women were impelled to walk naked through the streets to illustrate their point that the land was naked.

Prone to see the Devil's handiwork in every misadventure that befell them, the Puritan leaders declared that the country was being invaded by an "accursed and pernicious sect of hereticks" and took measures to protect themselves in much the same spirit and with the same weapons that they later employed against witches. The Reverend Increase

Mather, an authority on demonology, warned that the Quakers were under "the strong delusions of Satan" and that therefore Christians should "dread to come among such creatures, lest haply the righteous God suffer Satan to take possession of them also." Accordingly, in 1656, the bodies of two Quaker women were searched for telltale signs of witchcraft. Although the charge could not be made to stick, the two women were banished from the colony.

As the number of these unwelcome visitants increased, so did the severity of the punishment inflicted upon them. Quakers were branded, whipped from town to town and driven from the colony; if they returned and were convicted of heresy for the third time they were ordered to have their tongues bore through with a red-hot iron. The Puritan authorities tried to sell the children of Quakers to the sugar plantations in the West Indies but the plan fell through because no shipmaster would take them aboard. Any person found in possession of a book containing the "develish opinions" of the Quakers was fined, and to speak in favor of them or their beliefs was made punishable by fine, imprisonment and banishment. Finally, in 1658, acting upon the Biblical injunction, "If thy brother entice thee to serve other gods, thou shall surely put him to death," the New England Confederation recommended that any Quaker who returned to New England after having been banished should be executed.

So eager was the Reverend John Wilson of Boston to begin the work of purifying the land that he said he would gladly "carry fire in one hand and faggots in the other, to burn all the Quakers in the world." Yet nothing stopped the Quakers: joyously they sought martyrdom at the hands of the Puritans. The pertinacity with which the Quakers offered themselves for sacrifice was matched by the ruthlessness of the Puritans in removing these "pests" from the world. By 1661, six Friends, including one woman, had been sent to the gallows and many more were awaiting trial. Governor Endicott was prepared to carry on to the last Quaker; in his opinion, the Quakers were persecuting the Puritans by intruding upon their privacy.

As for liberty, Endicott pointed out that the Quakers had the liberty to stay away from Massachusetts. He said:

The Quakers died not because of their other Crimes, how capital soever, but upon their superadded presumptuous and incorrigible contempt of authority. . . . They would not be restrained but by Death.

At this juncture, in response to the Quakers' pleas, Charles II intervened in their behalf by ordering all future trials of Quakers to be transferred to England. Even though Charles persecuted Quakers in England by fines, imprisonment and deportation to the plantations, he disapproved of New Englanders' methods of disposing of the Quaker menace, particularly since they acted without royal authority. Because the Quakers suffered more spectacularly in New than in Old England, Boston, in the annals of the Society of Friends, figures as the "bloody town" despite the fact that far more members of the Society perished in English prisons than died on the gallows in the Puritan metropolis.

The clergy and magistrates of Massachusetts Bay were no respecters of the ordinances of an English king, especially when those ordinances seemed to conflict with a clear directive from the Bible. Nevertheless, in the case of the Quakers, they yielded, not so much, however, to royal authority as to public opinion at home. For it had become plain that the people had had enough of killing, particularly when for every Quaker that fell two took his place. One man, Wenlock Christian, under sentence of death as a heretic, had to be reprieved because of the unexpected squeamishness shown by the public toward taking human life.

Although Quakers continued to be whipped in many parts of Massachusetts, after 1674 they were permitted to live peaceably in Boston provided that they, like all other citizens of Massachusetts, paid taxes for the support of the Congregational churches. By this time, many Puritans had begun to feel the force of the truism that their own experience ought to have taught them—persecution merely redoubles the zeal of those who believe that they act under divine inspiration. "I am verily persuaded," said the Reverend Cotton Mather, "these miserable Quakers would in a little while (as we have now seen) have come to nothing, if the civil magistrate had not inflicted any civil penalty upon them." It had proved impossible to seal off Massachusetts from all outside contagion, and the royal charter of 1691 deprived the Congregational churches of some of their most jeaously-guarded privileges.

For the Quakers, the finding of a refuge against oppression was far more urgent than it had been for the English Puritans in the 1630's. Yet in establishing West Jersey, Delaware and Pennsylvania, William Penn did not think solely of his unfortunate co-religionists; while admitting that the plight of the Friends was uppermost in his mind, the scope of his idealism embraced all mankind. The Quaker colonies in the New World offered refuge to all those persecuted for cause of conscience and other "plain and well intending people."

While William Penn's ultimate objective was similar to that of the New England Puritans—in Pennsylvania he hoped to reproduce true primitive Christianity—he chose a very different route to the millennium from that taken by John Winthrop and the Reverend John Cotton. Penn's "Holy Experiment" was an effort to create an orderly, harmonious and righteous Christian society without an established church and without a secular government empowered to compel conformity to any creed. He assumed that the essence of Christianity was so simple, plain and unmistakable, and could be apprehended so readily with the aid of the "inner light," that there was no need of coercion: true Christianity throve in freedom but perished when force was brought to bear upon men's consciences. The acceptance of religious diversity as an inevitable by-product of religious freedom was the way to "the happy life of concord."

Once this principle had been accepted, Penn expected that an awareness of the indwelling spirit of God would permeate every aspect of life, including the government.

Penn therefore did not hesitate to promise settlers in the Quaker colonies the full measure of civil liberty—a representative assembly and all other "rights of Englishmen." He said:

> Let men be good, and the government cannot be bad; if it be ill, they will cure it. But if men be bad, let the government be never so good, they will endeavour to warp and spoil it to their turn.

While "Soul Liberty" supplied the principal key with which Penn proposed to unlock the door of Heaven upon Earth, he recognized the necessity of providing for the more mundane necessities of life. To that end, he offered land to all comers on easy terms—contingent, however, upon the payment of a quit rent in perpetuity to himself and his heirs. In these respects, Penn's vision of the good life was similar to that of Thomas Jefferson's: political and religious liberty combined with economic security based upon land ownership. Penn devoted much of his capital and energy to creating the conditions in which this life could be led.

Voltaire once said that "were there but one religion in England, its despotism would be fearful; were there but two, they would cut each other's throats; but there are thirty, and they live in peace and happiness." If the diversity and multiplicity of religious sects made for religious freedom, Pennsylvania was a far better example than was England. For in the Quaker colony, Roman Catholics, Jews and representatives of almost every Protestant sect took advantage of Penn's invitation to enjoy the blessings of religious freedom and cheap land. As early as 1690, the household of Daniel Pastorious, the founder of Germantown, consisted of Lutherans, Presbyterians, Anglicans, Anabaptists, Roman Catholics and one Quaker. "Africa never more abounded with New Monsters," exclaimed a clergymen of the Church of England, "than Pennsylvania does with New Sects." Despite the fact that, by 1750, there were more Quakers in Pennsylvania than in all of Great Britain, they were a minority group in Pennsylvania.

Much of this religious diversity was owing to the heavy immigration from Germany that occurred in the eighteenth century. Religious persecution and economic privation in Germany, together with Penn's skilful advertising of the felicity awaiting settlers in Pennsylvania, led large numbers of Lutherans, Dunkers, Moravians, Pietists and Schwenkfelders to seek land and religious liberty in the Quaker colony. Many of these sects held pacifistic and quietistic views closely akin to those of the Quakers. Unlike the Friends, however, some sought to attain purity by withdrawing from the world.

The first true religious communities in America were the work of these German sectarians. Conrad Beissel, a Dunker, gathered together the Ephrata Community where the members, renouncing the flesh and holding marriage to be unclean, lived as brothers and sisters. The Moravians founded Bethlehem on a semicommunistic basis. Although personal property was permitted, members were required to labor upon the communal lands.

Although the early Quakers often trembled, shouted and quaked under the stress of the Spirit, by the beginning of the eighteenth century, these physical manifestations had subsided into "Quaker silence." Increasingly, Quakers tended to regard the inner light as a gradual and progressive heightening of awareness of the Creator and His goodness rather than a sudden illumination. Thus the Friends adopted the position of the seventeenth century Puritans, whom they had once condemned.

Potentially, the Quaker doctrine of the inner light was even more destructive of a hierarchical, organized church than was the Puritans' belief in the autonomy of each congregation and the right of every man to read the Bible and to follow the dictates of his conscience. But the Society of Friends was saved from dissolution by the countervailing principle that decreed that the collective inspiration of the meeting was superior to the inspiration of any individual and by the Quakers' emphasis upon group activity. From the beginning, Quakerism was based upon the principle of mutual aid and brotherhood; as a result, the Society never failed to take care of its own poor and unfortunates, and special committees and associations were organized for such benevolent purposes as aiding the Indians and Negro slaves. Nor did the Quakers wholly dispense with churchly organization: monthly, quarterly and yearly meetings of the Society were held, presided over by Elders and Overseers. Each of these meetings represented a progressively larger area, culminating in the yearly gathering in which the whole country was represented. Moreover, as a result of their custom of traveling throughout the country, the Quakers not only extended the geographical boundaries of the faith but also made its practices more uniform.

Insofar as the outward life of the people was concerned, the moral code of Pennsylvania would have satisfied even the most straight-laced Puritan. There was a strong Puritan strain in William Penn—indeed, the Puritans and the Quakers were in closer agreement upon what constituted a truly Christian life than either side cared to admit. Despite his devotion to "Soul Liberty," Penn had no more intention than had John Winthrop of permitting people to do as they pleased. In his first *Frame of Government*, Penn recommended that cards, dice, May games, masques, revels, bull-baiting, cock-fighting, bear-baiting and stage plays be prohibited. For Penn, as for the Puritans, the Bible was an infallible touchstone in these and all other matters. Penn asked rhetorically:

How many plays did Jesus Christ and his apostles recreate themselves at? How many pieces of riband, and what feathers, lacebands, and the like did Adam and Eve wear in paradise, or out of it?

The Quakers stopped short of reverting entirely to a state of nature but the Pennsylvania Assembly did enact Penn's wishes regarding sports and finery in dress and provided fines and imprisonment for violators. In this quest for holiness, the Pennsylvania Quakers so flagrantly violated the Rights of Englishmen that the English government finally stepped in. In 1709, the Pennsylvania Blue Laws were disallowed by the Privy Council in London on the ground that they restrained "her Majesty's Subjects from Innocent Sports and Diversions."

But the abrogation of their laws by the British government did not cause the Quakers to relax their vigilance against sin. Constant surveillance over family and private life was the rule in Philadelphia as it was in Boston. Since William Penn and his followers believed that the inner light enabled every man to distinguish between right and wrong, there was less excuse for misconduct in Pennsylvania than in the Puritan colonies, where the depravity of human nature was accepted as one of the irrefutable facts of life.

Bibliography

Adams, Brooks. *The Emancipation of Massachusetts.* Boston: Houghton Mifflin Co. 1962.

Covey, Cylcone. *The American Pilgrimage.* Stillwater, Okla.: Oklahoma State University Press, 1960.

Etten, Harry van. *George Fox and the Quakers.* New York: Harper Torchbooks, 1959.

Rothermund, Dietmar. *The Layman's Progress.* Philadelphia: University of Pennsylvania Press, 1961.

Tolles, Frederick B. *Meeting House and Counting House; the Quaker Merchants of Colonial Philadelphia.* Chapel Hill, N. C.: University of North Carolina Press, 1948.

SPORTS AND RECREATIONS

BETWEEN the Puritans, Pietists, Quakers, Presbyterians, Baptists and the other religious groups that regarded most of the normal diversions of Englishmen as shameful, immoral and a waste of precious time, there was little chance for sports and recreation in colonial America. And, indeed, Elizabethan music, games, rural festivals and dances did not flourish in the American environment. The village culture of Old England could not be successfully transplanted to the dispersed farms and plantations of the South; and in New England, where village life existed, the Puritans would not permit the recreational side of this culture to gain a foothold.

Moreover, most people came to the English colonies to acquire land, pursue a trade or practice a particular kind of religion. Consequently they had little time or inclination for fun and games. Secondly, the conditions of life imposed by the frontier—and during the seventeenth century most of the Atlantic seaboard fell within this category—militated against recreation and leisure. True, the early Virginians spent a good deal of their time bowling on the green and roistering in the tavern at Jamestown when they ought to have been tilling the fields and building houses, but their fate was not calculated to encourage other Americans to follow their example. Finally, when, as a result of hard work and thrift, Americans were finally in a position to relax from their labors, along came Benjamin Franklin to remind them insistently that "time is money."

The Puritans carried their aversion to pagan holidays and merrymaking in general to include Christmas, Good Friday and Easter. In 1644, Christmas was officially abolished by an act of the English Parliament, then controlled by Puritans. New Englanders made it a point to work on the traditional Christian holy days, just as they ostentatiously ate meat on Fridays. A Puritan would no more celebrate Christmas than he would attend Mass or dance round the Maypole; in either case, he thought that he was jeopardizing his chances of salvation. Even eating mince pie on Christmas day was frowned upon—it might be construed as a form of commemoration. On Christmas Day, 1621, when some servants at Plymouth took the day off for sports and other entertainment, William Bradford confiscated their "implements" and informed them that, while it ran against *their* consciences to work on Christmas, it was against *his* conscience that they should make merry on that day. Since Bradford was governor of the colony, the promptings of his conscience prevailed. In 1640, Massachusetts imposed a fine of five shillings upon anyone who observed Christmas by fasting, feasting or refusing to work. Unless Christmas fell on Sunday, the meetinghouses remained closed. In some parts of rural New England, Christmas was not observed until after the Civil War.

In partial compensation, the Puritans designated certain days for religious observances. Unhappily, however, for lovers of good cheer, the Jehovah of the Puritans seemed more often disposed to wreak His displeasure with mankind than to express His satisfaction with the work going on below. As a result, most of the Puritans' rites consisted of fasting and prayer, in which the people, reproved and chastened by the Almighty's wrath, sought to determine the reason for their punishment and to beg forgiveness for their sins.

Yet not all was gloom and foreboding: the Puritans and Pilgrims gave Americans Thanksgiving. At first, Thanksgiving was held to commemorate any auspicious event: in Massachusetts Bay, for example, the first Thanksgiving was held on July 8, 1630, to render thanks for the safe arrival of the fleet carrying John Winthrop and company to New England. Despite the Puritans' antipathy toward pagan celebrations, in the course of time Thanksgiving became essentially a harvest festival.

Although births and marriages occasioned little festivity, the Puritans really spread themselves when it came to observing the demise of friends and relatives. A Puritan funeral was a social as well as a religious event: the deceased was commemorated by a reunion of friends and kinfolk, feasting, and the bestowal upon the mourners of gifts such as scarves, gloves and gold rings that put the bereaved to heavy expense. Funerals tended to become an opportunity for the conspicuous display of wealth even more than of grief. In 1717, at the funeral of Andrew Belcher, 90 dozen pairs of gloves were distributed among the mourners: "None of any figure but what had gloves sent 'em," recorded Samuel Sewall in his diary. In 1738, Governor Belcher of Massachusetts gave 1,000 gloves in honor of his wife; not to be outdone, Peter Faneuil, a wealthy Boston merchant, sent out 3,000 gloves as a mark of respect for his uncle.

In colonial America the Puritan ethic was not confined to New England Congregationalists. Especially during the seventeenth century, the Puritan concept of what constituted the good (by which the Puritans meant "holy") life transcended denominational lines, theological differences and provincial boundaries.

Nowhere was this underlying unity of thought and purpose more strikingly exemplified than in the Sabbatarian laws enacted by the legislatures of the various colonies. These laws created the Puritan Sabbath—the principal contribution of the English Puritans to the Calvinistic ethic. Before the English Puritans came to power in the 1640's, Englishmen had been permitted, after attending church, to engage in Maypole dancing, archery, bowling on the green, vaulting, and other sports. Even in Geneva, some recreation was allowed on the Sabbath after church services—John Calvin himself occasionally played at bowls—but the English Puritans tried to improve upon Calvin's "School of Christ" by outlawing all forms of recreation on the Sabbath.

Their reading of the Bible persuaded them that God had ordained that His Day be kept holy—which, to the Puritans, meant churchgoing, family prayer, meditation and Bible reading. On this, of all days, the true Christian must keep his mind and heart upon God and therefore only those activities which contributed to that end were tolerated.

In New England, the Puritan ideal of the godly Sabbath was fully realized. The day (it began on Saturday night and ended at sundown on Sunday) was made so sacrosanct that no labor (cooking, cleaning house or making beds came under the ban), travel, recreation, "wanton Dallyances," or even "unnecessary and unseasonable walking in the streets and fields" were permitted. In New London, Connecticut, John Lewis and Sarah Chapman were charged in court with "sitting together on the Lord's Day, under an apple tree in Goodman Chapman's Orchard." In 1656, Captain Kemble of Boston was condemned to sit two hours in the stocks for "lewd and unseemly behavior." His offense consisted in kissing his wife in public on the Sabbath after he had returned to Boston from three years at sea.

Travelers never ceased to be astonished by the rigor with which these Sabbatarian laws were enforced in New England. Writing in the 1730's, Joseph Bennett, an English traveler, remarked:

Their observation of the sabbath (which they rather choose to call by the name of the Lord's Day, whensoever they have occasion to mention it)—is the strictest kept that ever I yet saw anywhere. On that day, no man, woman, or child is permitted to go out of town [Boston] on any pretence whatsoever; nor can any that are out of town come in on the Lord's Day. The town being situated on a peninsula, there is but one way out of it by land; which is over a narrow neck of land at the south end of the town, which is enclosed by a fortification, and the gates shut by way of prevention. There is a ferry, indeed, at the north end of the town; but care is taken by way of prevention there also. But, if they could escape out of the town at either of these places, it wouldn't answer their end: for the same care is taken, all the country over, to prevent travelling on Sundays; and they are as diligent in detecting of offenders of this sort, all over the

New England Government, as we in England are of stopping up of highways,—more; and those that are of the Independent persuasion refrain any attempt of this kind, in point of conscience. And as they will by no means admit of trading on Sundays, so they are equally tenacious about preserving good order in the town on the Lord's Day; and they will not suffer any one to walk down to the water-side, though some of the houses are adjoining to the several wharfs; nor, even in the hottest days of summer, will they admit of any one to take the air on the Common, which lies contiguous to the town, as Moorfields does to Finsbury. And if two or three people, who meet one another in the street by accident, stand talking together,—if they do not disperse immediately upon the first notice, they are liable to fine and imprisonment; and I believe, whoever it be that incurs the penalties on this account, are sure to feel the weight of them. But that which is the most extraordinary is, that they commence the sabbath from the setting of the sun on the Saturday evening; and, in conformity to that, all trade and business ceases, and every shop in the town is shut up: even a barber is finable for shaving after that time. Nor are any of the taverns permitted to entertain company; for, in that case, not only the house, but every person found therein, is finable. I don't mention this strict observation of the Lord's Day as intended rather to keep people within the bounds of decency and good order than to be strictly complied with, or that the appointment of this duty was only by some primary law since grown obselete; but that it is now in full force and vigor, and that the justices, attended with a posse of constables, go about every week to compel obedience to this law.[1]

Early Virginia was not far behind Massachusetts in proscribing Sunday sports and amusements. Governor Dale issued edicts prohibiting, among other things, bowling on the green, dancing, fiddling, card-playing, hunting and fishing. This kind of interference in the private lives of the colonists might have been expected from a Puritanical martinet like Governor Dale, but one of the first acts of the Virginia House of Burgesses in 1619 was to adopt laws compelling idle persons to work, forbidding gaming at cards and dice, regulating drinking and dress, and closing

[1] Joseph Bennett, *History of New England* (Vol. V of *Proceedings of the Massachusetts Historical Society, 1880–1862*) (Boston, 1862), pp. 115–16.

the colony to actors. In 1629, the Burgesses forbade the profanation of the Sabbath by working or traveling, and ordering or even permitting servants to work on the Lord's Day was declared to be a punishable offense. In Virginia, drinking, swearing, gambling or quarreling were always deemed more reprehensible if they occurred on the Sabbath.

Sabbatarian laws were enacted in all the non-Puritan colonies. In 1656, for example, the government of New Netherlands prohibited on the Sabbath any form of labor, recreation and amusement. The governor tried to enumerate the proscribed activities: "frequenting tavern or tippling houses, dancing, playing ball, cards, tricktrack, tennis, cricket, or ninepins, going on pleasure parties in a boat, car, or wagon, before, between, or during divine service." Maryland, where Puritan influence was strong, decreed that the Sabbath should be kept holy, and even after the Church of England was made the established church of the colony, the Sabbatarian laws remained in force.

In 1712, a barber was arrested in Phialdelphia for cutting hair on the Sabbath, but 20 years later Gottlieb Mittelberger, a German who settled temporarily in Pennsylvania, reported that the Sabbatarian laws, particularly in the country districts, had been allowed to lapse:

In the province of Pennsylvania, especially in the city of Philadelphia, the Sabbath-breakers who buy and sell on Sunday, when there is no necessity for doing so, are fined £5, or 30 florins each. Even a baker who bakes bread and sells it in his shop on Sundays or holidays is fined 30 florins. A merchant trading on Sundays has still less claim to indulgence. Grinding flour is forbidden under the same penalty. A waggoner who needlessly drives into the fields or even across the country must pay the same penalty, because driving is held to be his everyday occupation, just like any other.

Nevertheless, because of the numerous religious denominations and sects, there is great confusion. Sunday is very badly kept, especially in the rural districts, where most country folk pay little attention to it. Apostle-days and holidays are not observed at all. And, as I reported before, because the inhabitants are widely scattered and often live far from the churches, many a father holds divine service for his family in his house. Many other people plough, reap, thresh, hew or split wood, and the like. And thus Sunday is disregarded by many, especially since for want of an annual calendar many do not even know when Sundays fall. And thus the young people especially grow up like Indians or savages, without the necessary knowledge of divine things.[2]

Although Charleston, South Carolina, bore the reputation of being the gayest metropolis in British America, in the 1780's a German traveler found that, on the Sabbath, Charleston outwardly resembled Boston:

No shop may keep open, no sort of game or music is permitted, and during the church service watchmen go about who lay hold upon any one idling in the streets, (any not on urgent business or visiting the sick), and compel him to turn aside into some church or pay 2 shillings 4 pence; no slave may be required to work on this day.[8]

True, during the colonial period, these laws were not everywhere and at all times enforced with equal rigor. In the eighteenth century, for example, nonattendance at church was not so severely punished in Virginia as in Massachusetts. Indeed, after 1705, it was possible in Virginia to miss church for as long as one month at a time without incurring any penalty; for a longer period of absence, the offender was subject to a fine of 50 pounds of tobacco. Moreover, the Sabbath became a day marked less by outward piety than by visiting, dining and other forms of conviviality, and by the transaction of business. Philip Vickers Fithian, just out of Princeton, observed in Virginia "rings of Beaux chatting before & after Sermon on Gallantry" and planters "assembling in crowds after Service to dine & bargain":

A Sunday in Virginia dont seem to wear the same Dress as our Sundays to the Northward. Generally here by five o'Clock

[2] Gottlieb Mittelberger, *Journey to Pennsylvania*, edited by Oscar Handlin and John Clive (Cambridge, Mass.: Harvard University Press, 1960), p. 80.

[8] J. D. Schoepf, *Travels in the Confederation, 1783–1784* (2 vols., Philadelphia: W. J. Campbell, 1911), Vol. II, p. 222.

on Saturday every Face (especially the Negroes) looks festive & cheerful. All the lower class of People, & the Servants, & the Slaves, consider it as a Day of Pleasure & amusement, & spend it in such Diversions as they severally choose. The Gentlemen go to Church to be sure, but they make that itself a matter of convenience, & account the Church a useful weekly resort to do Business. 1. Before the Service giving & receiving letters of business, reading Advertisements, consulting about the price of Tobacco, Grain &c, & settling either the lineage, Age, or qualities of favourite Horses. 2. In the Church at Service, prayers read over in haste, a Sermon seldom under & never over twenty minutes, but always made up of sound morality, or deep studied Metaphysicks. 3. After Service is over three quarters of an hour spent in strolling round the Church among the Crowd, in which time you will be invited by several different Gentlemen home with them to dinner.

Nevertheless, William Byrd, a Virginia planter who spent a good part of his life in London as a man-about-town, felt that no good could come of traveling on the Sabbath:

A northwest wind having cleared the sky, we were now tempted to travel on a Sunday, for the first time, for want of more plentiful forage, though some of the more scrupulous amongst us were unwilling to do evil, that good might come of it, and make our cattle work a good part of the day in order to fill their bellies at night. However, the chaplain put on his casuistical face, and offered to take the sin upon himself. We therefore consented to move a Sabbath day's journey of three or four miles, it appearing to be a matter of some necessity.

. . . However, we found plainly that traveling on the Sunday, contrary to our constant rule, had not thriven with us in the least. We were not gainers of any distance by it, because the river made us pay two days for violating one. Nevertheless, by making this reflection, I would not be thought so rigid an observer of the sabbath as to allow of no work at all to be done, or journey to be taken upon it. I should not care to lie still and be knocked on the head, as the Jews were heretofore by Antiochus, because I believed it unlawful to stand upon my defense on this good day. Nor would I care, like a certain New England magistrate, to order a man to the whipping post, for daring to

4 Philip Vickers Fithian, *Journal and Letters*, edited by H. D. Farish (Williamsburg, Va., 1945), p. 220.

ride for a midwife on the Lord's day. On the contrary, I am for doing all acts of necessity, charity, and self-preservation, upon a Sunday as well as other days of the week. But, as I think our present march could not strictly be justified by any of these rules, it was but just we should suffer a little for it.[5]

On another occasion, when Byrd lost a pair of gold buttons while traveling on Sunday, he accounted himself properly punished for his transgression.

Sabbatarian laws have proved to be one of the most durable vestiges of seventeenth-century Puritanism. Today, 37 states of the Union restrict Sunday commerce in varying degrees; and in many areas, local laws prohibit organized sport. But in this respect, Great Britain has left the United States far behind. The Lord's Day Observance Society—a body from which, it has been said, the Almighty receives regular advice—is one of the most powerful and successful pressure groups in England.

If the Puritans' insistence upon hard work and thrift were essential to the survival of a frontier community, their insistence upon one day of surcease from labor was no less essential to the well-being of the community. But while Sunday was observed as a day of rest from physical labor, the Puritan soul was given on that day a thorough workout. In New England, the Puritans gave free rein to their passion for listening to sermons. To them, a sermon based upon Biblical texts was the means by which God spoke to the hearts of men and initiated the regenerative process that ultimately brought an assurance of salvation. In consequence, not content with one sermon, the Puritans instituted a second sermon on Sunday afternoon and a lecture on religious topics on Thursday night. Altogether, five or six hours of each week were spent in the meetinghouse, so cold in winter that even the flames of hellfire conjured up by the minister might have been welcomed by the half-frozen congregation.

On their voyage across the Atlantic, a group of Puritans was regaled with at least one sermon, and on some days as

[5] William Byrd, *A Journey to the Land of Eden and Other Papers* (New York: Macy-Masius, 1928), pp. 192–93.

many as three sermons, each day for ten weeks. One passenger was caught fishing on the Lord's Day. When called to account for this transgression, he protested that "he did not know when the Lord's Day was; he thought every day was a sabbath day for, he said, they did nothing but pray and preach all the week long." Two Dutchmen who visited Boston in the 1680's reported that prayers lasting two hours were held for a sick minister "after which an old minister delivered a sermon an hour long," which was followed by more prayers and psalm-singing. In the afternoon, three or four hours were devoted to prayer, three ministers relieving each other alternately; when one was exhausted, another took his place on the pulpit.

Bibliography

Dulles, Foster Rhea. *America Learns To Play: A History of Popular Recreation. 1607–1940*. New York: Appleton-Century Co., 1940.

Quinn, Arthur H. *A History of the American Drama*. New York: Crofts Co., 1922.

LIFE ON A
SOUTHERN PLANTATION

IT was a far remove from the Jamestown of John Smith to the Virginia Tidewater of William Byrd II. The struggling settlement on the James River proved to be the embryo of a society distinguished by large concentrations of wealth, Negro slavery and the plantation system of agriculture. This ascent to power and affluence was made possible by tobacco: as King Charles I said, Virginia was "founded upon smoke." Tobacco provided the economic foundation for an aristocracy that vied with that of Great Britain in the size of its estates, its pretensions to refinement and culture, and the conspicuous display of wealth.

Almost without exception, the Southern aristocracy was self-made. It was the product of brains and energy applied in an environment where these qualities, with luck added for good measure, were richly rewarded. From the beginning, America belonged to the optimists who were not afraid to go into debt and wait for the country to grow up —always provided, of course, that they were not wiped out in a depression. Most of the important families of eighteenth-century Virginia took their rise from the lesser English squirearchy or, more commonly, from a middle- or lower-class immigrant. Richard Lee, who arrived in Virginia in 1640 as a poor immigrant, became one of the wealthiest men in the colony, and the first William Byrd was the son of a London goldsmith. In general, the upper echelon of Southern society was composed of active, shrewd and enterprising men whose wealth, when transmitted to succeeding generations, gave Southern society its aristocratic tone. Often it was the descendants of horny-handed pioneers who traced their family genealogy back to exiled Cavaliers.

Unlike the New England Puritans, the Virginia and Maryland planters did not aspire to live in accord with some pattern laid up in Heaven. Instead, they chose a more mundane example—the way of life of the English landed gentry. They chose their models from the most polished representatives of that order—Roger de Coverley rather than Squire Western—who lived upon their estates but who were equally at home in the *bon ton* of London. The planters had no intention of becoming boorish rustics: they even deliberately cultivated a London accent "without which," it was said, "no Englishman, of what constitution soever he be, can make any tolerable figure."

But the resemblance was never more than superficial: the necessity of living with and disciplining a large population of Negro slaves made the way of life of the Chesapeake planter very different indeed from that of the English squires. Nevertheless, Negro slavery, upon which the Southern economy and social structure were built, provided a good life for those on the top. The planters constituted a wealthy minority in the midst of a large population of yeoman farmers, poor whites and enslaved Negroes. In addition to savoring the sweetness of life peculiar to the eighteenth century, the Southern planters among other Americans, were also given the unique sense of power that comes from the absolute ownership of human beings.

Geography likewise imposed a pattern upon life in Virginia. The existence of four major rivers, navigable to oceangoing ships for a considerable distance, flowing into the Chesapeake, inevitably dispersed the commerce of the colony over a wide area. Every considerable plantation boasted its own dock and warehouses. As a result, instead of being concentrated in seaports, much of the import and export trade of the Cheaspeake region was conducted in small stations located on the waterways.

The dispersal of the plantations over a wide area and

the desire of every large tidewater planter to make his plantation a port of call for oceangoing ships retarded the development of towns in Virginia and Maryland. The Virginia Assembly attempted to remedy this state of affairs by passing laws ordering the erection of towns, but these centers of trade and commerce refused to spring into being at the behest of the Burgesses. Because of the absence of towns, a solid middle class of artisans and tradesmen failed to develop in the Chesapeake region. To a large degree, Negro slaves served as artisans and in the eighteenth century, the representatives of English and Scottish mercantile houses assumed the functions once exercised by the planters themselves.

In Virginia and Maryland, the profits made in agriculture tended to be ploughed back into land, slaves and the amenities of life. Until the middle of the eighteenth century, the cultivation of tobacco was so profitable that it absorbed almost all the energy and capital of the Chesapeake planters. In consequence, land became the honorific form of wealth: it conferred social esteem and political power whereas merchandizing came to be held in contempt. By 1776, while lawyers and "Gentlemen of taste and fortune" abounded in Virginia, there was no native-born business class. "Up from Business" might well have been the motto of these great landed patricians.

More than any other group in colonial America, the Southern planters practiced conspicuous expenditure on borrowed money: they were the first Americans to establish a way of life based upon credit. They tended to spend their money before they received it; they lived on next year's crop and the year beyond that; and English merchants were always ready to advance them credit—with land and slaves as security. It was said of them that they never disputed a bill and never paid one "until, like their Madeira, it had acquired age." But they paid a penalty for this easy credit: by the time of the American Revolution, Thomas Jefferson described the Chesapeake planters as "a species of property annexed to certain English mercantile houses." These debts, like family heirlooms, descended from father to son, constantly increasing by the force of compound interest.

Had this borrowed capital been put to productive use, it would have redounded to the benefit of the borrower but, instead, much of it was devoted to the nonproductive embellishments of genteel living. Striving to imitate the English country gentry, the Chesapeake planters slipped insensibly deeper and deeper into debt. On the other hand, so long as the credit lasted and until the books were balanced—and many planters did not deign to keep accurate accounts—the Chesapeake planters made a splendid show. Their mansion houses, filled with fine furniture, paintings and plate, never ceased to astonish English travelers, who had expected to find America a raw wilderness. The First Gentlemen of Virginia rode in phaetons emblazoned with coats of arms and attended by Negro slaves on horseback. They wore silver-hilted swords—but purely for ornamental purposes: when they dueled, as the code of honor required, they used pistols.

Robert Beverly reproached his fellow Virginians for their dependence upon British manufactured goods and their neglect of home manufacturers:

They have their Cloathing of all sorts from England, as Linnen, Woollen, Silk, Hats, and Leather. Yet Flax, and Hemp grow no where in the World, better than there; their Sheep yield a mighty Increase, and bear good Fleeces, but they shear them only to cool them. The Mulberry-Tree, whose Leaf is the proper Food of the Silk-Worm, grows there like a Weed, and Silk-Worms have been observ'd to thrive extreamly, and without any hazard. The very Furs that their Hats are made of, perhaps go first from thence; and most of their Hides lie and rot, or are made use of, only for covering dry Goods, in a leaky House. Indeed some few Hides with much adoe are tann'd, and made into Servants Shoes; but at so careless a rate, that the Planters don't care to buy them, if they can get others; and sometimes perhaps a better manager than ordinary, will vouchsafe to make a pair of Breeches of a Deerskin. Nay, they are such abominable Ill-husbands, that tho' their Country be over-run with Wood, yet they have all their Wooden Ware from England;

their Cabinets, Chairs, Tables, Stools, Chests, Boxes, Cart-
Wheels, and all other things, even so much as their Bowls, and
Birchen Brooms, to the Eternal Reproach of their Laziness.[1]

In vain, moralists rebuked the planters for aping upper-
class Englishmen "in every Foppery, Luxury and Recreation." The Southern grandees continued to act upon the
un-Puritan assumption that life was given to be enjoyed—
with due regard, of course, to the penalties likely to be
visited upon wrongdoing in the next world. The Reverend
Jonathan Boucher of Maryland remarked that the planters:

really have the Art of Enjoying Life, I think in a Manner to
be envied. They live well and dress well, all without any
Labour & almost without any Concern of their own.

For this reason, English travelers usually felt more at
home among the Cheseapeake planters than anywhere else
in America. Lord Adam Gordon, a member of the British
Parliament who visited Virginia in 1765, was charmed
by what he saw:

I have had an opportunity to see a good deal of the Country,
and many of the first people in the Province and I must Say
they far exceed in good sense, affability, and ease, any set of
men I have yet fallen in with, either in the West Indies, or on
the Continent, this in some degree may be owing to there being
most of them educated at home [in Great Britain], but cannot
be altogether the cause, since there are amongst them many
Gentlemen, and almost all the Ladies, who have never been out
of their own Province, and yet are as sensible, conversable and
accomplished people, as one would wish to meet with.

Upon the whole, was it the case to live in America, this
Province, in point of Company and Climate, would be my choice
in preference to any, I have yet seen; the Country in general
is more cleared of wood, the houses are larger, better and more
commodious than those to the Southward, their Breed of Horses
extremely good, and in particular those they run in their Car-
riages, which are mostly from thorough bred Horses and

[1] Robert Beverly, *The History and Present State of Virginia,* edited by
Louis B. Wright (Chapel Hill: University of North Carolina Press,
1947), p. 295.

country Mares—they all drive Six horses, and travel generally from 8 to 9 Miles an hour—going frequently Sixty Miles to dinner—you may conclude from this their Roads are extremely good—they live in such good agreement, that the Ferries, which would retard in another Country, rather accelerate their meeting here, for they assist one another, and all Strangers with their Equipages in so easy and kind a manner, as must deeply touch a person of any feeling and convince them that in this Country, Hospitality is every where practised.

. . . Their Women make excellent Wives, and are in general great Breeders. It is much the fashion to Marry young and what is remarkable in a Stay I have made of near a Month in the Province—I have not heard of one unhappy couple.[2]

Since the Chesapeake gentry spent much time at home— a room of the mansion-house was reserved as an office— the father fully participated in family life. Having a man constantly underfoot may have been one of the unacknowledged trials of Southern womanhood. The reading aloud of novels, presenting plays in which all members of the family took part, singing and instrumental music, family prayers and other religious devotions provided cohesion to the family. William Byrd II found time to walk in his garden, play billiards with his wife and supervise the education of his children—but, of course, Byrd made a practice of rising at five o'clock in the morning.

As in New England, the Southern family was a patriarchy. A wealthy planter held sway over a large number of dependents, including his children's tutor and a housekeeper. But George Washington made sure that Mrs. Forbes, the housekeeper at Mount Vernon, did not consider herself a member of the family. He said:

Mrs. Forbes will have a warm, decent and comfortable room to herself, to lodge in, and will eat of the Victuals of our Table, but not sit at it, at any time, *with us*, be her appearance what it may: for if this was *once admitted,* no line satisfactory to either party, perhaps, could be drawn thereafter.

Even though Virginia and Maryland lacked large com-

[2] N. D. Mereness, *Travels in the American Colonies* (New York: Macmillan Co., 1916), p. 405.

mercial centers—Baltimore did not become an important seaport until the American Revolution—they did have thriving political and social headquarters. Williamsburg and Annapolis, the capitals of the two tobacco provinces, served as meeting places for the legislatures, the courts and social life. Since the worlds of fashion and of politics were identical, the opening of the court sessions the summoning of the legislatures and the Christmas holidays converted these little towns into scenes of gaiety, fashion, business and politics. Most of the leading families of Virginia lived within 50 miles of Williamsburg, and few neglected the opportunity to frolic with their friends and relatives and to patronize the milliners, tailors, shoemakers, coachmakers, silversmiths, jewelers, cabinet-makers and wigmakers who provided the luxury goods and services demanded by the planters.

Whenever a considerable number of members of both sexes came together in Virginia, dancing was almost certain to follow. Passionately fond of dancing, Virginians jigged and reeled until the small hours, only to rise and begin again the next day. Balls, especially those given to celebrate weddings, sometimes lasted for three days of almost uninterrupted dancing, drinking and feasting. In 1727, Governor Gooch of Virginia boasted that there was not an ill dancer among the ladies and gentlemen in the province, and ten years later a dancing school was opened at William and Mary College.

Philip Vickers Fithian described in his diary how Robert Carter, his family and friends spent an evening at his estate, Nomini Hall:

When the candles were lighted we all repaired, for the last minuet, into the dancing Room; first each couple danced a Minuet; then all joined as before in the country Dances, these continued till half after Seven when we played *Button*, to get Pawns for Redemption; here I could join with them, and indeed it was carried on with sprightliness, and Decency; in the course of redeeming my Pawns, I had several Kisses of the Ladies! Early in the Evening came colonel Philip Lee, in a traveling

Chariot from Williamsburg. Half after eight we were rung into Supper; The room looked luminous and splendid; four very large candles burning on the table where we supp'd, three others in different parts of the Room; a gay, sociable Assembly, & four well instructed waiters! [8]

Nicholas Cresswell, a young Englishman, found Virginia dancing did not conform to his ideas of decorum:

Saturday, June 7th, 1775.   Alexandria, Virginia
Last night I went to the Ball. . . . Here was about 37 ladies dressed and powdered to the life, some of them very handsome and as much vanity as is necessary. All of them fond of dancing, but I do not think they perform it with the greatest elegance. Betwixt the Country dances they have what I call everlasting jigs. A couple gets up and begins to dance a jig (to some Negro tune) others comes and cuts them out, and these dances always last as long as the Fiddler can play. This is sociable, but I think it look more like a Bacchanalian dance than one in a polite assembly. Old Women, Young wives with young children in the lap, widows, maids and girls come promiscuously to these assemblies which generally continue till morning. A cold supper, Punch, Wines, Coffee and Chocolate, but no Tea. This is a forbidden herb. The Men chiefly Scotch and Irish. I went home about two o'clock, but part of the company stayed, got drunk and had a fight.[4]

Although Thomas Jefferson lamented that he had been born in a country where music was little known or appreciated, it was beginning to find an increasing number of devotees. Skill upon the violin, flute, French and German horns was accounted a gentlemanly accomplishment, while ladies were expected to display their talents upon the spinet, harpsichord and pianoforte. Robert Carter of Nomini Hall spent several hours every day practicing upon musical instruments. The formal balls and impromptu dances to which Virginians were addicted put a high premium upon musical ability. For example, the music for a ball given by Richard Lee that lasted from Monday to Saturday and in which 70 ladies and gentlemen took part,

[8] Philip Vickers Fithian, *Journals and Letters,* edited by H. D. Farish (Williamsburg, Va.: Colonial Williamsburg Press, 1945), pp. 42–48.
[4] *The Journal of Nicholas Cresswell 1774–1777* (New York: Dial Press, 1924), pp. 52–53.

was provided by two overworked violins and a French horn.

Royal birthdays, Governor's balls, weddings and funerals afforded the planters an opportunity for conviviality. Durand of Dauphine, a Frenchman who came to Virginia in the 1680's, left this description of a wedding:

There were at least 100 Persons invited, several of them of good estate, and some ladies, well dressed and good to look upon. Although it was the month of November, the feast was spread under the trees. It was a delightful day. We were 80 at the first table and were served so abundantly of meat of all sorts that I am sure there was enough for a regiment of 500 men, provided only it was not recruited in Languedoc, Province, or Dauphine.

. . . During the rest of the day and all the night the company drank, smoked, sang and danced. They had no wine; their liquors were beer, cider and punch, the latter a mixture made in a great bowl. They put in three portions of beer, three portions of brandy, three pounds of sugar, some nutmeg and cinnamon, stir them well together and as soon as the sugar is melted they drink it. When one punch is being consumed another is brewing. As for me, I did not drink anything but beer. The cider made me sick and I do not like sugar. It is the custom of the country to serve only one meal on these occasions, at two o'clock in the afternoon. They do not provide beds for the men, those available being reserved for the women and girls; so about midnight, after I had seen the party in full frolic, some being already under the table, I went to sleep in a chair near the fire. The master of the house observed me and hospitably lead me into one of the rooms reserved for the women and girls, where there were four or five beds made up either on the floor or on feather matrasses. Collecting all their covers, he laid me out a bed on the floor, saying that he did not dare spread it in the hall because these drunken fellows would fall over me and keep me from sleeping. The frolic lasted all night. When it was day I got up, and found the whole company stretched about like dead men. A little later the bridegroom appeared, gave me a good breakfast, and then sent me back to my lodging, in the boat with his slaves.[5]

[5] Durand of Dauphine, *A Frenchman in Virginia* (Privately Printed, 1923), pp. 32–35.

Cockfighting was one of the most popular pastimes among the Southern gentry and common people. Josiah Quincy, Jr., of Boston recoiled from a sport he regarded as cruel, barbarous and a waste of precious time:

I spent yesterday chiefly with young men of fortune: they were gamblers and cock-fighters, hound-breeders and horse-jockies. To hear them converse, you would think that the grand point of all science was properly to fix a gaff and touch with dexterity the tail of a cock while in combat. He who won the last match, the last main, or last horse-race assumed the airs of a hero or German potentate. The ingenuity of a Locke or the discoveries of a Newton were considered as infinitely inferior to the accomplishments of him who knew when to shoulder a blind cock or start a fleet horse.[6]

Southerners of high and low degree spent much of their time in the saddle. It was said that they would walk four miles to get their horse in order to ride a mile. A Frenchman observed:

Even when they live not five hundred yards from the church, they [Virginians] mount their horses to go there. The women ride like the men, always at a canter. I was astonished how they held themselves on.

In South Carolina a traveler remarked that horses were so numerous "that you seldom see any body travel on foot, except *Negroes*, and they oftener on horseback; so that when a Taylor, a Shoemaker, or any other Tradesmen, is obliged to go but 3 Miles from his House, it would be extraordinary to see him travel on foot." Even Thomas Jefferson, scholar that he was, managed to spend three hours a day on horseback. Indeed, so addicted were Americans to riding that it was feared they might lose their powers of locomotion. "Nobody walks—everybody rides," was a complaint applicable to the colonial period as well as to the twentieth century.

[6] *The Journal of Josiah Quincy* (Vol. XLIX of the *Proceedings of the Massachusetts Historical Society*) (Boston, 1916), p. 467.

Among all classes in the Chesapeake area, horse racing was a popular pastime. Clergymen of the Church of England frequented these functions and, along with their parishioners, placed their bets. In Maryland, the climax of the social season were the horse races held at Annapolis; the local Jockey Club, composed of the gentry of the town and neighboring country, imported pure-blooded horses from England. To the pleasures of the turf were joined those of the hunt. In order that the planters might emulate the English squires, a few red foxes were brought over from England but they left their pursuers behind and disappeared into the vastness of the American forest. In consequence, the Virginia gentry had to content themselves with such sports as deer-stalking, fishing, fowling, and hunting hares and wild horses.

Both men and women gambled at cards. Mrs. Thomas Jefferson had a long run of bad luck but George Washington gallantly lost money—perhaps to put the ladies in good humor. Gambling, at the horse track, card table, and dicing board, threatened to become the bane of both sexes. In William Byrd III love of gaming became an overmastering passion: a contemporary described him as "never happy but when he has the box and Dices in his hand." Byrd ran through the large estate he had inherited from his father (on one occasion, he was compelled to sell four hundred Negro slaves to pay his gambling debts) and committed suicide in 1777.

From the great landed proprietors to the small tobacco-grower, Southern planters were renowned for the hospitality they showed travelers: "They are not easy," remarked a newcomer to Maryland, "till you give them an Opportunity to show you a kindness." In fact, they took such delight in entertaining visitors that innkeepers frequently complained that the competition from private houses was putting them out of business. In part, this concern for the well-being of total strangers was owing to the isolation in which the planter lived, to their eagerness for news of the outside world, particularly of England, and to the relative ease of entertaining guests when Negro slaves provided the answer to the Servant Problem.

In South Carolina, the planters often posted Negro slaves along the road with instructions to invite travelers to stop for refreshment and lodging. George Washington compared his house at Mount Vernon to "a well resorted tavern, as scarcely any strangers who are going from north to south, or from south to north do not spend a day or two at it." Washington took pride in the fact that many of his guests were "people of the first distinction."

As a way of dissipating a fortune, Southern hospitality ranked close to betting on the horses or gambling at cards. In one year, the Carters of Nomini Hall, aided by their numerous guests, consumed 27,000 pounds of pork, 20 beavers, 550 bushels of wheat, 4 hogsheads of rum and 150 gallons of brandy. Twenty-eight fires were kept burning all winter at the Hall. George Washington, who did not lightly disburse a shilling, complained that his guests were eating and drinking him into insolvency.

Durand of Dauphine marveled at the lavishness of the food and drink dispensed by the planters:

Mr. Wormeley is so beloved and esteemed in these parts that all the gentlemen of consideration of the countryside we traversed came to meet him, and as they rode with us, it resulted that by the time we reached Col. Fitzhugh's we made up a troop of 20 horse. The Colonel's accomodations were, however, so ample that this company gave him no trouble at all; we were all supplied with beds, though we had, indeed, to double up. Col. Fitzhugh showed us the highest hospitality. He had store of good wine and other things to drink, and a frolic ensued. He called in three fiddlers, a clown, a tightrope dancer and an acrobatic tumbler, and gave us all the divertisement one would wish. It was very cold but no one thought of going near the fire because they never put less than the trunk of a tree upon it and so the entire room was kept warm.

. . . The frolic continued well into the afternoon of the second day. It then became necessary for us to withdraw if ever we were to cross the river. Colonel Fitzhugh was hospitable to the last. He not only brought a quantity of wine and bowls of punch down to the shore, there to serve a parting glass, but he lent us his sloop.[7]

Yet the life of a Chesapeake planter was not wholly devoted to sports, entertaining guests and provincial politics. The time and energy of successful planters were absorbed by the task of overseeing the affairs of his plantation, transacting business with British merchants, parish duties, and in ministering to the needs of their families and servants. William Byrd II described his life at Westover, his principal estate, as that of a patriarch surrounded by his flocks and herds, his bondmen and bondwomen. But Byrd did not pretend that he enjoyed a life of leisured ease. "I must take care," he said, "to keep all my People to their Duty, to set all the Springs in motion and to make every one draw his equal Share to carry the Machine forward." Besides managing his plantations, Byrd was concerned in mining, surveying, settling immigrants on his lands, land speculation (he died possessed of 179,440 acres of land in Virginia and Maryland), and dabbling in science. The early morning hours of each day he spent in reading Greek, Hebrew and Latin, surrounded by one of the largest libraries in colonial America.

Bibliography

Beatty, R. C. *William Byrd of Westover*. Boston: Houghton Mifflin Co., 1932.

Bridenbaugh, Carl. *Seat of Empire: The Political Role of Eighteenth-Century Williamsburg*. Williamsburg: Colonial Williamsburg, 1950.

———. *Myths and Realities: Societies of the Colonial South*. Baton Rouge: Louisiana State University Press, 1952.

Craven, Wesley Frank. *The Southern Colonies in the Seventeenth Century*. Baton Rouge: Louisiana State University Press, 1949.

Davis, Richard Beale (editor). *William Fitzhugh and His Chesapeake World, 1676–1701*. Chapel Hill: University of North Carolina Press, 1963.

Merrens, Harry Roy. *Colonial North Carolina in the Eighteenth Century*. Chapel Hill: University of North Carolina Press, 1964.

[7] Durand of Dauphine, *op. cit.*, pp. 68, 70.

Morgan, Edmund S. *Virginians at Home: Family Life in the Eighteenth Century*. Williamsburg: Colonial Williamsburg, 1952.

Schlesinger, Arthur M. *The Aristocracy in Colonial America* (Vol. 47 of the "Proceedings of the Massachusetts Historical Society"). Boston: Massachusetts Historical Society, 1962.

Sydnor, Charles S. *Gentlemen Freeholders: Political Practices in Washington's Virginia*. Chapel Hill: University of North Carolina Press, 1952.

Wertenbaker, Thomas J. *Patrician and Plebian in Virginia*. New York: Russell and Russell, 1958.

———. *The Planters of Colonial Virginia*. Princeton: Princeton University Press, 1922.

Wright, Louis B. *The First Gentlemen of Virginia: Intellectual Qualities of the Early Colonial Ruling Class*. San Marino, Calif.: Henry Huntington Library, 1940.

SOCIAL RANK
AND DRESS

FROM their European background, the first settlers brought a highly developed sense of class or, as they termed it, rank. Each rank in society was given a distinctive form of address, dress and other indicators of status. When they arrived in the New World, these transplanted Europeans did not attempt to create forthwith a new egalitarian society; instead, they tried to introduce into their unique environment the social stratification they had known in Great Britain and Europe. Long-established custom dictated that yeoman farmers were called "goodmen"; gentlemen were saluted as "mister"; members of the Governor's Council and other high officials bore the title of "Esquire" and their wives were entitled to be called "madam." The upper class was referred to as "the better sort," whereas ordinary people were called "the meaner sort." in 1651, the General Court of Massachusetts officially sanctioned the division of the inhabitants into "the better class"; "those above the ordinary degree"; and "those of mean condition."

With only one exception, the leaders of the expeditions that colonized Virginia in 1607–11 were "persons of quality." The roster included such knights, barons, lords and the younger brothers of nobles as Sir Thomas Gates, Bartholomew Gosnold, Edward Maria Wingfield, Baron de la Warr, and George Percy. No one supposed that the common people of England would be willing to venture their lives in the New World unless they were led by aristocrats. John Smith, the only commoner in this goodly company, was never able to overcome the feeling among his fellow colonists that he had no right to command because he was not a gentleman born.

The founders of Puritan New England were certain that a hierarchical society was essential to the realization of God's Will upon earth. Said John Winthrop:

> God Almightie in his most holy and wise providence·hath so disposed of the condition of mankind, as in all times some may be rich, some poore, some high and eminent in power and dignitie; others meane and in subjection.

Instead of protesting against these inequalities, Winthrop continued, men ought to accept them as part of the Divine plan for the better ordering of human society. Viewed in this light, inequality of wealth was expected to teach the rich and mighty "not to eate up the poor, nor the poore and dispised rise upp against their superiours and shake off their yoeake." In short, the rich would learn mercy and justice from their good fortune while the poor would learn resignation from the hardships and mean condition God had seen fit to impose upon them.

Of course, in this dispensation, the burden of adjusting to God's Will as regards the distribution of wealth fell upon the poor. Yet the Puritans, because they saw God's hand in everything—including their place in the social structure—insisted that all of low degree yield obedience to their superiors in wealth, godliness and education. A disobedient servant, a social agitator or a poor man who did not show proper respect for his betters was regarded as a contemner of God's holy ordinances. The Reverend Increase Mather asked:

> You that are servants, . . . have you been guilty of stubborn, disobedient carriage towards your Masters, though God in his word tells you that you ought to be obedient to them with fear and trembling?

Manifest on every hand in everyday life, social distinctions did not cease within the Puritan meetinghouses. Seats were arranged according to "dignity, age and estate."

Pews, in particular, were an emblem of social rank; in the eighteenth century, partitions were often erected to ensure complete privacy to their occupants. A separate gallery at the rear of the meetinghouse was assigned to servants.

As a being apart from the general run of mankind, a gentleman was hedged with laws both human and divine. In early Virginia, the courts ordered those who denigrated their social superiors to suffer 20 to 100 lashes. Corporal punishment was rarely inflicted upon gentlemen: in 1623, the Virginia House of Burgesses declared that persons of quality were exempt from whipping—a form of chastisement to which the common people were subject upon slight provocation. Even death did not erase social distinctions: whereas "the lower sort of people" were buried in the churchyard, planters and their families were laid to rest in private burial places upon their estates.

Because it was based upon recently acquired wealth, the American aristocracy never found it easy to make good its claims to superior merit and to command the unquestioning deference of the people. Unlike the patricians of older societies, American aristocrats lacked the sanctions characteristic of a post-feudal society: ancient lineage, inherited wealth in land, and centuries of social preeminence. Here, then, was the dilemma of American aristocrats, whether they were Southern planters or Northern merchants: how to assert in an emerging democratic society the pretensions usually associated with birth. Said Governor Francis Nicholson of Virginia in 1703:

This generation know too well from whence they come, and the ordinary sort of planters that have land of their own, though not much, look upon themselves to be as good as the best of them [the would-be aristocrats], for he knows, at least has heard, from whence these mighty Dons derive their originals . . . and that he or his ancestors were their equals if not superiors.[1]

---

[1] Thomas Wertenbaker, *Patrician and Plebeian in Virginia* (New York: Russell and Russell, 1958), p. ii.

Even so, the Southern planters enjoyed a large measure of social prestige and political power. This circumstance was owing not only to the patterns of behavior brought from the Old World but, more importantly, to the fact that the patricians of the South made themselves the spokesmen of popular causes in their colonies—usually taking the side of the province against the exercise of power by the British government. Public service was regarded by the rich and educated as an obligation, and the people elected them to office in the expectation that they would represent the interests of the whole community. Politics in Virginia usually took the form of a contest between aristocrats for public office. But if Virginia was ruled by an oligarchy of wealthy planters, it was also true that this oligarchy enjoyed the confidence, respect and political support of the people.

Devereaux Jarrett, who was born in Virginia in 1732, the son of a carpenter, described how he was brought up to regard the planter aristocrats:

We were accustomed to look upon, what were called *gentle folks,* as beings of a superior order. For my part, I was quite shy of them, and kept off at a humble distance. A *perriwig,* in those days, was a distinguishing badge of *gentle folk*—and when I saw a man riding the road, near our house, with a wig on, it would so alarm my fears and give me such a disagreeable feeling, that, I dare say, I would run off, as for my life. Such ideas of the differences between *gentle* and *simple,* were, I believe, universal among all of my rank and age. . . .

My parents neither sought nor expected any titles, honors, or great things, whether for themselves or children. Their highest ambition was to teach their children to read, write and understand the fundamental rules of arithmatic. I remember also that they taught us short prayers, and made us very perfect in repeating the *Church Catechism.* They wished us all to be brought up in some honest calling, that we might earn our bread, by the sweat of our brows, as they did.[a]

[a] Devereaux Jarrett, "The Autobiography of Devereaux Jarrett," *William and Mary Quarterly* (Third Series, IX, 1952), p. 361.

William Byrd II, one of the First Gentlemen of Virginia, felt that in marriage class lines ought to be strictly observed:

> The widow smiled graciously upon me, and entertained me very handsomely. Here I learned all the tragical story of her daughter's humble marriage with her uncle's overseer. Besides the meanness of this mortal's aspect, the man has not one visible qualification, except impudence, to recommend him to a female's inclinations. But there is sometimes such a charm in that Hibernian endowment, that frail woman cannot withstand it, though it stand alone without any other recommendation. Had she run away with a gentleman or a pretty fellow, there might have been some excuse for her, though he were of inferior fortune: but to stoop to a dirty plebeian, without any kind of merit, is the lowest prostitution. I found the family justly enraged at it; and though I had more good nature than to join in her condemnation, yet I could devise no excuse for so senseless a prank as this young gentlewoman had played.[8]

Most Americans dressed in the English style: in clothing, as in other matters, the ideal was to be as much like an Englishman or Englishwoman as possible. Even the Puritans were indistinguishable by their clothing from other Englishmen of their period—which meant that they wore breeches that reached below the knee, long-sleeved linen shirts, white linen collars, long stockings and leather shoes. The type of hat that has become the trademark of the Pilgrim Fathers—a black cone decorated with a silver buckle—did not come into use until the French Revolution. Although they eschewed ornaments—silver buckles and decorated buttons were condemned as vanities—they wore gray and light-brown cloth rather than the funereal black in which they are usually depicted.

When they could afford it and their rank permitted, the Puritans wore on festive occasions clothing of brilliant hues. William Brewster, one of the elders at Plymouth, cut a dashing figure in "a paire of greene drawers." The inven-

[8] William Byrd. *A Journey to the Land of Eden and Other Papers* (New York: Macy-Masius, 1928), pp. 318–19.

tory of Governor William Bradford's estate revealed that he had a coat with silver buttons, a cloth coat faced with taffety, a pair of black breeches and a red waistcoat, one black and one colored hat, and twenty-one pair of shoes. Had they worn their best go-to-meeting clothes, the Pilgrims would have made quite a splash of color when they landed at Plymouth Rock. Certainly the Indians had no reason to believe that the Pilgrims shunned bright colors: when they entertained Massasoit, the Indian chief, in Plymouth, they brought out a green rug with three or four gaily colored cushions.

During the seventeenth century, all the colonies enacted a large amount of legislation regulating the kind and quality of clothing that could be worn by people of different ranks. These laws had a twofold purpose: to prevent ill-considered expenditure upon finery and to preserve the distinctions between the various groups within the social hierarchy.

So fond of finery were some Puritans that within a few years of the settlement of Boston, it was found necessary to prohibit by law the wearing of silver, gold and silk laces, ruffs, girdles and beaver hats. The English fashion of slashing the sleeves in order that a fabric of another color might show through the opening was carried to such lengths that the General Court of Massachusetts ordered that no man or woman should wear clothing with more than one slash on each sleeve and that "no garment shall be made with short sleeves, whereby the nakedness of the arme may bee discovered."

But the Puritans always found it easier to pass a law against something they disliked than to enforce it. In his *Journal,* Governor John Winthrop recorded how the ladies successfully defied the magistrates:

The court, taking into consideration the great disorder general through the country in costliness of apparel, and following new fashions, sent for the elders of the churches, and conferred with them about it, and laid it upon them, as belonging to them, to redress it, by urging it upon the consciences of their people, which they promised to do. But little was done about it; for

diverse of the elders' wives, etc. were in some measure partners
in the general disorder.[4]

The Puritans were torn between their conviction that
plain, unadorned apparel was prescribed for God's People
and their equally strong conviction that differences in dress
must be maintained between classes. William Brewster of
Plymouth declared that he could not abide sinners who
"would haughtily and proudly carry and lift up themselves,
being risen from nothing and having little else in them to
commend them but a few fine clothes or a little riches more
than others." In this spirit, the Massachusetts General
Court decreed in 1651 that those who affected a style of
dress above their station in life should be punished for their
temerity:

Although several declarations and orders have been made by
this court against excess in apparel, both of men and women,
which have not taken that effect as were to be desired, but on
the contrary, we can not but to our grief take notice that intolerable excess and bravery hath crept in upon us, and especially
amongst people of mean condition, to the dishonor of God, the
scandal of our profession, the consumption of estates, and altogether unsuitable to our poverty; and, although we acknowl-
edge it to be a matter of much difficulty, in regard to the blind-
ness of men's minds and the stubborness of their wills, to set
down exact rules to confine all sorts of persons, yet we cannot
but account it our duty to commend unto all sorts of persons
the sober and moderate use of those blessings which, beyond
expectation, the Lord hath been pleased to afford unto us in this
wilderness; and also to declare our utter detestation and dislike, that men or women of mean condition should take upon
them the garb of gentlemen, by wearing gold or silver lace, or
buttons, or points at their knees, or to walk in great boots;
which, though allowable to persons of greater estates, or more
liberal education, yet we can not but judge it intolerable in
persons of such like condition:
It is therefore ordered by this court, and the authority
thereof, that no person within this jurisdiction, nor any of their
relations depending upon them, whose visible estates, real and

[4] John Winthrop, *The History of New England, 1630–1649* (2 vols.,
Boston: Little Brown, 1853), Vol. I, p. 331.

personal, shall not exceed the true and indifferent value of two hundred pounds, shall wear any gold or silver lace, or gold and silver buttons, or any bone lace above two shillings per yard, or silk hoods, or scarfs, upon the penalty of ten shillings for every such offense, and every such delinquent to be presented by the grand jury.[5]

One woman, haled into court for overdressing, went free when she proved that her husband was in the 200-pound bracket.

The increasing prosperity of the colonies and the rise of a class of wealthy merchants and planters eager to emulate the English aristocracy made it impossible to preserve the standards of dress and manners of the first generation of settlers. While Americans resisted the tyranny of the English government they submitted cheerfully to the tyranny of English fashions. William Eddis marveled at the rapidity with which the latest London styles were adopted on the other side of the Atlantic:

> The quick importation of fashions from the mother country is really astonishing. I am almost inclined to believe, that a new fashion is adopted earlier by the polished and affluent Americans, than by many opulent persons in the great metropolis: nor are opportunities wanting to display superior elegance. We have varied amusements and numerous parties, which afford to the young, the gay, and the ambitious, an extensive field to contend in the race of vain and idle competition. In short, very little difference is, in reality, observable in the manners of the wealthy colonist and the wealthy Briton. Good and bad habits prevail on both sides the Atlantic.[6]

Among the fashions imported from England was the wearing of wigs. Despite the sanctity attached by the original Puritans to a closely cropped head, late in the seventeenth century English fashions began to overcome the force even of Biblical injunctions. In his *Diary*, Samuel Sewall of Boston, recorded how he remonstrated with a young Bostonian who had succumbed to the craze for wigs:

[5] John B. Dillon, *Oddities of Colonial Legislation* (Indianapolis, 1879), pp. 27–28.
[6] William Eddis, *Letters from America* (London, 1792), pp. 112–13.

Tuesday, June 10, 1701. Having last night heard that Josiah Willard had cut off his hair (a very full head of hair) and put on a Wigg, I went to him this morning. Told his Mother what I came about, and she call'd him. I inquired of him what Extremity had forced him to put off his own hair, and put on a Wigg? He answered, none at all. But said that his Hair was straight, and that it parted behinde. Seem'd to argue that men might as well shave their hair off their head, as off their face. I answered men were men before they had hair of their faces, (half of mankind have never any). God seems to have ordain'd our Hair as a Test, to see whether we can bring our minds to be content to be at his finding; or whether we would be our own Carvers, Lords, and come no more at him . . . Pray'd him to read the Tenth Chapter of the Third book of Calvins Institutions. . . . Told him that it was condemn'd by a Meeting of Ministers at Northampton in Mr. Stoddards house, when the said Josiah was there. . . . He seem'd to say would leave off his Wigg when his hair was grown. I spake to his Father of it a day or two after: He thank'd me that had discoursed his Son, and told me that when his hair was grown to cover his ears, he promis'd to leave off his Wigg. If he had known of it, would have forbidden him. His Mother heard him talk of it; but was afraid positively to forbid him; lest he should do it, and so be more faulty.[7]

While the wearing of wigs did not, as some Puritans apprehended, call down lightning bolts from Heaven upon the head of the offender against "God's Laws," it certainly brought down thunder from the pulpits. In some quarters, the Indian uprising under King Philip that, in 1676–77, took the lives of hundreds of New Englanders was attributed to the Lord's displeasure upon seeing His People disporting themselves in wigs.

But defections appeared within the ranks of the clergy themselves. Even the Reverend Cotton Mather appeared before his congregation in a periwig. Among the upper class, the fashion was embraced eagerly; a wig became *de rigueur* and no gentleman would be seen without one in public. In the towns, even children and servants wore them. With the passage of time, wigs became increasingly

[7] *Samuel Sewall's Diary*, edited by Mark Van Doren (New York: Macy-Masius, 1927), pp. 161–62.

elaborate and expensive: it was not only the original cost—which might run as high as 250 dollars—but the upkeep of a wig that made this fashion a serious financial burden.

If fashion was a tyranny, it at least had the merit of changing frequently. About the middle of the eighteenth century, powdered wigs began to lose favor, largely because King George II decided that they were a nuisance. Thereupon men allowed their hair to grow long, powdered it liberally and either queued it or tied the tail in a small silk bag.

Dressing was a serious and exacting business to which gentlemen devoted fully as much time as did women. Included in every gentleman's toilette were cosmetics, pomatum, perfume and powder. He was expected to appear in public in a cocked hat, ruffled shirt, embroidered frock coat, knee breeches, silk hose, and pumps with silver or gold buckles.

Attired in a lavender jacket and lilac-colored breeches, with frills of lace on his cuffs and shirt front, John Hancock cut a dashing figure. To watch Hancock flourish the lace at his cuffs and sneeze daintily when taking snuff was deemed a richly rewarding experience by all aspirants to the *bon ton*. Long before he gained renown as a patriot, Hancock achieved fame as a Macaroni—the name bestowed upon foppish Englishmen who returned from the Grand Tour affecting wasp waists, diamond buckles, two watches, silk stockings, a vast amount of lace and braid, a diminutive hat, and a cane and a sword.

Although the laws governing dress fell into desuetude, the distinctions between classes in this regard became more pronounced as the eighteenth century progressed. The colonial *bon ton* was confined to the privileged few: the great majority of Americans dressed like the farmers they were. Instead of wigs, they wore their hair long and tied in the back with a ribbon; if they wore buckles on their shoes, they were of brass; instead of lace, they used a plain linen neckband; and instead of breeches and pumps, they wore trousers, homespun stockings and cowhide shoes. The

50 gentlemen who were reputed to have taken part in the Boston Tea Party did not adopt by way of disguise anything as elaborate as Indian feathers and paint: they simply put on the trousers and jackets worn by the common people.

The Quakers were only slightly more successful than were the New England Puritans in resisting the beguilements of high living and the conspicuous display of wealth. As late as 1740, the only public clock in Philadelphia had no dial because the Quakers considered it to be a superfluity. Quakers wore no cuffs or buttons on their coats and the Yearly Meeting of Friends decried the "immodest fashion of hooped petticoats," "bare necks" and "shoes trimmed with gaudy colors." Yet about 1730, when the Quakers began to adopt the "Quaker Oats" costume with which they are associated, it was observed that, while the well-to-do still retained the plain garb enjoined by George Fox, they insisted upon the most expensive materials.

The only distinctive costume worn by Americans during the colonial period came from the frontier and it was inspired by the Indians. The frontiersmen's ideal was to look as much like an Indian brave as possible and still preserve the proprieties. Unlike some Frenchmen who lived among the Indians and led them into battle against the English settlers, the frontiersmen did not go so far as to strip off their clothing and go naked except for a breechclout; instead, they adopted a costume consisting of leather breeches and leggings, a fringed deerskin shirt, a round coonskin cap, and a belt from which sometimes was suspended an Indian's scalp. Armed with rifles, tomahawks and long-bladed knives, they presented a spectacle calculated to make an Indian blanch under his war-paint. For, however fearsome was the Indians' paint, it did not actually kill anyone, whereas the frontiersmen's rifle was the most accurate and deadly small arm in the world.

On many parts of the frontier, both men and women dressed drably and meanly: even their Sunday clothes were often nondescript hand-me-downs. "How the Polite People of London stare," said the Reverend Charles Woodmason, whose parish was on the Carolina frontier, "to see the Females (many very pretty) come to Service in their Shifts and a short petticoat only, barefooted and bare legged— Without Caps or Handkerchiefs—dress'd only in their Hair, Quite in a State of Nature." The men appeared in shirts and long trousers, without shoes or stockings. As for the children, they were permitted to run half-naked in the Indian fashion.

The eighteenth century witnessed the emergence of women in the full panoply of fashion. In the previous century, women wore numerous petticoats, a hood and white neckcloth, and a bodice resembling an outside corset laced in front and back. But the whirl of London fashion in which American women as well as men were caught up, decreed around 1700 that women should be encased in stiff whalebone stays, surrounded by voluminous hoop petticoats six feet in diameter (for which special doors and stairways had to be built), and their stature increased by high-heeled shoes and elaborately coiffured hairdos. They wore long gloves and, on formal occasions, masks to protect their complexions. A woman of fashion also had several fans, each suited to a particular purpose: a ball, a wedding and a funeral. A coquette adept in the use of a fan hardly needed to speak: her fan spoke more eloquently than words. The spectator remarked:

There is an infinite variety of motions to be made use of in the fluttter of a fan. There is the angry flutter, the modest flutter, the timorous flutter, the confused flutter, the merry flutter, the amorous flutter. . . . There is scarce any emotion in the mind which does not produce a suitable agitation in the fan.[8]

Built of wire, lace, ribbons, beads, jewels and feathers, women's headdresses were marvels of structural engineering. By 1720, so lofty had become these pinnacles that it was almost impossible to sleep without ruining the effect:

[8] *The Spectator* (8 vols., New York: R. Worthington, 1883), Vol. II, pp. 201–02.

at this point, women took to wearing wigs. By 1770, however, the coiffure had reappeared in even more exaggerated form—a vogue that lasted until the French Revolution abruptly cut it short.

With the high headdress came the low-cut dress. Indeed, in the eighteenth century, American women seemed on the point of achieving the topless gown when this promising line of development was arrested by a change in fashion. During his American travels, Brissot de Warville sat down to dinner with seven or eight women, "all," he observed, "dressed in great hats, plumes, &c. Two among them had their bosoms very naked. I was scandalized at this indecency among republicans." Ordinarily, the reaction of American males was quite different. Philip Vickers Fithian, observed with regret:

She [Elizabeth Lee] was pinched up rather too near in a long pair of new fashioned Stays, which, I think, are a Nuisance both to us & themselves. For the late importation of Stays which are said to be now most fashionable in London, are produced upwards so high that we can have scarce any view at all of the Ladies Snowy Bosoms; & on the contrary, they are extended downwards so low that whenever Ladies who wear them, either young or old have occasion to walk, the motion necessary for Walking must, I think cause a disagreeable Friction of some part of the body against the lower Edge of the Stays which is hard & unyielding. I imputed the Flush which was visible in her Face to her being swathed by *Body & Soul & limbs* together.[9]

It was the French, not the American, Revolution that brought about democracy in dress. Knee breeches were replaced by trousers; James Monroe was the last President of the United States to wear the garb that had once been the hallmark of the aristocrat. A side effect of this democratization of dress was that the male animal was deprived of his resplendent plumage and turned into a drab, lackluster creature, arrayed in a garb of black, grey or brown.

[9] Philip Vickers Fithian, *Journals and Letters,* edited by H. D. Farish (Williamsburg: Colonial Williamsburg Press, 1945), pp. 171–72.

Despite this handicap, the poor, broken butterfly continues to court the female of the species.

Bibliography

Earle, Alice Morse. *Costume of Colonial Times.* New York: Macmillan Co., 1894.

Schlesinger, Arthur M. *The Aristocracy in Colonial America* (Vol. 47 of the "Proceedings of the Massachusetts Historical Society"). Boston: Massachusetts Historical Society, 1962.

Singleton, Esther. *Social New York under the Georges, 1714–1776.* New York: Appleton Co., 1902.

LIFE IN THE
COLONIAL CITIES

DURING the seventeenth and eighteenth centuries, Americans were a mobile people, but their mobility took the form of moving from one farm to another, not from a farm to the city. In consequence, even the Northern commercial colonies were decidedly rural in character: by 1776, although approximately 108,000 people resided in cities, the population of the colonies had grown so rapidly that the proportion of people living in cities had actually declined from the beginning of the century. Only about one of twenty Americans was an urban dweller. No one dreamed that the time would come when "how to keep 'em down on the farm" would be a national problem.

Small as was the urban population of the colonies, in comparison to that of the rural areas, its influence upon American life was out of all proportion to its numbers. For the cities—of which Boston, New York, Philadelphia, Charleston and Newport were the most important—served as distributing centers for British and European culture as well as for imported merchandise: the latest fashions both in dress and ideas reached the American people chiefly through the medium of the colonial seaports. These cities not only transmitted the European Enlightenment across the Atlantic but also helped to create a kind of Enlightenment that was peculiarly American. They provided the best education available in the colonies; they contained most of the educated men in British America; and they furnished a considerable part of the audience for plays, readers of books and newspapers, and patrons of the arts. Whatever opportunities existed in the colonies for the advancement of learning, whether in science, literature or the arts, they were found chiefly in the cities.

The conditions of urban life required more cooperative action than was demanded of those who lived on farms and plantations. Many urban problems—health, sanitation, police protection and fire prevention—could be met only by communal effort. At the same time, classes were more sharply demarcated in the cities than in the rural areas and there were more glaring contrasts between rich and poor. Finally, the cities were centers of manufacturing as well as of commerce: such industries as hatmaking, tailoring, shoe-making, furniture making, printing, engraving, shipbuilding and housebuilding flourished in these urban centers.

Of these cities, Philadelphia was the most populous. Boston, long the largest, began about 1740 to grow less rapidly than its rivals. New York did not take the lead until early in the nineteenth century; Newport, which owed its prosperity in part to the slave trade, suffered a severe set-back by the curtailment of that trade after the American Revolution; and Charleston, South Carolina, the only true metropolis in the Southern colonies, was a center of gaiety and elegance as well as of commerce.

The rapidity with which these cities grew in size, wealth, and commercial importance never ceased to amaze travelers, particularly those who returned after an absence of several years. Within 18 years of its founding, Philadelphia had a population of over ten thousand people; and by the middle of the eighteenth century it had become one of the principal cities in the English-speaking world.

Lord Adam Gordon was astonished by the wealth and populousness of the City of Brotherly Love:

The City of Philadelphia is perhaps one of the wonders of the World, if you consider its Size, the Number of Inhabitants, the regularity of its Streets, their great breadth and length, their cutting one another all at right Angles, their Spacious publick and private buildings, Quays and Docks, the Magnificence and diversity of places of Worship (for here all Religions who profess the Name of Christ, are tolerated equally) the plenty of provisions brought to Market, and the Industry of all its Inhabitants, one will not hesitate to Call it the first Town in America, but one that bids fair to rival almost any in Europe. It is not an hundred years since the first tree was cut where the City now Stands, and at this time it consists of more than three thousand Six hundred Houses. It is daily encreasing, and I doubt not in time, will reach all the way from River to River,—the great and foreseeing Founder of it, Mr. Penn having wisely laid out the Space so far, which is daily taking and filling. I must not pass over two foundations here, which do them much honour; their College for education of youth, and their Hospital for the reception of all Sick persons whatever, including Lunaticks, which is supported by the benefactions of the Charitable and well disposed Subscribers.[1]

Lord Adam Gordon's praise was not fulsome: by 1765, Philadelphia boasted more of the amenities of urban life than did any provincial English city. The streets and sidewalks were paved with brick and were illuminated by lamps that were lit every night except when the moon shone (the Quakers disliked redundancy in any form); a regular night watch was instituted in 1751 to preserve order, call out the time of night and the state of the weather; and fire protection was in the hands of a company of 30 volunteers organized by Benjamin Franklin, the man responsible for most of these civic improvements. Philadelphia had 50 booksellers, compared with 42 in Boston, attesting to the keen intellectual interests of the townspeople. The Library Company of Philadelphia, founded in 1731, and the American Philosophical Society, dating from 1743, were two of the leading institutions in colonial America dedicated to the advancement of learning.

While some visitors complained that all the streets and houses of Philadelphia looked alike and found fault with William Penn's severely rectangular city plan—"nothing could be gloomier than this uniformity," remarked a Frenchman, "unless it be the sadness of the inhabitants, most of whom are Quakers or Puritans"—others regarded

[1] Newton D. Mereness, *Travels in the American Colonies* (New York: Macmillan Co., 1916), pp. 410–11.

it as a masterpiece of planning, fit to be the metropolis of an empire. Benjamin Franklin said that, if an atheist existed in the universe, upon seeing Philadelphia he would be converted to a belief in the existence of a Deity—"a town where everything is so well arranged." Contemplating the vice and disorder of Europe, Voltaire once expressed the wish that he might end his days in Philadelphia. But another Frenchman, who knew Philadelphia well, predicted that Voltaire would have soon returned to Paris:

> The gravity of the Quakers would have appeared to him a gloomy pedantry; he would have yawned in their assemblies and been mortified to see his epigrams pass without applause.

Philadelphia was also ahead of other colonial cities in traffic control and street cleaning and lighting. But in all these departments of city living, much remained to be done. Almost everywhere, garbage disposal was entrusted to hogs, and the hogreeve who patrolled the streets was an important official. Urban water supply and sanitation were primitive: most city houses had an outdoor privy and well, often in unhealthy juxtaposition.

In view of the complaints registered by later generations of English travelers that they did not hear the English language spoken properly in any part of the United States, it is noteworthy how many Englishmen remarked during the colonial period upon the Purity of Americans' speech. Lord Adam Gordon—not a man to be easily pleased in such matters—observed that in Philadelphia "the propriety of Language here surprized me much, the English tongue being spoken by all ranks, in a degree of purity and perfection, surpassing any, but the polite part of London."

By the middle of the eighteenth century, Boston would have been unrecognizable to its Puritan founders, who had dreamed of making it a "City Upon a Hill." Travelers commented upon the elegance, the urbanity and the lack of prudery exhibited by the social leaders of the Puritan metropolis.

Joseph Bennett, an English traveler, considered Boston to be one of the liveliest places in British America:

What they call the Mall is a walk on a fine green Common adjoining the south-west side of the town. It is near half a mile over, with two rows of young trees planted opposite to each other, with a fine footway between, in imitation of St. James's Park; and part of the bay of the sea which encircles the town, taking its course along the north-west side of the Common,—by which it is bounded on the one side, and by the country on the other,—forms a beautiful canal, in view of the walk.

Their rural diversions are chiefly shooting and fishing. For the former, the woods afford them plenty of game; and the rivers and ponds with which this country abounds yield them great plenty, as well as variety, of fine fish.

The government being in the hands of dissenters, they don't admit of plays or music-houses; but, of late, they have set up an assembly, to which some of the ladies resort. But they are looked upon to be none of the nicest in regard to their reputation; and it is thought it will soon be suppressed, for it is much taken notice of and exploded by the religious and soberest part of the people.

There are several families in Boston that keep a coach, and pair of horses, and some few drive with four horses; but for chaises and saddle-horses, considering the bulk of the place, they outdo London. They have some nimble, lively horses for the coach, but not any of that beautiful large black breed so common in London. Their saddle-horses all pace naturally, and are generally counted sure-footed; but they are not kept in that fine order as in England. . . . When the ladies ride out to take the air, it is generally in a chaise or chair, and then but a single horse; and they have a negro servant to drive them. The gentlemen ride out here as in England, some in. chairs, and others on horseback, with their negroes to attend them. They travel much the same manner on business as for pleasure, and are attended in both by their black equipages. . . .

For their domestic amusements, every afternoon, after drinking tea, the gentlemen and ladies walk the Mall, and from thence adjourn to one another's houses to spend the evening,— those that are not disposed to attend the evening lecture; which they may do, if they please, six nights in seven, the year round. But, notwithstanding plays and such like diversions do not obtain here, they don't seem to be dispirited nor moped for want of them; for both the ladies and gentlemen dress and appear as gay, in common, as courtiers in England on a coronation or birthday. And the ladies here visit, drink tea, and indulge every little piece of gentility, to the height of the mode; and neglect the affairs of their families with as good a grace as the finest ladies in London.[2]

Until late in the eighteenth century, New York City retained much of the outward aspect of the Dutch town it had once been. Many of the houses were built of brick in the Dutch style, and many of the inhabitants preserved the old Dutch ways. On the other hand, as the headquarters of the British Army in North America, New York City was exposed to strong influence from the mother country. Moreover, young New Yorkers occasionally journeyed to London, where they acquired, among other things, at least a veneer of English manners. Once returned, a traveler could "boast the honour of having been several times drunk in London." After a brief sojourn in England, another New Yorker, it was observed:

can move a Minuet after the newest fashion in England; can quiver like a butterfly; is a perfect connoisseur in dress; and has been author to all the new cock'd hats and scatches in town; has learnt the art of address from the gentility at Covent Garden, which by Jove, he swears has ruined his constitution. Amongst the accomplished beaux, he has learned those elegant expressions, *Split me, Madam; by Gad, Dam me;* and fails not to use them on all occasions. So entirely is he taken up with England, that he always mentions guineas when he speaks of money.[3]

The hub and center of the social life of the cities was the tavern, the principal social institution of colonial America. There were taverns of every degree, from low grogshops to elaborate establishments that catered to gentlemen only.

[2] Joseph Bennett, *History of New England* (Vol. V of *Proceedings of the Massachusetts Historical Society,* 1860–62) (Boston, 1862), pp. 124–26.
[3] Esther Singleton, *Social New York Under the Georges* (New York: Appleton, 1902), p. 374.

Each tavern had its regular clientele. They provided a place where newspapers could be read, business transacted, shipping news and prices discussed, and companionship sweetened by a glass of ale. All the clubs—fraternal, philanthropic and convivial—that abounded in the cities, met in taverns. A gentlemen living in a colonial city could, if his inclinations ran that way, spend each of six nights a week at a different club and still not exhaust the possibilities of dining and drinking in congenial company. The patron saints of England, Ireland and Scotland—St. George, St. Patrick and St. Andrew—were commemorated by their countrymen in fraternal organizations. Even St. Nicholas, "otherwise called Santa Claus," had a separate club; Masonic clubs existed in all the cities, and there were a host of drinking societies. By 1770, Americans had begun to organize clubs dedicated to the American titular saint— Saint Tammany.

As William Eddis described it, the meetings of the Tammany Society of Annapolis, Maryland, were lively affairs.

There are few places where young people are more frequently gratified with opportunities of associating together than in this country. Besides our regular assemblies, every mark of attention is paid to the patron Saint of each parent dominion; and St. George, St. Andrew, St. Patrick, and St. David, are celebrated with every partial mark of national attachment. General invitations are given, and the appearance is always numerous and splendid.

The Americans on this part of the continent, have likewise a Saint, whose history, like those of the above venerable characters, is lost in fable and uncertainty. The first of May is, however, set apart to the memory of Saint Taminay [Tammany], on which occasion the natives wear a piece of a buck's tail in their hats, or in some conspicuous situation. During the course of the evening, and generally in the midst of a dance, the company are interrupted by the sudden intrusion of a number of persons habited like Indians, who rush violently into the room, singing the war song, giving the whoop, and dancing in the stile of those people; after which ceremony a collection is made, and they retire well satisfied with their reception and entertainment.[4]

Nevertheless, some of the most stimulating conversation, as well as some of the heaviest drinking, took place in these clubs. Colonial union was fostered by the presence in American cities of educated men who were able to meet on common intellectual ground—often over a glass of port —visitors from other parts of the continent. Dr. Alexander Hamilton had no difficulty in finding congenial company in the tavern-clubs of New York, Philadelphia and Boston, where the conversation ranged over such subjects as science, literature, politics and the arts. But Hamilton, a man of delicate constitution, who undertook a Grand Tour of the Northern colonies in the hope of restoring his health, frankly acknowledged that he could not keep up with the drinking:

> The people of New York at the first appearance of a stranger are seemingly civil and courteous, but this civility and complaisance soon relaxes if he be not either highly recommended or a good toper. To drink stoutly with the Hungarian Club, who are all bumper men, is the readiest way for a stranger to recommend himself, and a sett among them are very fond of making a stranger drunk. To talk bawdy and to have a knack at punning passes among some there for good sterling wit. Govr. Clinton himself is a jolly toper and gives good example and, for that one quality, is esteemed among these dons.[5]

Because of their close connection with the morals of the community, taverns were the most closely regulated form of business enterprise in colonial America. The tavern keeper was told by the law what he could charge for food, drink and lodging and how much liquor he could serve to each customer. In New England, a guest could spend only a limited time in "tippling" unless he was a traveler, but even travelers were prohibited from accompanying their potations with dancing, loud singing, etc. The law required

[4] William Eddis, *Letters from America* (London: 1792), pp. 114–15.
[5] Carl Bridenbaugh (ed.), *Gentleman's Progress. The Itinerarium of Dr. Alexander Hamilton* (Chapel Hill: University of North Carolina Press, 1948), p. 88.

the tavern keeper to see that his guests did not drink after nine o'clock in the evening or become "bereaved or disabled in the use of his understanding."

In Puritan New England, the position of a tavern keeper was much sought after. Mine host of a public house was a man of standing in the community—only men of exemplary morals need apply. The man who presided over the bar of the Cambridge tavern was a deacon in the local church, and when he retired he was succeeded by his son.

With the growth of a waterfront population of sailors, longshoremen, shipyard laborers and rope-walk workers, the character of the tavern and of the tavern keeper underwent a marked change. Sin, suppressed in its more blatant manifestations, simply went underground—and usually into a tavern. In the genial, smoke-filled and rum-impregnated atmosphere of these hostelries, many citizens found a few hours' escape from the constraints of Puritanism. By the middle of the eighteenth century, John Adams declared that in taverns "the money, health, modesty of most that are young and of many old are wasted; here diseases, vicious habits, bastards and legislators are frequently begotten." The innkeeper, no longer a pillar of the Establishment, became a power in local politics. Much of the preliminary groundwork of the American Revolution was laid in the smoke-filled rooms of colonial taverns.

In 1690, there were in Boston 54 taverns licensed to sell strong drink. Nor was there any necessity for a citizen of Philadelphia to go thirsty: in 1745, Benjamin Franklin counted over 100 public houses, most of which were located in the section of the city popularly known as "Hell-Town," where fur traders, sailors and other transients were relieved of their cash. Franklin was concerned lest the taverns and other drinking places would, by their very numbers, "impoverish one another as well as the Neighbourhoods they live in, and, for want of better Customers, may, thro' Necessity, be under greater Temptations, to entertain Apprentices, Servants and even Negroes."

As a member of the Grand Jury, Franklin drew up a report on moral conditions in Philadelphia:

The Grand Jury observe with great Concern the vast Number of Tipling Houses within this City, many of which they think are little better than Nursuries of Vice and Debauchery, and tend very much to encrease the Number of our Poor. They are likewise of Opinion, that the profane Language, horrid Oaths and Imprecations, grown of late so common in our Streets, so shocking to the Ears of the sober Inhabitants, and tending to destroy in the Minds of our Youth, all Sense of the Fear of God and the Religion of an Oath, owes its Increase in a great Measure to those disorderly Houses. The Jury therefore beg Leave to recommend it to the Court, to fall on some Method of limiting or diminishing the Number of Publick Houses, and preserving Good Order in such as shall be licenced for the future.[6]

In the Northern provinces, the winter season ushered in a round of festivities. Wherever the Church of England was established, Christmas was observed with feasting and merrymaking. Winter also provided an opportunity for ice-skating and sleigh-riding, two of the most popular recreations in the North.

For pleasure-bent New Yorkers, one of the favorite excursions was "the little town of Harlem," chiefly inhabited by Dutch-speaking farmers. After 1765, Ranelagh Gardens and Vauxhall, places of amusement modeled upon the London resorts of the same names, provided New Yorkers with concerts, fireworks displays and dancing. Nor were the other amenities of genteel living lacking: on Long Island, where many wealthy New Yorkers had country houses, horse races were held twice a year.

The gayest and most leisured society in colonial America was found in Charleston, South Carolina. It was celebrated for its splendid mansions, its elegant women, its balls, theater and concerts, its numerous gentlemen's clubs and its horse races. In 1762, the St. Cecilia Society, America's oldest musical society, was founded in Charleston. During the winter and spring seasons, the Society's orchestra, consisting of professional and amateur musicians, gave fortnightly performances. Open-air concerts were also held at the Orange Gardens.

[6] Benjamin Franklin, *Papers*, edited by L. W. Labaree and W. J. Bell (5 vols., New Haven: Yale University Press, 1961), Vol. 3, p. 10.

Thanks to the Huguenots who came to Charleston early in the eighteenth century, French influence was stronger than in any other American city. The young of both sexes were educated *"à la mode"* by French tutors and dancing masters. But Charleston's closest ties were with London, whence came the furniture, silver, books and fabrics that graced the houses of "Gentlemen of Taste and Fortune."

Charleston's social tone was set by an aristocracy of planters, merchants and professional men. It was a society composed mainly of *nouveaux riches,* for the prosperity of the city and of Lowland Carolina was based upon rice and indigo, the cultivation of which was not introduced until the eighteenth century, and rapidly expanding trade with Britain and the West Indies. As a result, South Carolina presented the spectacle of a fluid society in which individuals competed strenuously for wealth and social prestige. In 1773, the *South Carolina Gazette* said of the people of the province:

Their whole Lives are one continual Race in which everyone is endeavoring to distance all behind him; and to overtake or pass by, all before him; everyone is flying from his inferiors in Pursuit of his Superiors, who fly from him, with equal alacrity. . . . Every Tradesman is a Merchant, every Merchant is a Gentleman, and every Gentleman one of the Noblesse.

We are a Country of Gentry. . . . We have no such Thing as a common People among us: The better Sort of Gentry, who can aim at no higher, plunge themselves into Debt and Dependence, to preserve their Rank.

One of the strongest aversions felt by the Puritans—and they were a people with many aversions—was toward the theater. Had they had their way, the Elizabethan theater would have been suppressed as an abomination in the sight of God. This abhorrence of plays and players endured long after the American Revolution. In 1750, an attempt to stage a play in Boston nearly resulted in a riot; and in 1759 the New Hampshire House of Representatives denied a troupe of actors permission to enter the colony on the ground that plays had "a peculiar influence on the minds of young people and greatly endanger their morals by giving them a taste for intriguing, amusement and pleasure." As late as 1824, President Timothy Dwight of Yale warned the student body that "to indulge a taste for playgoing means nothing more or less than the loss of that most valuable treasure the immortal soul."

To evade the laws against the presentation of plays, dramatic works were billed under innocuous, morally uplifting names. In Rhode Island, for example, an attempt was made to present *Othello* as "a series of Moral Dialogues depicting the Evil Effects of Jealousy and other Bad Passions, and Proving that Happiness can only Spring from the Pursuit of Virtue." In Philadelphia, the Southwark Theater was called "the Opera House" and a play was called "Spectaculum Vitae" [Spectacle of Life]. *Hamlet* appeared as "a moral and Instructive Tale as exemplified in the History of the Prince of Denmark" and *The School for Scandal* became "a Comic Lecture in five Parts on the Pernicious Vice of Scandal."

Virginia and Maryland did not have laws against the theater but neither did they have large population centers where it could flourish. Nevertheless, plays were given at Williamsburg as early as 1716, with students from William and Mary College as actors.

Because the theater required comparatively large audiences of well-to-do, cultured and, at least in this regard, un-Puritanical people, it was most successful in cities like New York and Charleston, South Carolina. New York City had a theater as early as 1732; Charleston's was established four years later. Despite the opposition of a large segment of the Quaker community, a theater was built in Philadelphia in 1754. A few years later, when an attempt was made to outlaw the theater in Philadelphia, its defenders pointed out that it was located in a section of the city "where but very few, and those of the worst Sort, resided, that no Nuisance might arise therefrom."

In spite of its unsavory location, the Philadelphia theater, thanks to Hallam's Company of Comedians, enjoyed the most professional acting and stage designing in British

America. Lewis Hallam, a London actor-manager, brought his troupe to Philadelphia in 1754. Eight years later, the Hallam Company began regular tours of the colonies with a repertoire including the tragedies of Shakespeare and Addison and the comedies of Farquhar and Steele.

In polite circles in New York, Philadelphia, Annapolis, Williamsburg and Charleston—but not in Boston—plays and players provided an engrossing subject of conversation. A few Americans even tried their hand at writing plays. The first-produced drama written by an American was Thomas Godfrey's *The Prince of Parthia,* staged in Philadelphia in 1767. Parthia was far removed from Philadelphia, but Godfrey's play was equally remote from the real Parthia: it was wholly English in tone and manner. It was not until Major Robert Roger's *Ponteach* (Pontiac), published in England in 1766 but probably not produced on the stage until much later, that American themes took their place in dramatic literature.

Bibliography

Bowes, Frederick P. *The Culture of Early Charleston.* Chapel Hill: University of North Carolina Press, 1942.

Bridenbaugh, Carl. *Cities in the Wilderness.* New York: Ronald Press, 1938.

———. *Cities in Revolt: Urban Life in America, 1743–1776.* New York: Ronald Press, 1955.

Bridenbaugh, Carl and Jessica. *Rebels and Gentlemen: Philadelphia in the Age of Franklin.* New York: Reynal and Hitchcock, 1942.

LIFE ON THE FRONTIER

TRAVELERS who remarked upon the similarity in dress and manners of the inhabitants of the colonial seaports with those of English cities were hardly prepared for the conditions they encountered on the frontier. Here there was little to remind them of the civilized amenities of the Old World: a raw clearing in the wilderness, a log cabin, a few hogs, cattle and chickens, and a patch of corn were often the only visible signs of white occupation. And yet, in the beginning, all Americans were frontiersmen and the experience of confronting Nature in the raw was written over and over again by successive generations.

Most of the people who composed the first wave of settlers—the true frontiersmen—came not to make permanent homes but to stake out claims to the land, build a log cabin, and, after the Indians had been "pacified," to sell out to newcomers seeking land for farming. The frontiersmen repeated this process over and over, always moving a little farther west ahead of the pursuing farmers. Usually the frontiersman did not cut down the trees around his cabin, instead, he simply stripped the trees and planted hills of corn in the dead forest. It was therefore left to the farmer to clear the land, but by that time the frontiersman was making his second or third remove west. This kind of pioneering did not enrich the frontiersmen: often they staked their lives against formidable odds for a small profit.

Benjamin Franklin put land speculation high on the list of the Ways to Wealth. As Franklin pictured it, frontiersmen and other land speculators could not lose: everything they bought, particularly in the unsettled parts of the country, was certain to go up in price:

Land being cheap in that Country, from the vast Forests still void of Inhabitants, and not likely to be occupied in an Age to come, insomuch that the Propriety of an hundred Acres of fertile Soil full of Wood may be obtained near the Frontiers, in many Places, for Eight or Ten Guineas, hearty young Labouring Men, who understand the Husbandry of Corn and Cattle, which is nearly the same in that Country as in Europe, may easily establish themselves there. A little Money sav'd of the good Wages they receive there, while they work for others, enables them to buy the Land and begin their Plantation, in which they are assisted by the Good-Will of their Neighbours, and some Credit. Multitudes of poor People from England, Ireland, Scotland and Germany, have by this means in a few years become wealthy Farmers, who, in their own Countries, where all the Lands are fully occupied, and the Wages of Labour low, could never have emerged from the poor Condition wherein they were born. . . .

The writer of this has known several Instances of large Tracts of Land, bought, on what was then the Frontier of Pensilvania, for Ten Pounds per hundred Acres, which after 20 years, when the Settlements have been extended far beyond them, sold readily, without any Improvements made upon them, for three Pounds per Acre.[1]

The Noble Savage was the creation of the eighteenth century; the American frontiersman had to wait until the next century for his literary apotheosis. Before James Fenimore Cooper, the frontiersman was usually depicted as a ne'er-do-well who had drifted to the frontier because he was rejected by the orderly, hardworking society of the settled areas. Cultured colonists in the seaport towns recoiled from these "white barbarians," so alien in every respect to the ideals of the eighteenth century.

George Washington considered frontiersmen to be "a parcel of barbarians and an uncouth set of people." In 1748, he wrote a friend:

[1] Oscar Handlin (ed.), *Readings in American History*, (New York: Alfred A. Knopf, Inc., 1957), pp. 50–52.

Since you received my letter in October last, I have not slepp'd above three nights of four in a bed, but, after walking a good deal all the day, I lay down before the fire upon a little hay, straw, fodder, or bearskin, which ever is to be had, with man, wife, and children, like a parcel of dogs and cats; and happy is he, who get the berth nearest the fire. . . . I have never had my clothes off, but lay and sleep in them, except the few nights I have lay'n in Frederick Town.[2]

To Crèvecoeur, the true American was a farmer who lived in a settled, orderly community. He was not willing to admit that frontiersmen were really Americans, as he defined the breed:

Now we arrive near the great woods, near the last inhabited districts; there men seem to be placed still farther beyond the reach of government, which in some measure leaves them to themselves. How can it pervade every corner; as they were driven there by misfortunes, necessity of beginnings, desire of acquiring large tracts of land, idleness, frequent want of economy, ancient debts; the re-union of such people does not afford a very pleasing spectacle. When discord, want of unity and friendship; when either drunkenness or idleness prevail in such remote districts; contention, inactivity, and wretchedness must ensue. There are not the same remedies to these evils as in a long established community. The few magistrates they have, are in general little better than the rest; they are often in a perfect state of war; that of man against man, sometimes decided by blows, sometimes by means of the law; that of man against every wild inhabitant of these venerable woods, of which are come to disposses them. There men appear to be no better than carnivorous animals of a superior rank, living on the flesh of wild animals, when they can catch them, and when they are not able, they subsist on grain. He who would wish to see America in its proper light, and have a true idea of its feeble beginnings and barbarous rudiments, must visit our extended line of frontiers where the last settlers dwell, and where he may see the first labours of settlement, the mode of clearing the earth, in all their different appearances; where men are wholly left dependent on their native tempers, and on the spur of uncertain industry, which often fails when not sanctified by the

[2] W. C. Ford (ed.), *The Writings of George Washington* (14 vols., New York: G. P. Putnam's Sons, 1889–93), Vol. 1, p. 7.

efficacy of a few moral rules. There, removed from the power of example and check of shame, many families exhibit the most hideous parts of our society. They are a kind of forlorn hope, preceding by ten or twelve years the most respectable army of veterans which come after them. In that space, prosperity will polish some, vice and the law will drive off the rest, who uniting again with others like themselves will recede still farther; making room for more industrious people, who will finish their improvements, convert the loghouse into a convenient habitation, and rejoicing that the first heavy labours are finished, will change in a few years that hitherto barbarous country into a fine fertile, well regulated district. Such is our progress, such is the march of the Europeans toward the interior parts of this continent. In all societies there are off-casts; this impure part serves as our precursors or pioneers; my father himself was one of that class, but he came upon honest principles, and was therefore one of the few who held fast; by good conduct and temperance, he transmitted to me his fair inheritance, when not above one in fourteen of his contemporaries had the same good fortune.

Forty years ago this smiling country was thus inhabited; it is now purged, a general decency of manners prevails throughout, and such has been the fate of our best countries.[3]

The only exceptions Crèvecoeur admitted to his generalization that, on the frontier, men degenerated into semisavages were the Moravians, Quakers and Congregationalists. He attributed their immunity to the fact that they settled in communities and thereby preserved their religion, fellowship and respect for law and order. These men, he observed with satisfaction, lived like farmers and preferred the wholesome food they raised on their own land to the gamey meat of wilderness animals.

Certainly the frontier exerted a powerful attraction upon the adventurous, the discontented and those in search of "a purer air of freedom." Young rebels went west and worked off their belligerence and frustrations upon the Indians: one of the status symbols on the frontier was a belt loaded with Indian scalps. For social misfits the frontier afforded a refuge against the vagrancy and compulsory-labor laws of the more civilized parts of the coun-

[3] J.Hector St. John de Crèvecoeur, *Letters from an American Farmer* (New York: F. P. Dutton and Co., 1926), pp. 46–47.

try. Many frontiersmen were uncouth, belligerent, disorderly, lazy and shiftless. Nevertheless, whatever their moral shortcomings, they found on the frontier "the utmost enjoyment of liberty and independency." James Madison believed that the paramount reason that so many of his countrymen went west was that they were "irresistibly attracted by that complete liberty, that freedom from bonds, obligations, duties, that absence of care and anxiety which characterize the savage state." In short, the frontier served as outdoor therapy for the neuroses produced by civilization.

Life on the frontier was a constant challenge that required an unquenchable optimism and the utmost in courage, self-reliance, and the capacity for enduring hardship. Even Crèvecoeur, despite his low opinion of the morals and manners of the frontier people, paid tribute to their fortitude and resourcefulness:

> He that is just arrived and sees a fine, smooth plantation with a good house or a flourishing orchard, and hears that the proprietor pays but a small tax, immediately thinks: this man is too happy. His imagination presents him with such images and ideas as are suggested to him by what he has seen in Europe. He sees not that sea of trouble, of labour, and expense which have been lavished on this farm. He forgets the fortitude, and the regrets with which the first emigrant left his friends, his relations, and his native land. He is unacquainted with the immense difficulties of first settlement, with the sums borrowed, with the many years of interest paid, with the various shifts these first people have been obliged to make use of. The original log-house, the cradle of the American, is now gone, and has made room for the more elegant framed one. Is there no credit to be given to these first cultivators who by their sweat, their toil, and their perseverance have come over a sea of three thousand miles to till a new soil? [4]

Sometimes this escape from the tensions of civilization and its attendant problems took the form of an escape from work. It was this aspect of pioneering that particularly struck travelers who visited the Carolina frontier. Janet Schaw, a "Lady of Quality," attributed the indolence of

[4] J. Hector St. John de Crèvecoeur, *Sketches of Eighteenth-Century America* (New Haven: Yale University Press, 1925), pp. 88–89.

the people to the baneful effect of overindulgence in New England rum:

> . . . Nature holds out to them every thing that can contribute to conveniency, or tempt to luxury, yet the inhabitants resist both, and if they can raise as much corn and pork, as to subsist them in the most slovenly manner, they ask no more; and as a very small proportion of their time serves for that purpose, the rest is spent in sauntering thro' the woods with a gun or sitting under a rustick shade, drinking New England rum made into grog, the most shocking liquor you can imagine. By this manner of living, their blood is spoil'd and rendered thin beyond all proportion, so that it is constantly on the fret like bad small beer, and hence the constant slow fevers that wear down their constitutions, relax their nerves and infeeble the whole frame. Their appearance is in every respect the reverse of that which gives the idea of strength and vigor, and for which the British peasantry are so remarkable. They are tall and lean, with short waists and long limbs, sallow complexions and languid eyes, when not inflamed by spirits. Their feet are flat, their joints loose and their walk uneven. These I speak of are only the peasantry of this country, as hitherto I have seen nothing else, but I make no doubt when I come to see the better sort, they will be far from this description. For tho' there is a most disgusting equality, yet I hope to find an American Gentleman a very different creature from an American clown.[5]

Poverty, indolence and ignorance in the midst of the bounties of Nature—such was North Carolina as depicted by William Byrd II in his *History of the Dividing Line* and *Journey to the Land of Eden*. The western inhabitants of that colony provided Byrd with an opportunity for the display of his talents for ridicule and satire. In Byrd's account, the North Carolinians appear as the inhabitants of Lubberland. Among the many causes of mortality in that province, Byrd excluded overwork. No man, he remarked, ever died of *that* malady. The aversion of the backwoodsman to labor seemed to him comparable to the lilies of the field—although the resemblance ended there. They were, Byrd remarked, "slothfull in everything but getting Chil-

[5] Janet Schaw, *Journal of a Lady of Quality*, edited by Charles M. Andrews (New Haven: Yale University Press, 1922), p. 153.

dren." When not engaged in that pursuit, they dozed in the sun, sat on rail fences and chawed and, at rare intervals, summoned up enough energy to do a little hoeing in the corn patch. Household chores, tending the children and doing most of the farm work they left to their wives; seemingly they had adopted the Indians' theory that women, by their transgressions, had laid the curse of work upon the world and that therefore it was their duty to shoulder the burden. An Indian brave considered *his* duty done when he helped strap the load on his squaw's back.

It never occurred to William Byrd that the listless, apathetic dullards he described were the victims of hookworm and deficiency diseases such as pellagra; indeed, it was not until the twentieth century that the physical rehabilitation of the poor whites began. Byrd was content to accept the theory, widely accepted in his time, that an indulgent climate combined with too much rum aggravated the Carolinians' natural tendency toward sloth.

If material equality existed anywhere in America, it was on the pristine frontier, where the leveling influences of the wilderness were most strongly felt. Yet these pioneers were not seeking economic equality. Like other Americans, they wanted a chance to raise themselves above the general level and, if possible, to become rich. On the frontier, "equality" often meant not equality of circumstances among individuals but equality between the western and the eastern sections of the country. The frontier, in short, was a society of expectant capitalists. All that the pioneers asked was equal political rights and an equal chance to exploit the natural resources of the region and to profit from the increment in land values.

In this free-for-all, competitive society, inequalities manifested themselves very quickly. Land speculation led to the concentration of large holdings in the hands of a few wealthy men or land companies. Often even before the pioneers arrived, title to the land had passed into the possession of speculators—with the result that the frontiersmen were obliged to squat upon soil to which they had no legal claim. Moreover, the discrepancy between the various kinds of people drawn to the frontier—the drifters and ne'er-do-wells together with the ambitious and enterprising —tended to produce the very inequalities from which some pioneers hoped to escape. Among its other functions, the frontier brought to the fore able and energetic individuals —and they formed the nucleus of a frontier aristocracy.

Bibliography

Crane, Verner W. *The Southern Frontier, 1670–1732.* Durham: Duke University Press, 1928.

Eaton, Clement. *A History of the Old South.* New York: Macmillan Co., 1949.

Tunis, Edwin. *Frontier Living.* Cleveland: World Publishing Co., 1961.

Wright, Louis B. *The Atlantic Frontier. Colonial American Civilization, 1607–1763.* New York: A. A. Knopf, Inc., 1947.

BLACK AND WHITE LABOR
IN COLONIAL AMERICA

IN colonial America, a considerable part—in some areas the major part—of the labor force was not free. Most of the people who came to America from Great Britain and Europe paid their passage across the Atlantic by agreeing to sell their labor for a term of from four to seven years. These "indentured servants" and "redemptioners" were bound by contract to serve the individuals who bought their labor; they could not legally leave his employ and they were obliged to work under conditions prescribed by their master. No social stigma attached to this form of servitude: the servants had rights that could be enforced in the courts and they became free after serving their term. As freemen, they were entitled to their "freedom dues," consisting of a suit of clothes, agricultural tools and, in some colonies, 50 acres of land.

Once he had attained freedom, the white American workingman, particularly if he were skilled, could be sure of receiving the highest wages in the world. Moreover, there were always more jobs available than workers to fill them; only the unemployable were without work. In consequence, the American workingman not only commanded high wages, but, equally important, he commanded respect and even deference from his employers. Crèvecoeur was one of the first to observe among the forces working for democracy in the colonies the special status enjoyed by the American workingman:

As to labour and labourers,—what difference! When we hire any of these people we rather pray and entreat them. You must give them what they ask: three shillings per day in common wages and five or six shillings in harvest. They must be at your table and feed, as you saw it at my house, on the best you have. . . .

Last year Mr. ———, the first man in our country, our first judge and assemblyman, received in harvest a large company from the town of ———. He immediately ordered two tables in two different rooms, for he always eats with his work-people. The reapers, perceiving the new distinction which he was going to establish, quitted him after having made very severe reflections, and it was not without great difficulties that he was enabled to finish his harvest with his own people.[1]

Indentured servants and redemptioners were so eager to partake of the bounties of freedom that many ran away before their term of service was completed. Since their objective was to become free and independent American farmers, few of those who served their full term were content to remain as tenants or hired hands. As a result, while the system of indenture proved to be an excellent method of peopling the colonies, it failed to satisfy the need for a permanent labor force.

Because of the plenitude and cheapness of land, a permanent labor force necessarily meant an unfree labor force. The first to suffer enslavement in America at the hands of white men was the Indian. When Europeans reached the New World, they supposed that the aborigines would provide an almost inexhaustible supply of forced labor. Christopher Columbus, observing that the natives of Hispaniola were the most gentle, docile and amiable creatures that he had ever seen, concluded that they would make splendid slaves.

But the American Indians failed to realize their conquerors' high hopes: when enslaved, the natives obstinately refused to work, ran away, or died. Even though the English colonists expended far more effort upon enslaving the Indians than upon converting them to Christianity, it was

[1] J. Hector St. John de Crèvecoeur, *Sketches of Eighteenth-Century America* (New Haven: Yale University Press, 1925), pp. 82–83.

all to no avail. Nevertheless, Indian slaves were put on the market for what they would bring. In 1676, after New Englanders had suppressed an uprising of Indians under King Philip, chief of the Wamapanoag Indians and leader of the most formidable war waged against the whites in New England, most of the captives, including King Philip's wife and child, were sold into slavery in the West Indies. In the continental colonies the price of Indian slaves remained depressed and after every war with the natives the market was glutted. In 1708, for example, there were 1,400 Indian and 2,000 Negro slaves in South Carolina, but the redskins brought only half the price that the blacks commanded.

Recognizing the impracticability of forcing Indians to work on farms and plantations and the impossibility of preserving peace so long as captives were sold into servitude, most of the English colonies took action early in the eighteenth century to prevent the enslavement of the tribesmen. Gradually Indian slavery faded away—as did, indeed, the Indian himself.

The Indians' insistence upon remaining free men—preferring, as Patrick Henry put it on another occasion, death to slavery—had a direct bearing upon the lives of millions of black Africans. Since America itself could not furnish a labor force sufficient to the needs of the white newcomers, they turned perforce to the black continent.

Here they found a seemingly inexhaustible supply of workers who were precluded by the color of their skin and their servile status from leaving the employ of their masters and becoming free and independent farmers. The beneficiaries of this traffic in black flesh were not merely the planters and the slave traders: virtually every branch of industry was animated by the Black Man with the Hoe. His labor produced the principal staples of the British mercantilist empire: tobacco, sugar, rice, cotton and indigo. Black Africa, in the words of an eighteenth-century economist, "carried the empire."

While the black slaves were concentrated in the South, the institution of slavery existed in all the English colonies.

In Northern cities, a considerable number of slaves were held as laborers and house servants: as early as 1715, of Boston's 12,000 inhabitants, approximately 2,000 were Negro slaves and in 1740 almost one quarter of the population of New York City was colored. Except among the Quakers and kindred German religious sects, little stigma was attached to the holding of slaves by whites: the clergy of the Church of England owned slaves and they were accepted as a form of endowment for colonial churches. When the Reverend Cotton Mather of Boston was presented with a slave by his congregation, he piously recorded the event in his diary as "a smile from Heaven." The first English slaver, Captain John Hawkins, was a devout Christian whose slave ship was named *Jesus;* and Captain John Newton, an eighteenth-century slaver, composed the hymn "How Sweet the Name of Jesus Sounds" while waiting in his ship off the African coast for a cargo of slaves.

Especially when they worked in large gangs under the supervision of an efficient overseer, slaves produced a handsome profit for their owners. John Woolman, a Pennsylvania Quaker, tried to calculate the debt, including compound interest. that masters owed their slaves by withholding the wages fairly owing them; if his computations were correct, the slaveowners might have ended by changing places with the slaves. Certainly every effort was made by the slaveowners to ensure that they received a comfortable margin of profit from the labor of their slaves. Although there was a steady increase in the market price of slaves, the cost of maintaining them remained minimal. Black fieldhands wore the cheapest and coarsest cloth available, the so-called Negro cloth, and they were provided with a blanket only once every three years. Their diet consisted of rice, corn, beans, pork and molasses and, on special occasions, herring and meat. Nor was all the food consumed by slaves provided by the master: on many plantations, they were allotted plots of ground on which to raise garden vegetables for their own use or to sell in the market.

White workers, free or indentured, did not often choose

to compete with black slave labor. It generally followed that, as the slave population increased, the number of white laborers tended to decrease. Whereas during the 1670's, approximately 1,500 white indentured servants arrived annually in Virginia, by 1720 this flow of workers had subsided to a mere trickle. By the middle of the eighteenth century, black slaves had preempted most of the skilled as well as the unskilled trades in the South: they served as coopers, carpenters, blacksmiths, ironworkers and artisans of every kind. Thomas Jefferson operated on his plantation at Monticello a small nail factory in which the "hands" were Negro slave children, and George Washington used slave girls to manufacture woolen, cotton and linen cloth. Thus, by reason of the versatility of the slave himself, Negro slavery tended to produce the conditions that ensured its survival by eliminating competing forms of labor.

Like white indentured servants and redemptioners, Negro and Indian slaves were called "servants." A slaveowner referred to his "servants" or his "people," never to his "slaves." Nevertheless, there was an unbridgeable gulf between white and black servants. Unlike a white servant, a Negro slave was bound for life, his children inherited his status, and he was regarded as belonging to a race inferior and apart. A slave possessed only such rights as were granted him by law whereas a white servant enjoyed all the rights appertaining to a freeman except those of which he was temporarily deprived by law or contract.

Even so, a white skin was no protection against exploitation in colonial America. When black slaves and white indentured servants were held by the same master, it was often the whites for whom the least consideration was shown. After all, the term of service of an indentured servant was of comparatively short duration and he could make trouble if he did not receive his "freedom dues." Some masters, therefore, did not permit humanitarian considerations to prevent them from getting as much labor as possible out of an indentured servant before his term ran out. Because a Negro slave's term expired only with his life, it was to the master's advantage to prolong the slave's existence and to keep him in good working condition.

The hours of labor of black and white servants did not greatly differ in colonial America. In the Northern colonies, a 14-hour day for apprentices and journeymen was not uncommon. On Southern plantations where white servants worked alongside Negro slaves, they often did the same kind of work and put in the same number of hours in the field. By an act of the South Carolina legislature, hailed as a humanitarian measure, servants could not be forced to work more than 15 hours a day.

Apologists for slavery often compared the working conditions of the slaves with those of the "laboring poor" of Great Britain and Europe—to the disadvantage of the latter. The Reverend Jonathan Boucher of Maryland was certain that the slaves, even though their spiritual welfare was neglected, enjoyed a higher standard of living than did lower-class Englishmen:

Nothing is easier than to excite compassion by declamations against slavery. Yet I have seldom heard or read things of this sort which carried much conviction to my mind. The condition of the lower classes of mankind everywhere, when compared with that of those above them, may seem hard; yet on a fair investigation, it will probably be found that people in general in a low sphere are not less happy than those in a higher sphere. I am equally well persuaded in my own mind that the negroes in general in Virginia and Maryland in my time [1759–75] were not upon the whole worse off nor less happy than the labouring poor in Great Britain. Many things respecting them no doubt were wrong; but this is saying no more than might be said of the poor of these kingdoms. . . . Slavery is not one of the most intolerable evils incident to humanity, even to slaves; I have known thousands of slaves as well-informed, as well-clad, as well-fed, and in every respect as well off as nine out of ten of the poor in every kingdom of Europe are. Nor is the possession of slaves so desirable an acquisition as may be imagined: if a wrong be done them, as I question not there is, in making them slaves, their owners are probable sufficiently punished by the unpleasant nature of their services. I remember a gentleman of Virginia, the owner of many slaves, used to say that the passage of Scripture in which the difficulty of a rich man's entering into the Kingdom of Heaven is spoken of must certainly have alluded to those who were rich in slaves.[2]

Colored house servants were usually better treated than fieldhands, and the slaveowner himself was generally more humane than was the overseer he hired to get out the crop. If the overseer's salary was based upon the amount of tobacco, rice or indigo he produced, the slaves were likely to be pushed to the limit of their endurance. Worst of all, they were sometimes hired out to contractors whose sole purpose was to get the work done as quickly and as cheaply as possible without regard to the welfare of the workers.

In both the Northern and Southern colonies there were slaveowners who took seriously their duty to their slaves and prided themselves upon their Christian charity. Southerners, in particular, always insisted that slavery could be beautiful and pointed to their old Negro "Mammy" as proof of the essential benevolence of the institution. A fixture in many households, the colored "Mammy" often took as much pride in and felt almost as much affection for the white children she had raised as she did toward her own offspring; and for her and other faithful servitors, the white family often felt an affection that went far toward erasing the barriers of race and status. There was, in truth, a humane side to slavery and the relationship between the two races was not wholly a matter of fear and servility on one side and cruelty and oppression on the other.

Even so, the slave's best protection against incapacitating mistreatment by a cruel master was the fact that he was a valuable piece of property, with a cash value on the auction block. Moreover, a brutal master was likely to incur social opprobrium: in the best slaveholding circles self-command was expected of every master no matter how egregiously he was provoked by the disobedience or laziness of his slaves. And yet no institution ever placed a heavier responsibility upon the self-restraint and the conscience of individuals. Slavery conferred power virtually unchecked by law; and whether that power was used for good or for

[2] Jonathan Boucher, *Reminiscences of an American Loyalist* (Boston: Houghton Mifflin Co., 1925), pp. 97–98.

ill, benevolently or cruelly, was left almost wholly to the slaveowner himself. In effect, this meant that men who had risen in the world by giving free rein to their acquisitive instincts were vested with the almost absolute ownership of human beings. The agricultural system of the Old South, no more than the later industrial system of the North, did not bestow wealth and power upon the gentle, the meek and the compassionate. Composed largely of self-made men and their immediate descendants, the Southern slaveowning aristocracy of the colonial period set less store by human values, as exemplified in Negro slaves, than did the more seasoned and patriarchal society of nineteenth-century Virginia.

William Byrd II had no kind words for slavery, an institution he regarded as injurious to whites as well as to blacks. He said:

> They [slaves] blow up the pride and ruin the industry of our white people, who, seeing a rank of poor creatures below them, detest work for fear it should make them like slaves.

And, because a great mass of enslaved blacks always posed the threat of servile war, he would have liked to see the British Parliament "put an end to the uncristian traffic of making merchandize of our fellow creatures."

Yet Byrd, like his fellow planters, was a captive of the system: he could not forego slave labor without injuring his competitive position as a tobacco producer. Therefore he manned his plantations with hundreds of blacks and maintained a large staff of household servants at Westover.

Although Byrd considered himself to be a kind and indulgent master who watched carefully over the health and well-being of his slaves and ministered to them when they fell ill, his *Secret Diary* reveals that he sometimes whipped his black "servants" on slight provocation. Byrd justified this treatment on the ground that, where many Negroes were held together in servitude, their owners were compelled to be severe: "Numbers," he observed, "make them insolent and then foul means must do what fair will not."

Accordingly, he resorted to foul means for such offenses as spilling water on the couch, "for doing nothing," "for not doing their business on pretense of sickness," "for drinking all day Sunday," for running away, and for stealing hogs. In October, 1710, while staying at Williamsburg, he recorded this incident in his diary: "I went to my lodgings but my man was gone to bed and I was shut out. However I called him and beat him for it." He vented his anger with a whip against Moll "for doing everything wrong" and again for "a hundred faults"; and Anaka was whipped "for stealing the rum and filling the bottle up with water."

Despite William Byrd's readiness to use the lash, the slaves at Westover might well have prayed to be delivered from the wrath of their mistress to the relative mercy of their master. For Lucy Byrd, a neurotic woman with a pronounced sadistic streak, derived deep satisfaction from inflicting punishment; for her, the bare back of a slave provided a ready outlet for the release of tensions and frustrations. The following entries in his diary disclose that Byrd was often obliged to protect the blacks from the ungovernable fury of his wife:

[July 15, 1710:] My wife against my will. caused little Jenny to be burned with a hot iron, for which I quarreled with her.

[February 27, 1711:] In the evening my wife and little Jenny had a great quarrel in which my wife got the worst but at last by the help of the family Jenny was overcome and soundly whipped.

[December 31, 1711:] My wife and I had a terrible quarrel about whipping Eugene while Mr. Mumford was there but she had a mind to show her authority before company but would not suffer it, which she took very ill.

[March 2, 1712:] I had a terrible quarrel with my wife concerning Jenny that I took away from her when she was beating her with the tongs. She lifted up her hands to strike me but forbore to do it. She gave me abundance of bad words and endeavored to strangle herself, but I believe in jest only. However after acting a mad woman a long time she was passive again.

[May 22, 1712:] My wife caused Prue to be whipped violently notwithstanding I desired not, which provoked me to have Anaka whipped likewise who had deserved it much more, on which my wife flew into such a passion that she hoped she would be revenged of me. . . . My wife was sorry for what she had said and came to ask my pardon and I forgave her in my heart but seemed to resent, that she might be the more sorry for her folly.

[September 12, 1712:] My wife had a good a great [sic] quarrel with her maid Prue and with good reason: she is growing a most notable girl for stealing and laziness and lying and everything that is bad.[8]

Philip Vickers Fithian described how an overseer of a Virginia plantation exercised his ingenuity at the expense of the blacks who were entrusted to his care:

When I am on the Subject, I will relate further, what I heard George Lees's Overseer, one Morgan, say the other day that he himself had often done to Negroes, and found it useful. He said that whipping of any kind does them no good, for they will laugh at your greatest Severity; But he told us he had invented two things, and by several experiments had proved their success.

For Sullenness, Obstinacy, or Idleness, says he, Take a Negro, strip him, tie him fast to a post; take then a sharp Curry-Comb, & curry him severely till he is well scrap'd; & call a Boy with some dry Hay, and make the Boy rub him down for several Minutes, then salt him, & unlose him. He will attend to his Business (said the inhuman Infidel) afterwards!

But savage Cruelty does not exceed His next diabolical Invention—To get a Secret from a Negro, says he, take the following Method—Lay upon your Floor a large thick plank, having a peg about eighteen inches long, of hard wood, & very Sharp, on the upper end, fixed fast in the plank—then strip

[8] *The Secret Diary of William Byrd of Westover, 1709–1712*, edited by Louis B. Wright and Marion Tingling (Richmond: The Dietz Press, 1941), pp. 56, 68, 205, 307, 462, 494, 533, and 582–83.

the Negro, tie the Cord to a staple in the Ceiling, so that his foot may just rest on the sharpened Peg, then turn him briskly around, and you would laugh (said our informer) at the Dexterity of the Negro, while he was relieving his Feet on the sharpen'd Peg! [4]

The Reverend Francis Le Jau, a missionary of the Church of England, discovered that in South Carolina the planters were unwilling to permit their slaves to be converted to Christianity. In at least one instance, the message of Christianity seems not to have penetrated among the master race:

Few Masters appear Zealous or even pleased with what the Missionaries try to do for the Good of their Slaves. They are more Cruel Some of them of late Dayes than before. They hamstring, maim & unlimb those poor Creatures for Small faults. A man within this Month had a very fine Negroe baptized. Sensible, Carefull & good in all Respects who being wearyed with Labour & fallen asleep had the Mischance to lose a parcell of Rice which by the Oversetting of a Periogua fell into a River. The man, tho Intreated by the Minister of the Parish, who is Brother Maule and some Persons of the best Consideration among us to forgive the Negroe, who had Offended only through Neglect without Malice, thought fit to keep him for several Dayes in Chains, & I am told muffled up that he might not Eat, & Scourged him twice a Day, and at Night to put him into a hellish Machine contrived by him into the Shape of a Coffin where he could not Stirr. The punishment having continued Several Dayes & Nights and there being no Appearance when it should End, the poor Negroe through Despair Ask't one of his Children for a knife & manacled as he was Stabb'd himself with it. I am told this is the 5th Slave that the Same man has destroyed by his Cruelty within 2 or 3 Yeares, but he is only an hired Overseer. The Owner of the Slaves lives out of this Province. I own I see everybody almost angry at So much Barbarity. Yet he pretends to go to Church, and they look upon the Man as Guilty of Murder, and So do great many of my Acquaintance who tho not So Barbarous take no Care

[4] Philip Vickers Fithian, *Journals and Letters, 1767–1774* (Williamsburg: Colonial Williamsburg Press, 1934), pp. 50–51.

at all of the Souls of their Slaves, and as little as they can of their bodies.[5]

While white Americans were divided in opinion regarding the advisability of permitting slaves to be exposed to Christian teachings, they were in almost complete agreement that the education of slaves constituted a serious functioning, the slave system required docility, obedience and abjectness, and no one supposed that these qualities were inculcated by education. A black who could read and write was regarded as a potential leader of a servile revolt; in a slave, education in any degree was esteemed a dangerous thing. For this reason, South Carolina imposed a fine of 100 pounds upon anyone found guilty of teaching a slave to write or employing him to write. The laws of that province made it a more heinous offense to educate a slave than to kill him.

This large population of ignorant and debased blacks took a subtle revenge upon the master race. In 1774, it was observed that South Carolina gentlemen, once noted for the purity of their diction and the correctness of their London accent, were beginning to talk like Negroes.

Unsanctioned by English law and unknown in England itself, Negro slavery was the "peculiar institution" of the American colonies. The laws and customs governing this institution were developed by Englishmen living overseas; each colony had its own slave code, the provisions of which were gradually developed over a considerable period of time. These codes differed markedly as regarded the severity of the restraints and punishments imposed upon the slaves. But everywhere the effect of these laws was to make the Negro slave a mere chattel. By virtue of this legal definition of the slave's status, "the Masters or owners," a colonist observed, "have as good a Right to and title to them, during their lives, as a Man has to a horse or Ox, after he has bought them." In Virginia, during the eighteenth century, it

---

[5] Frank J. Kingberg (ed.), *The Carolina Chronicle of Dr. Francis Le Jau. 1706–1717* (Los Angeles: University of California Press, 1956), pp. 129–30.

was gravely debated whether Negro slaves were real estate or personal property. It made little difference to the slaves for in neither case could they expect to be treated like human beings.

A slave accused of a crime enjoyed none of the safeguards erected by the common law; in his case, the procedures designed to protect the rights of the individual were wholly dispensed with in the interests of executing summary justice. A slave could be arrested, tried and condemned upon the testimony of only one witness and, after 1692, a jury trial was not required in Virginia even in capital cases. Negroes, Indians and convicts could not bear witness against a white man, although the law permitted them to testify against each other.

The South Carolina slave code was based upon the principle that Negroes "are of barbarous, wild, savage natures, and such as renders them wholly unqualified to be governed by the laws, customs and practices of this province." This point of view pervaded the relations between the two races in the province: the roads were constantly patrolled by companies of horsemen and even while going to church South Carolinians carried arms. Eternal vigilance against a potential internal enemy who might strike at any moment was the price paid by the whites for keeping large numbers of blacks in servitude.

By English law, the murder of a master by his servant was punished by hanging, beheading, drawing and quartering. In the colonies, the full treatment was meted out to black slaves guilty of murdering their masters. In 1755, for example, two of the slaves of Captain John Codman of Boston, a cruel man with an ungovernable temper, having previously burned down their master's house in the hope that the resulting financial loss would compel him to sell them, poisoned him with arsenic. The two slaves were tried for murder and found guilty. Phillis, the woman who had administered the poison, was burned to death in Cambridge; the man, Mark, was hanged and his body was suspended in chains on the Cambridge Common. It remained there for several years.

This spectacle was not uncommon in the American colonies. In 1767, four Virginia Negroes found guilty of conspiring to murder an overseer were hanged, their heads cut off and put on public display. One of the first things seen by Nicholas Cresswell, a young Englishman, on his arrival in Virginia in 1774 was the quarter of a Negro hanging from a pole.

On the other hand, the killing of a Negro slave by a white man was not a punishable offense. Although early in Virginia's history two white men were hanged for the murder of slaves, in 1753 the crime was reduced to manslaughter and carried no punishment whatever. As for whipping a slave to death, this was not usually regarded as indictable. In 1705, an act of the Virginia legislature forbade the "immoderate" correction of disobedient slaves but no penalty was inflicted upon the master if the slave died under this treatment unless it was proved upon the oath of a credible white witness that the Negro was killed, "wilfully, maliciously or designedly." A mere error of judgment regarding the capacity of the slave to absorb punishment was not an indictable offense. In South Carolina, to *steal* a slave was punishable by death, but to *kill* him was only finable. New Yorkers enjoyed equal immunity from prosecution. In 1735, John van Zandt of New York City horsewhipped his slave to death for having violated the curfew. The coroner's jury handed in the verdict that "the correction given by the master was not the Cause of his Death, but that it was by the Visitation of God."

Denied the Rights of Man, Negro slaves might reasonably have laid claim at least to the Rights of Animals. Yet in Virginia a person who cruelly beat a horse was subject to a fine whereas if he beat a slave unmercifully the law remained silent. Nevertheless, the law, in its majesty, began to take cognizance of the human quality of the Negro. In 1769, it was forbidden in Virginia to castrate slaves for any offense other than a rape or attempted rape upon a white woman.

In the Northern colonies, particularly in the areas where Negroes were heavily outnumbered by whites, both slaves

and free Negroes generally fared better than in the tobacco, rice and indigo producing regions of the South.
Among Northerners, a Negro was apt to be more an object of curiosity than a resentment or fear; they did not
compete with whites for jobs and, outside of the seaport
towns, there was no danger of a slave insurrection or of
racial strife in any form. Free Negroes took part in the
westward movement and they found on the frontier a
closer approximation to equality with whites than anywhere
else in colonial America.

Madame Knight, a doughty New England schoolmarm
who, in 1704, traveled overland from Boston to New
York, complained that there was altogether too much
social equality between whites and blacks in Connecticut:

> They Generally lived very well and comfortably in their
> families. But too Indulgent (especially the farmers) to their
> slaves: suffering too great familiarity from them, permitting
> them to sit at Table and eat with them, (as they say to save
> time,) and into the dish goes the black hoof as freely as the
> white hand. They told me that there was a farmer lived near the
> Town where I lodged who had some difference with his slave,
> concerning something the master had promised him and did
> not punctually perform; which caused some hard words be-
> tween them; But at length they put the matter to Arbitration
> and Bound themselves to stand to the award of such as they
> named—which done, the Arbitrators Having heard the Allega-
> tions of both parties, Order the master to pay 40 shillings to
> black face, and acknowledge his fault. And so the matter ended:
> the poor master very honestly standing to the award.[6]

Barbé-Marbois, the French chargé d'affaires in Philadelphia, optimistically supposed that the racial problem was
in the process of solution in Pennsylvania:

> Pennsylvania and almost all the United States north of it are
> a peaceful and happy refuge for negroes. Examples of severity
> are rare. Slaves are here regarded as being part of the family;
> they are assiduously cared for when they are sick; they are well

[6] Madame Sarah Knight, *The Private Journal of a Journey from
Boston to New York in the Year 1704* (Albany: F. H. Little,
1865), pp. 53–54.

fed and clothed. They attach themselves to their masters, whose children they regard as their own. Several women of my acquaintance have brought to them daily the children of their negroes, caress them, feed them, have them play with their own children. While traveling, I have often happened to spend the night in the houses of Dutch or Germans. In the morning the negro wakes them, crying "Get up, master, it is time for us to go to work." The master gets up, they eat a light breakfast, work together, and dine together like equals. They are clothed in the same way, and the slave can be recognized only by his color.[7]

And yet there was a darker side to slavery in the Northern colonies. The bloodiest repression of American Negroes during the colonial period took place not in Virginia or in South Carolina, but in New York City.

During the early spring of 1741, a series of fires, some of them certainly the work of arsonists, broke out in New York City. Most of the public buildings in Fort George, together with several houses on Broadway, were destroyed. Suspicion was immediately directed against the black slaves, most of whom lived on upper Broadway, and especially against some Negroes who had recently been captured aboard a Spanish ship. Being members of the crew, these Spanish Negroes were freemen but the British Admiralty Court in New York ordered them sold into slavery. They were immediately bought by New Yorkers, but they proved to be troublesome slaves because they kept insisting, contrary to the decision of the Admiralty Court, that they were freemen. The fact that one of the houses that had gone up in flames was owned by a New Yorker who had bought one of these "Spanish Negroes" was enough to incriminate them in the public mind. In order to clinch the case against them, the city authorities offered a reward of 100 pounds and a free pardon to anyone who would give evidence against the incendiaries.

At this moment a tavern owner whose place of business was frequented by Negroes was accused of receiving stolen

[7] Barbé-Marbois, *Our Revolutionary Forefathers. The Letters of François, Marquis de Barbé-Marbois* (New York: Duffield & Co., 1929), p. 156.

goods. His white servant, a sixteen-year-old tavern wench named Mary Burton, gave evidence against her master. With the offer of 100 pounds going begging, Mary Burton made a try for it by unfolding a plot that made the judge's and jurors' hair stand on end. Her master together with a white prostitute and some Negro slaves, she asserted, had laid plans to burn the city, massacre the citizens and make off with the plunder to the Spanish West Indies.

New Yorkers had a way of dealing with Negro slaves who rebelled against their masters. In 1712, a number of blacks set fire to a house in New York and killed the whites as they hurried to extinguish the flames. For this crime, 21 slaves were executed: "some were burnt, others hanged, one broke on the wheel, and one hung alive in chains in the town." Those who were burned were roasted over a slow fire in order to prolong their torment for eight or ten hours. The royal governor of New York did not exaggerate when he assured his government that "the most exemplary punishment had been inflicted that could be possibly thought of."

The guilt of the Negroes seemed established beyond all doubt when the prostitute, accused by Mary Burton of having taken part in the plot, confessed under third-degree methods that it was all true. The Negro slaves implicated by Mary Burton were immediately brought to trial. They had no counsel and the weight of the testimony, including that of several Negro slaves, was wholly against them. While the accused cowered in the dock, the prosecution lawyers, including the Attorney General of New York, fulminated against "the monstrous ingratitude of the black tribe." After a few minutes' deliberation, the jury brought in a verdict of guilty as charged; indeed, had the jurors returned any other verdict they would not have been safe in New York. In passing sentence of death, the judge castigated the prisoners as "abject wretches, the outcasts of the nations of the earth."

The panic and the executions now began in earnest. Every black was under suspicion. Hundreds of white citizens fled to Harlem and the Bowery, at this time pleasant country villages where few Negroes lived; others, more courageous, mounted guard over their property day and night. The tavern owner, his wife and the prostitute were tried without benefit of counsel, found guilty and hanged. In June, 1741, six more Negroes were condemned to be burned at the stake. To save himself, one of the condemned men made a confession in which he implicated other Negroes. Five of the Spanish Negroes were tried, found guilty and sentenced to be burned. When, on June 19, 1741, the Lieutenant Governor of New York offered a full pardon to all who would confess, on or before July 1, to having participated in what was now called "the Negro Plot," scores of slaves availed themselves of the opportunity to save themselves from almost certain death. The prison was crowded with suspects awaiting trial, but the executioner was cheated of most of his victims because so many confessed.

One batch of condemned slaves, although they were given an opportunity to save themselves by confessing, steadfastly maintained their innocence until they were brought to the stake. At this point their resolution gave way and they admitted their guilt. But the crowd that had turned out to watch the execution was too large and its demands for vengeance too strong to permit the Negroes to escape by a last-minute confession: the sentence of the court was duly carried out and the Negroes were chained and burned at the stake.

The only thing that could have taken the peoples' minds off the "Negro Plot" was the disclosure of a "Papists' Plot." At this time, Great Britain was at war with Spain, a Roman Catholic power, and rumors were rife of Jesuit priests, doubling as Spanish spies, who were trying to infiltrate the country in the guise of teachers, dancing masters and private tutors. Presumably, inciting the slaves to revolt would be, from the Jesuits' point of view, a glorious way of weakening the military power of Great Britain and destroying the Protestant religion.

It only remained, therefore, to implicate "Papists" in the Negro Plot. This was done by little Mary Burton, who had made the original accusation against the Negroes, her master and the prostitute. She now swore that John Ury, an itinerant teacher who had recently arrived in New York, was actually a Roman Catholic priest who had promised absolution to the blacks who took part in the projected uprising. Ury, it was charged, had made a ring with chalk on the floor "which he made the negroes stand round, and put their left foot in, and he swore with a cross in his hand, to burn and destroy the town, and to cut their masters' and mistresses' throats."

This farrago was enough to put Ury in prison charged with having been one of the main movers of the "Negro Plot." Having no counsel, Ury conducted his own defense, but it proved to be an uphill fight, for the Roman Catholic Church was actually on trial and Ury was compelled to bear the guilt not only of the "Negro Plot" but of St. Bartholomew's, the Gunpowder Plot, and the atrocities committed by the Duke of Alva in the Netherlands. Under the accumulated odium incurred in the course of centuries of heresy-hunting and with most of the people demanding that a "Papist" follow the publican and the prostitute to the gallows, Ury was convicted and sentenced to be hanged. Upon the scaffold he delivered a speech protesting his innocence and affirming his belief in God. When his body was cut down, a day of Thanksgiving was proclaimed "for the deliverance of His Majesty's subjects here from the destruction wherewith they were so generally threatened by the late execrable conspiracy." Mary Burton, the savior of the white Protestants of New York, received her promised reward of 100 pounds.

But danger still lurked on Long Island, where the discovery of another "Negro Plot" resulted in several arrests and the execution of one slave. Mary Burton, grown brazen with success, began to accuse people of unimpeachable respectability in New York City of having conspired with the Negroes. She might well have rested content with her handiwork: 150 people taken into custody; four whites hanged; thirteen Negroes burned to death and eight hanged; and over 80 Negroes transported to the West Indies where they experienced the most oppressive and brutal exploitation of human beings known in the Western Hemisphere.

After the panic had run its course, some New Yorkers realized that they had been caught up in the same kind of hysteria that had gripped Salem Village during the witchcraft trials. Whatever the degree of truth in the original charges, the contradictions, inconsistencies and patent fabrications accepted by the court as valid evidence, the perversions of law and the inflammatory harangues of the public prosecutors made the trials a travesty of justice. As in Salem Village, superstition tended to destroy itself by its own excesses, and public opinion in time turned against those who had whipped up the frenzy.

Bibliography

Aptheker, Herbert. *American Negro Slave Revolts.* New York: International Publishers, 1939.

Brackett, Jeffrey R. *The Negro in Maryland.* Baltimore: The Johns Hopkins Press, 1889.

Donnan, Elizabeth (editor). *Documents Illustrative of the Slave Trade to America.* 2 vols. Washington, D. C.: U. S. Government Printing Office, 1930–35.

Greene, L. F. *The Negro in Colonial New England.* New York: Columbia University Press, 1942.

Hurd, J. C. *Law of Freedom and Bondage.* 2 vols. New York: J. Van Nostrand Co., 1858–62.

Morris, Richard B. *Government and Labor in Early America.* New York: Columbia University Press, 1946.

O'Callaghan, E. B. (editor). *Documents Relating to the Colonial History of New York.* 14 vols. New York: Weed and Parsons, 1853–82.

Smith, Abbot Emerson. *Colonists in Bondage.* Chapel Hill: University of North Carolina Press, 1947.

Taylor, Joe Gray. *Negro Slavery in Louisiana.* Baton Rouge: Louisiana Historical Association, 1963.

WAYS OF MAKING
A LIVING

ALTHOUGH the great majority of Americans lived by farming, they were far from being the most efficient and productive farmers in the world. Indeed, it was the low crop yield per acre from their farms and plantations that most frequently impressed British and European travelers:

. . . The Europeans coming to America found a rich, fine soil before them, laying as loose between the trees as the best bed in a garden. They had nothing to do but to cut down the wood, put it up in heaps, and to clear the dead leaves away. They could then immediately proceed to plowing, which in such loose ground is very easy; and having sown their grain, they got a most plentiful harvest. This easy method of getting a rich crop has spoiled the English and other European settlers, and induced them to adopt the same method of agriculture as the Indians: that is, to sow uncultivated grounds, as long as they will produce a crop without manuring, but to turn them into pastures as soon as they can bear no more, and to take on new spots of ground, covered since ancient times with woods, which have been spared by the fire or the hatchet ever since the Creation. This is likewise the reason why agriculture and its science is so imperfect there that one can travel several days and learn almost nothing about land, neither from the English, nor from the Swedes, Germans, Dutch and French; except that from their gross mistakes and carelessness of the future, one finds opportunities every day of making all sorts of observations, and of growing wise by their mistakes. In a word, the grain fields, the meadows, the forests, the cattle, etc. are treated with equal carelessness; and the characteristics of the English nation, so well skilled in these branches of husbandry, is scarcely recognizable here. We can hardly be more hostile toward our woods in Sweden and Finland than they are here: their eyes are fixed upon the present gain, and they are blind to the future.[1]

Generally speaking, Americans engaged in an exploitative type of farming. The soil was exhausted by successive plantings of the same crop; then new lands were brought under cultivation and the same process was repeated. Because it was cheaper than labor, land was treated as an expendable commodity: it was seldom realized that it was also a perishable commodity.

The baneful results of this kind of agriculture were most clearly apparent in the Chesapeake Tidewater area. Once a region of mansion houses and great plantations, much of it had reverted to wilderness by 1812. John Randolph said that game was more abundant near his plantation at Roanoke than in Kentucky. Most of his neighbors had already moved west in search of new land.

Long before the Tidewater reached this state of impoverishment, most of the small planters had been driven from the region by the large landed proprietors, who, with their large plantations and gangs of Negro slaves, were able to produce tobacco and wheat more cheaply than were their small competitors. The farmers who remained in the Tidewater were for the most part tenants or sharecroppers. It was here that travelers from the Northern colonies first encountered large numbers of poverty-stricken white people, wearing ragged clothes and exhibiting in their wan, pinched appearance the effects of malnutrition and chronic disease.

Crèvecoeur, to whom the American farmer was the noblest creation of Nature, admitted that not all men could attain this state of beatitude. Only to the sober, the honest and the diligent, he said, was the prize given. A determinant of success to which Crèvecoeur attached much importance was national origin. "Out of twelve families of emigrants of his country," he observed, "generally seven Scotch will succeed, nine Germans and four Irish." Next in importance, Crèvecoeur placed a good wife: he who drew a blank in

[1] *The America of 1750. Peter Kalm's Travels in North America.* (2 vols., New York: Wilson, Erickson, 1937), Vol. I, pp. 307–08.

that lottery, he remarked, had little chance of becoming a true American farmer.

It was generally agreed that the Germans were the best farmers in colonial America. Despite the abundance of land, the German immigrants perpetuated the peasant attitude toward the soil. Moreover, wherever they settled, they sent down roots that attached them and, in many cases, their descendants to the land. Since they intended to live on their farms rather than to stake out a claim and sell at a profit, the Germans practiced crop rotation, intensive cultivation and used fertilizer rather than permit the land to lie fallow. As a result, the yield per acre of their farms was far greater than that of their neighbors. Dr. Benjamin Rush of Philadelphia said that one could always tell a German farm by its huge barn, the height of the fences, the extent of the orchard, the fertility of the fields, the luxuriance of the meadows "and a general appearance of plenty and neatness in everything that belongs to them." The size of their barns—"as large as palaces"—particularly impressed Crèvecoeur. "Many don't care much how they are lodged," he observed, "provided that they have a good barn and barn-yard and indeed it is the criterion by which I always judge of a farmer's prosperity."

Upon every score, the superiority of the Germans as agriculturalists seemed incontestable:

In settling a tract of land, they [Germans] always provide large and suitable accommodation for their horses and cattle, before they lay out much money in building a house for themselves. . . . The first dwelling house upon this farm is small and built of logs. It generally lasts the lifetime of the first settler of a tract of land; and hence, they have a saying, that "a son should always begin his improvements where his father left off," that is by building a large and convenient stone house.

They always prefer good land, or that land on which there is a large quantity of meadow land. From an attention to the cultivation of grass, they often double the value of an old farm in a few years, and grow rich on farms, on which their predecessors of whom they purchased them had nearly starved. They prefer purchasing farms with improvements to settling on a new tract of land.

In clearing new land, they do not girdle or belt the trees simply, and leave them to perish in the ground, as is the custom of their English or Irish neighbors; but they generally cut them down and burn them. In destroying underwood and bushes, they generally grub them out of the ground, by which means a field is as fit for cultivation the second year after it is cleared as it is in twenty years afterwards. The advantages of this mode of clearing, consists in the immediate product of the field, and in the greater facility with which it is ploughed, harrowed and reaped. The expense of repairing a plow, which is often broken, is greater than the extraordinary expense of grubbing the same field completely, in clearing.

They feed their horses and cows well, of which they keep only a small number, in such a manner that the former perform twice the labor of those horses, and latter yield twice the quantity of milk of those cows, that are less plentifully fed. There is great economy in this practice, especially in a country where so much of the labor of the farmer is necessary to support his domestic animals. . . . They keep their horses and cattle as warm as possible, in winter, by which means they save a great deal of their hay and grain, for these animals when cold, eat much more than when in a more comfortable situation.

The German farmers live frugally in their families, with respect to diet, furniture, and apparel. They sell their most profitable grain, which is wheat, and eat that which is less profitable, that is rye, or Indian corn. The profit to a farmer, from this single article of economy, is equal, in the course of a life-time, to the price of a farm for one of his children.

The German farmers have large or profitable gardens near their houses. These contain little else but useful vegetables. Pennsylvania is indebted to the Germans for the principal part of her knowledge in horticulture. There was a time when turnips and cabbage were the principal vegetables that were used in diet by the citizens of Philadelphia. This will not surprise those persons who know that the first settlers in Pennsylvania left England while horticulture was in its infancy in that country. Since the settlement of a number of German gardens in the neighborhood of Philadelphia, the tables of all classes of citizens have been covered with a variety of vegetables in every season of the year, and to the use of these vegetables in diet may be ascribed the general exemption of the citizens of Philadelphia from diseases of the skin.

... The wives and daughters of the German farmers frequently forsake for a while their dairy and spinning wheel, and join their husbands and brothers in the labor of cutting down, collecting and bringing home the fruits of the fields and orchards. The work of the gardens is generally done by the women of the family.[2]

To carry their produce to market, the Germans developed a special kind of wagon, the so-called Conestoga wagon, and a particularly powerful breed of horse that also bore the name of Conestoga. In the course of time, the Conestoga wagon became the prairie schooner.

Large-scale agriculture was not confined to the Southern colonies. In New Netherlands, the patroon system of landownership, unsuccessfully applied by the Dutch in an effort to build up the population of the colony, was continued in a modified form by the British after New Netherlands became New York. As a result, the area along the Hudson River became a region of large manorial estates where, almost without precedent in colonial America, thousands of tenants worked the lands of proprietors.

Similarly, during the eighteenth century, Rhode Island produced a kind of landowner that had no counterpart elsewhere in New England—the Narragansett planter. On their estates along the shore of Narragansett Bay, these planters operated stock and dairy farms and specialized in the breeding of fine riding horses, most notably the Narragansett Pacer. Narragansett cheese was exported to the Southern colonies; it was sold, along with a wide variety of other articles, by Benjamin Franklin in his shop in Philadelphia.

In all their varied activities—dairying, horsebreeding, and cattleraising—the Narragansett planters employed Negro slave labor. In 1758, there were over 5,000 Negro slaves in Narragansett County—the largest concentration of blacks

[2] Frank R. Diffenderffer, *The German Immigration into Pennsylvania* (In 2 parts, Lancaster: The Pennsylvania-German Society, 1900), Part II, pp. 120–23.

in rural New England. In purchasing slaves, the planters made use of the facilities afforded by nearby Newport, the great slave mart of the New England colonies.

Newport was also a fashionable watering place where the Narragansett planters hobnobbed with the vacationing South Carolina planters. Since these gatherings consisted almost entirely of *nouveaux riches,* it was difficult for anyone to assert family rank. In the absence of convincing genealogical evidence, degrees of gentility were ordinarily determined by the number of Negro slaves held on the plantation and accompanying the master and his family as body-servants. Here the Narragansett planters were at a disadvantage: the largest slaveowner among them could boast only 40 blacks.

Even so, the Carolina grandees, with their impressive entourages of blacks, did not disdain the entertainment provided by the Narragansett planters: the horse races held on the beaches and on the local track; the hunting parties; and the dinners and dances. With their fine mahogany and walnut furniture, their silver plate and evidences of their interest in art and literature, the planters of Rhode Island bore a closer resemblance to the Southern planters than did any other group of Northerners.

Animal husbandry was an important adjunct of the colonial farm: cattle, swine, sheep and fowl supplied much of the protein for the farmer and his family, while oxen and horses provided the motive power for plowing and transportation. Wherever frontier conditions prevailed—and this was as true of Jamestown as it was of Pittsburgh or any other wilderness settlement—domestic animals were permitted to run at large, protected only by the brand of their owner. Unfortunately, the Indians were no respecters of private property even when it was properly branded. Errant whites likewise had to be reckoned with: at Jamestown, hog stealing was punished by fine and whipping, and the crime became capital on the third offense. Social rank did not protect cattle rustlers: in 1630, Dr. Pott, who had recently retired from the governorship of Virginia, was found guilty of stealing his neighbors' livestock.

Farming was only one of the occupations carried on down on the farm. Each household was a sort of factory in the fields where a wide variety of crafts were pursued, all with a view to making the farmer and his family as self-sufficient as possible. Particularly during the winter months, when outdoor work was reduced to a minimum, every member of the family, including the children, labored at these household tasks. Everything from shoes to clothing to furniture was turned out on the farm itself. As Crèvecoeur said, to survive, a farmer had to be much more than a husbandman:

> The philosopher's stone of an American farmer is to do everything within his own family; to trouble his neighbors by borrowing as little as possible; and to abstain from buying European commodities. He that follows that golden rule and has a good wife is almost sure of succeeding. . . .
>
> However careful and prudent we are, the use of tea necessarily implies a great consumption of sugar. A northern farmer should never pronounce these two words without trembling, for these two articles must be replaced by something equivalent in order to pay for them, and not many of us have anything to spare.[3]
>
> If he [a farmer] is obliged to purchase many articles, then he works for others and not for himself; he is but a fool and a slave. His profits are so inconciderable that if they are uselessly expended, there remains nothing of his year's industry.[4]

Even though he practiced industry and frugality as strenuously as Benjamin Franklin recommended, an American farmer could hardly avoid going into debt. Since the outlay required for the purchase of land and farm implements often exceeded an individual's resources of cash, he was obliged to borrow—usually from the local storekeeper. As Crèvecoeur perceived, the chain of credit that gave the American farmer his start and sustained him in time of adversity began with the British merchants and manufacturers:

[3] J. Hector St. John de Crèvecoeur, *Sketches of Eighteenth-Century America* (New Haven: Yale University Press, 1925), pp. 104–06.

[4] *Ibid.*, p. 128.

A man must have a beginning, a certain capital without which he may languish and vegetate simply all the days of his life. The credit of England enables our merchants to trade and to get rich. The credit and wealth of the fathers enable our children to form new settlements. Were these two sources suspended only for ten years, you would soon see a death of enterprise, a spirit of inaction, a general languor diffuse itself throughout the continent. That bold activity, that spirit of emigration which is the source of our prosperity, would soon cease.

The number of debts which one part of the country owes to the other would greatly astonish you. The younger a country is, the more it is oppressed, for new settlements are always made by people who do not possess much. They are obliged to borrow, and, if any accidents intervene, they are not enabled to repay that money in many years. The interest is a canker-worm which consumes their yearly industry. Many never can surmount these difficulties. The land is sold, their labours are lost, and they are obliged to begin the world anew. . . .

It is vain to say: why do they borrow? I answer that it is impossible in America to till a farm without it.[5]

Thank God, I owe nothing, but I can tell you that there are not one hundred besides me in the country who can say that all they have is their own.[6]

A farmer was likewise dependent upon the help of his neighbors: rural society was based upon cooperation quite as much as upon rugged individualism. Crèvecoeur, who knew the life of an American farmer from firsthand experience, always emphasized the importance of mutual aid in a farming community.

While there was comparatively little rock-bound coast in New England, there was an uncommonly large amount of rock-bound farmland. One disillusioned settler wrote home that the Bay Colony was "builded upon rocks, sand and salt marshes"—and was promptly haled before the General Court charged with libeling God's own plantation. Many other New Englanders took one look at the land and went down to the sea in ships. The sea, in contrast to the land, offered an abundant harvest of fish and

[5] *Ibid.*, pp. 90–91.
[6] *Ibid.*, p. 92.

unlimited possibilities of adventure and moneymaking. By the 1640's, New England ships were trafficking in the Chesapeake, loading sugar in the West Indies and fighting Turkish corsairs in the Mediterranean. For Yankee skippers the world became a port of call.

Economically, New England was the most diversified part of British North America. True, during the colonial period, agriculture remained the most important occupation in New England and the export trade of the region was built upon its surplus corn, cattle and wheat, yet it was fish, lumber, shipbuilding and manufacturing that enabled New Englanders to enjoy a standard of living so high that it convinced some travelers that the Puritans really had arrived in the Promised Land. Both the bean and the cod were essential ingredients in New England's prosperity.

One of the manufactures of New England for which it became famous—and, in some quarters, infamous—was rum. The molasses from which this "hot and hellish liquor" was derived was brought from the West Indies to New England distilleries. Rum became not only a popular local drink but an article of trade with the Indians, with the fishermen on the Newfoundland Banks, and with the slave traders along the coast of West Africa. At the same time, a thriving trade sprang up with the Canary Islands, the Azores and Madeira, by which fish and agricultural surpluses were exchanged for wine. The Puritans, it would appear, scoured the earth for good things to drink. Certainly they accounted a good glass of wine or a nip of rum on a frosty night among the blessings vouchsafed to man by an otherwise stern and unrelenting Jehovah.

In addition to the rich merchant with his ships and well-stocked warehouses, New England produced the peddler—a man with a pack on his back who traveled the length and breadth of the colonies selling Yankee "notions." These prototypes of the traveling salesmen were welcomed in villages and isolated farmsteads where a stranger, much less a traveling salesman, was a rarity. Gradually the Puritan was evolving into the Yankee—a shrewd, bargain-hunting trader who dealt in everything from completely equipped merchant ships to wooden nutmegs. Wherever they traded—among the Southern planters, the slave merchants of the African coast and the West India sugar producers—Puritans acquired the reputation of being experts in the art of overreaching their customers. In the late seventeenth century, Ned Ward, an English writer, said that it was a proverb that "whosoever believed a New England Saint, shall be sure to be cheated. And he that knows to deal with their Traders, may deal with the Devil and Fear no Craft."

Bibliography

Bailyn, Bernard. *The New England Merchants in the Seventeenth Century..* Cambridge, Mass.: Harvard University Press, 1955.

Gray, L. C. *History of Agriculture in the Southern United States to 1860.* 2 vols. Washington, D. C.: U. S. Government Printing Office, 1933.

Heimann, Robert K. *Tobacco and Americans.* New York: McGraw-Hill Book Co., 1960.

Pares, Richard. *Yankees and Creoles: The Trade Between North America and the West Indies Before the American Revolution.* Cambridge, Mass.: Harvard University Press, 1956.

Weeden, W. B. *Economic and Social History of New England, 1620–1789.* 2 vols. Boston: Houghton Mifflin Co., 1890.

HOUSING

THE first Englishmen ashore in the New World threw up temporary shelters, moved into deserted Indian wigwams or lived in caves burrowed in sidehills. As soon as possible, however, they tried to reproduce the houses they had known in the Old World. This was not simply nostalgia: they knew no other way of building and most of the materials with which they were familiar were at hand. Accordingly, the settlers at Jamestown built small, dark, medieval-like cottages with steep thatched roofs and walls of wattle (woven willow or hazel branches) and mud. They were not satisfied until they had made Jamestown a replica of Stratford-on-Avon or some other small English country town, complete with church, alehouse and bowling green. By the same token, houses in New England were built with a second story protruding over the first or ground floor, not because this overhang made it easier to fight off Indians but because it was the current architectural fashion in England.

Thatched roofs proved highly inflammable, particularly since the chimneys in the early houses were built of wood or mud. In 1621, Governor William Bradford almost lost his life when the roof of a house in which he was lying ill caught fire. Seven years later, after several fires in which the whole town of Plymouth threatened to go up in flames, thatched roofs were prohibited. Even after houses were roofed with cedar shingles, fires were frequent in colonial towns and, because of the inadequate fire-fighting equipment, a single fire often spread over a wide area.

While the first settlers placed logs vertically in the ground to form a palisade for protection against the Indians, they did not build houses of logs. The log cabin—traditionally associated with the American frontier and the birthplace of several American presidents (some aspirants to that high office apologized for not having been born in a log cabin but pointed out that they really had not had any choice in the matter)—was introduced by the Finns and the Swedes around 1638 in New Sweden, on the banks of the Delaware River. As early as 1600, the French in Canada built log cabins of a different type of construction, but it had no influence on the English settlers. By the Swedish-Finnish method, the logs were split, deeply notched on both sides and the interstices "chinked" with a mixture of wood chips, clay and moss. The roof was usually made of bark. Since all of these materials were found in the forest, the log cabin was quickly adopted by the Scotch-Irish and the Germans who were engaged in pushing the frontier line westward. Besides its other attractions, the log cabin gave security against marauding Indians and, once the method of notching logs for houses had been mastered, it could be applied to the construction of blockhouses and other military defenses.

Under frontier conditions, whether on the seacoast or in the interior, oil paper or horn scraped so thin that light was admitted, served as window glass. But, as housing improved, glass windows were installed, although in seventeenth-century New England, because it was the English custom, casement windows with small, leaded, diamond-shaped panes were favored over solid sheets of glass.

Architectural style was largely determined by the national origin of the settlers themselves and the availability of the various kinds of construction materials. In New Netherlands, the Dutch were fond of building with brick, often in different colors, glazed and laid in checkers. Likewise, in Philadelphia, where clay was plentiful, houses were usually constructed of brick but without decorative coloring or design. The German farmers, the so-called Pennsylvania Dutch, constructed their dwellings of the stone found in the Pennsylvania countryside. One group of Germans, the

Moravians, insisted upon reproducing the traditional German half-timbered houses; as a result, Ephrata, Pennsylvania, resembled a medieval town.

Central heating being unknown, fireplaces provided the only warmth indoors. In New England, climate dictated that the chimney should be placed in the center of the house; the more indulgent climate of the South made it possible to place the chimneys and fireplaces at the ends of the house. But heating drafty, poorly insulated houses by means of fireplaces—even when each room contained a fireplace—was a frustrating experience. In his diary, the Reverend Cotton Mather recounted some of the hardships he underwent in his own study:

[January 23, 1697] I attempted, this Day, the Exercises of a secret FAST before the Lord. But so extremely cold was the weather, that in a warm Room, on a great Fire, the Juices forced out at the End of short Billets of Wood, by the Heat of the Flame, on which they were laid, yett froze into Ice, at their coming out. This Extremity of the Cold caused mee to desist from the purpose, which I was upon; because I saw it impossible to serve the Lord, without such Distraction, as was inconvenient.

[January 11, 1719–1720] 'Tis dreadful cold. My Ink-glass in my Standish is froze & splitt, in my very stove. My Ink in my very pen suffers a congelation: but my witt much more.[1]

In 1686, Samuel Sewall recorded that it was "so cold that the sacramental bread is frozen pretty hard, and rattles sadly into the places." Presumably the teeth of the worshipers were rattling no less sadly.

While everyone complained about the cold, the Germans did something about it. They built stoves of iron that, using the fireplace chimney as an outlet for the smoke, made a room comfortably warm even by modern American standards. The German iron stove gave Benjamin Franklin the idea for the so-called Franklin stove, which in its original form contained an air box through which air circulated and whence it was delivered hot and smokeless into

[1] *The Diary of Cotton Mather, edited by Worthington C. Ford* (2 vols., New York: Frederick Ungar, n.d.), Vol. I, p. 216; Vol. II, p. 581.

a room. With a Franklin stove, Americans could toast themselves all over, not simply on one side at a time, as they did when they hugged an old-fashioned fireplace.

To keep warm, the Dutch women of New Netherlands used the method traditional in Holland. Per Kalm, accustomed in his native Sweden to uncomfortably low temperatures, observed with interest how the Dutch managed in New Netherlands:

At this time of the year, since it was beginning to grow cold, it was customary for the women, all of them, even maidens, servants and little girls, to put live coals into small iron pans which were in turn placed in a small stool resembling somewhat a footstool, but with a bottom . . . upon which the pan was set. The top of the pan was full of holes through which the heat came. They placed this stool with the warming pan under their skirts so that the heat therefrom might go up to the *regiones superiores* and to all parts of the body which the skirts covered. As soon as the coals grew black they were thrown away and replaced by live coals and treated as above. It was almost painful to all this changing and trouble in order that no part should freeze or fare badly. The women had however spoiled themselves, for they could not do without this heat.

[In church] nearly everyone had her little container, with the glowing coals of which I have spoken before, under her skirt in order to keep warm. The negroes or their other servants accompanied them to church mornings carrying the warming pans. When the minister had finished his sermon and the last hymn had been sung, the same negroes, etc. came and removed the warming pans and carried them home.[2]

And yet the fireplace could not be dispensed with altogether, for there the cooking was done in iron pots suspended from a swinging iron crane. Kitchen equipment included some of the most costly items that went into the furnishing of a colonial house: brass and iron pots, kettles, skillets, pothooks, bellows and tongs. Meals were served on wooden or pewter plates and platters; not until

[2] Per Kalm, *Travels in North America* (2 vols., New York: 1937), Vol. 2, pp. 605, 624.

the eighteenth century did silver utensils appear—and then only in the houses of the well-to-do.

Only one house in the English colonies is reported to have had an inside bathroom, and it was strictly for bathing. The comparatively few Americans who took baths immersed themselves in water warmed by heated stones. More commonly, however, a basin of water sufficed for all necessary ablutions. Houses equipped with running water were a rarity. Even in the towns, privies were situated outdoors, usually in the garden; the Southern gentry constructed elaborately ornamented retreats and disguised them as pavilions. Commodes were provided in bedchambers and, in the houses of the well-to-do, servants took charge of all the sanitary arrangements.

The Reverend Francis Higginson described the kind of illumination used in the early houses of New England:

Although New England has no tallow to make candles of, yet by the abundance of the fish thereof it can afford oil for lamps. Yea, our pine trees, that are the most plentiful of all wood, doth allow us plenty of candles which are very useful in the house; and they are such candles as the Indians commonly use, having no other, and they are nothing else but the wood of the pine tree cloven into little slices something thin, which are so full of the moisture of turpentine and pitch, that they burn as clear as a torch.[3]

The tallow candle soon replaced the pine knots and later the spermaceti candle and the whale-oil lamp came on the market. While the spermaceti candle emitted much more light than did a tallow candle, it was too expensive for most householders. Whale oil was cheaper but it never succeeded in wholly displacing the tallow candle.

This kind of illumination was hard on the eyes of scholarly inclined Americans. Cotton Mather, among many other clergymen, surmounted this disadvantage: in the course of his career, he wrote over 400 books. But, since many Americans could not read and there was comparatively little reading matter available—newspapers did

[3] The Reverend Francis Higginson, *New England's Plantation* (London, 1630), pp. 11-12.

not appear until the eighteenth century—the absence of good lighting did not work the hardship it would have caused in a more literate age. During the early period of colonization, a few candles, together with the glow cast by the fireplace, were sufficient for eating, recreation and conversation.

Particularly during the seventeenth century, houses were sparsely furnished. Since so much had to be done—lands cleared, houses and barns built, wells dug—the settlers made do with the rudest sort of furniture. There were no rugs (considered too precious to be put on the floor, they were customarily used as table coverings); no upholstered chairs in which to take it easy after a hard day's work; no pictures, not even pinups, on the wall. Most of the furniture was homemade. It consisted of a table of hewn planks (they really "gathered round the board"), plain benches and a few chests. The bedstead was a rough frame supporting a straw mattress. Those who did not possess a bedstead slept on a pile of straw in the corner.

In March, 1631, when Thomas Dudley sat down in his house in Boston to write to the Countess of Lincoln, he apologized for his crabbed style of writing. He had, he explained, "no table, nor other room to write in, than by the fire side upon my knee, in this sharp winter; to which my family must have leave to resorte, though they break good manners, and make mee many times forget what I would say, and say what I would not." But such privations did not last long, particularly among the wealthier Puritans. The estate of Governor William Bradford, for example, included four leather chairs, "one great leather chair," two great wooden chairs, two stools and two spinning wheels. Myles Standish left his heir a frying pan, 16 pieces of pewter and several spinning wheels but, as befitted a military man, his estate consisted largely of weapons: a fowling piece, three muskets, four carbines, two small guns, a sword and a cutlass.

The 170 years that comprised the colonial period witnessed profound changes in every aspect of American life.

Nowhere was this change more evident than in the material comforts enjoyed by Americans. In housing, for example, the order of development was from a hovel to a mansion—and sometimes the mansion was built upon the very spot that had .given shelter to the first settlers. As the frontier was pushed westward, this process was repeated time after time. And yet, while fashionable ladies and gentlemen danced in ballrooms, dined upon costly plate and sat upon elegant furniture, pioneer families—sometimes only a few miles away—lived under conditions reminiscent of Jamestown.

This lavish style of living was most conspicuously exemplified by the Southern planters and Northern merchants. Their imported furniture was designed by Chippendale, Sheraton, Hepplewhite and the Adam brothers; their walls were covered with wainscot paneling or hand-painted wallpaper; their floors were decorated with rich Turkish carpets and their tables laden with silver punchbowls, urns and costly porcelain dishes. On festive occasions, rooms were illuminated with so many candles that a black slave or white servant had to be kept in attendance to replace the candles and snuff the wicks. By the end of the colonial period, some Americans lived far more luxuriously than the English country gentry whom they aspired to imitate.

While early-American architecture is generally divided into "Early American" and "Georgian" (1700–76), within these categories there evolved several distinctive styles, each reflecting a sectional variation. A New England colonial house belongs to a definite period of time and a geographical area; it existed only in the New England of that day. So with a Southern mansion such as William Byrd's Westover: only the eighteenth-century South could have produced it. But the "South," too, was subject to many regional differences: combining English and West Indian styles of architecture, the South Carolinians developed an individual urban architecture. Differences fully as marked appeared in the public architecture of the various sections and subsections.

As the plantation system developed, the "big house"

tended to be surrounded by an increasing number of smaller structures: storehouses, smokehouse, stable, workshops, slave quarters, kitchen, and housing for the overseer and his family. Sometimes even a school house was included. The plantation, in fact, resembled a small village and in many essentials it was wholly self-sufficient: slaves were trained as carpenters, blacksmith, cobblers and saddlers while slave women spun and wove homegrown flax into cloth. But for their luxuries, tools, and woolen cloth, the planters depended upon British sources of supply. As a result, the South made no important contribution to what is called "colonial furniture." This furniture was largely the creation of New Englanders, Dutch and Germans, whose specialties included the Windsor chair, the double chest, the secretary, the Dutch wardrobe and the elaborately decorated bridal chest.

Of the Southern mansions, one of the most magnificent was Rosewell, built by Mann Page. The central part of the building was three stories high, exclusive of a high basement, and it contained three wide halls, nine passages and 23 rooms. With its wings, the house had a frontage of 232 feet. In Northern towns, the Vassall (Longfellow) house and Mt. Pleasant in Philadelphia, with their high ceilings, wainscot paneling and air of spacious elegance, rank among the best examples of how the wealth and taste of the Northern merchant princes combined to produce architectural masterpieces.

"Every gentleman his own architect" might well have been the motto of wealthy Americans of the eighteenth century. Books on architecture not merely adorned their libraries: these books were studied, digested and used as guides when the colonists came to build their residences and public buildings. Andrew Hamilton, a Philadelphia lawyer, designed Independence Hall; William Price, a Boston art dealer, drew the plans for the Old North Church, Boston's first Georgian building; Peter Harrison, a Rhode Island merchant, inspired by Inigo Jones, the English architect, created the Synagogue, the Market and the Redwood Library in Newport; and Thomas Jefferson designed, among many other buildings, Monticello and the Virginia State House. It was the age of the gifted amateur.

Bibliography

Bridenbaugh, Carl. *Peter Harrison, the First American Architect.* Chapel Hill: University of North Carolina Press, 1949.

Downs, Joseph. *American Furniture in the Henry Francis du Pont Winterthur Museum.* New York: Macmillan Co., 1952.

Kimball, Sidney Fiske. *Domestic Architecture of the American Colonies and the Early Republic.* New York: Charles Scribner's Sons, 1922.

Shurtleff, Harold Robert. *The Log Cabin Myth: A Study of the Dwellings of the English Colonists in North America.* Cambridge, Mass.: Harvard University Press, 1939.

Waterman, Thomas T. *The Mansions of Virginia, 1706–1776.* Chapel Hill: University of North Carolina Press, 1946.

FOOD AND DRINK

TO establish settlements on the coast of North America required courage, perseverence—and corn. Without this staple the early colonists and the Western pioneers would have found conditions of life in the wilderness almost intolerable. Corn provided them with sustenance; it grew quickly and with comparatively little labor; and the Indians obligingly taught the whites how to plant, fertilize and grind corn, and even shared their favorite recipes for preparing it. The colonists made corn their staff of life and, for a time, a medium of exchange. In the course of time they improved its cultivation and invented new ways of preparing it. By mixing flour, milk and eggs, none of which was known to the Indians, with corn meal they produced johnnycake, "Indian pudding" and spoon bread.

Pumpkins and squash were also borrowed from the Indians, who had domesticated these native American vegetables. The potato, on the other hand, although indigenous to the Western Hemisphere, did not reach the English colonies until the eighteenth century. By that time, because of its popularity in Ireland, it was known as the "Irish potato."

While prospective immigrants to the colonies were warned by Benjamin Franklin and others not to expect that fully roasted fowls, ready for eating, would drop into their mouths, no one denied that food was far more abundant in America than in Europe. Wild game—turkeys, geese, deer and pigeons—were almost always available. Americans hunted these creatures with such abandon that they wholly exterminated the wild pigeon and almost succeeded in doing the same to the wild turkey. But so great was the plenty enjoyed by Americans that the disappearance of a species or two seemed of little consequence.

Every farm family, no matter how self-sufficient, had to buy its salt, sugar and spices. Since none of these commodities was produced in the continental English colonies —the salt came from Spain, the sugar from the West Indies and the spices from the Far East—they were expensive compared with the other items on Americans' tables. Yet they were essential to every household: lacking refrigeration, meat could be preserved only by the time-honored methods of salting, smoking or pickling. Even so, it was advisable to add pepper and other spices to preserved meat: they did wonders for lean, sinewy beef and mutton.

Affluent Americans, merchants as well as planters, followed the English custom of loading their tables with far more food than they or their guests could possibly eat. Even delicacies such as crabs, oysters, game and roast meat were served in excess; to get through the multitude of courses taxed even the most efficient digestive system. In colonial America, there was a conspicuous absence of lean and hungry looks; the portraits of colonial worthies are usually of sleek, obviously well-fed men and women already confronting the problem that, in an acute form, bedevils their twentieth-century descendants—weight.

One of the reports most calculated to discourage Britons and Europeans from going to America was that there was nothing but water to drink in that parched benighted region. The settlers at Jamestown complained that, when they asked for beer, they were given water—"which," they said, "is contrary to the nature of the English." In *New England's Prospect* (1634), William Wood tried to dispel the effect of these harrowing tales of privation by making out a case for New England water:

It is thought there can be no better water in the world, yet dare I not prefere it before good Beere, as some have done, but any man will choose it before bad Beere, Whey or Buttermilke.

Those that drink it be as healthful, fresh, and lustie, as they that drinke beere.

But Governor William Bradford candidly admitted that wholesome as was the water of Plymouth, it could never take the place of beer for a true-born Englishman. And John Hammond, the author of an early description of Maryland, declared that the best way to tell a good from a bad housewife was whether the family drank beer or water—only a "sloathful and careless" wife, he averred, would inflict water upon her husband.

William Penn, one of the most successful real-estate promoters in American history, did not make the mistake of telling prospective immigrants that they must drink water. Super-salesman that he was, he could not have sold *that* idea to Englishmen. Instead, Penn described the excellent beverages awaiting the newcomer to Pennsylvania:

Our Drink has been Beer and Punch, made of Rum and Water. Our Beer was mostly made of molasses, which well boyld, with Sassafras or Pine infused into it, makes very tollerable drink. But now they make Mault, and Mault Drink begins to be common, especially at the Ordinaries and the Houses of the more substantial People. In our great Town [Philadelphia] there is an able Man, that has set up a large Brew House, in order to furnish the People with good Drink, both there, and up and down the River.[1]

The widespread prejudice against water as a beverage had the endorsement of colonial physicians. Water, they pointed out, was often contaminated whereas beer, if properly brewed, was hygienic, nutritious and refreshing. But the colonists' aversion to water extended to bathing in it. Few Americans willingly exposed their entire bodies to this dubious liquid lest they contract colds, pneumonia and kindred ailments. Excessive indulgence in water, both internally and externally, was believed to have brought many an unwary American to his grave.

Although Puritanism has often been blamed for prohibi-

[1] Frank R. Diffenderffer, *The German Immigration into Pennsylvania* (Lancaster: The Pennsylvania-German Society, 1900), p. 27.

tion, the Puritans themselves would have indignantly denied the impeachment. They, together with virtually all other Americans, would have cried "tyranny" had the British government attempted to deprive them of their favorite beverage; indeed, a tax levied on molasses by Parliament led John Adams to remark that rum was an essential ingredient in the American Revolution. When the settlers found wild grapes, their first thought was of the wine they might produce; as early as 1629, a vineyard was planted at Salem. "No minister," it has been said, "called at the houses of his parishioners without being offered the cup of courtesy, nor did he decline with thanks"—unless the cup contained grape juice.

The Puritans had special prayers to be said during the brewing of beer; even so, Satan, apparently out of sheer deviltry, sometimes spoiled the mash. But this is not to say that the Puritans condoned overindulgence. Moderation was the ideal of the New England Puritans: the Reverend Increase Mather laid down the maxim:

Drink is in itself a good creature of God, and to be received with thankfulness, but the abuse of drink is from Satan; the wine is from God, but the Drunkard is from the Devil.

Anyone who drank to excess in Boston could expect to find his name posted publicly; and if he repeated the offense he himself was posted in the stocks or pillory and forced to wear the letter "D" for "Drunkard."

While the custom of wearing letters to designate the sin gradually fell into disuse, the sin itself did not show any signs of disappearing. Instead, during the eighteenth century, cheap rum became the American counterpart of the cheap gin that debauched the lower classes of England. The popularity of rum was deplored by William Byrd II, who, like other gentlemen, drank only the finest Madeira and Canary wine. He said:

That Diabolical Liquor Rum does more mischief to Peoples' Industry and Morals than any thing except Gin and the Pope.

. . . My Dear Country Men [Virginians] are fonder of it than they are of their Wives and Children, for they often sell the Bread out of their mouths, to buy Rumm to put in their own.

In New York, house builders demanded free liquor on the job as a fringe benefit and Byrd recorded that the governor of Virginia

made a bargain with his servants that if they would forbear to drink upon the Queen's birthday, they might be drunk this day. They observed their contract and did their divisions very well and get very drunk today.

Not all Americans joined William Byrd in condemning rum. During the French and Indian War and the War of American Independence, rations of rum, when available, were given the troops. Soldiers came to expect these rations and when they were not forthcoming, mutiny sometimes resulted. Per Kalm encountered an American officer who testified to the salutary effects of rum upon his men:

Major Roderfort told me that upon the Canada expedition he had observed that most of his soldiers who drank brandy for a time died; but those who drank rum were not hurt, though they got drunk with it every day for a considerable time.[2]

As Americans pushed westward, rum was superseded by whiskey as their favorite alcoholic drink. Whiskey was a product of the westward advance: denied easy access to Eastern markets, frontiersmen converted their grain into whiskey and sent it across the mountains to be sold for cash. But by no means all of this product went over the mountains: the hardships of life in the wilderness, it was said, could only be assuaged by copious quantities of whiskey and other distilled liquors. The Reverend Charles Woodmason found the stills on the Carolina frontier bubbling with raw whiskey and peach brandy. "In this Article," he remarked, "both Presbyterians and Episcopalians very

[2] Peter Kalm, *Travels in North America* (2 vols., New York: Wilson, Erickson, 1937), Vol. 1, p. 325.

charitably agree (viz.) That of getting Drunk."

Certainly there seemed to be no lack of occasions for a friendly glass: house-raisings, weddings, town meetings, militia days, court sessions and funerals. In New England, the raising of the meetinghouse was commemorated with barrels of rum and cider. At the sessions of the lower courts in Virginia, a gallon of brandy was provided to assist the justices in their deliberations. To prepare for a meeting of the Virginia Council, William Byrd ordered 20 dozen bottles of claret, 6 dozen bottles of sherry, Rhenish and Canary wines, and a quarter of a cask of brandy. In 1675, a Virginian provided in his will that because he had observed "the debauched drinking used at burials, tending to the dishonor of God and religion, my will is that no strong drink be provided or spent at my burial." When all else failed, the weather could be counted upon to provide reason for at least a small potation: in South Carolina it was a rule that "during the warm months one should think and work little, and drink much."

In most of the colonies, four times a year, the militia was mustered and put through its paces. Since militia duty was compulsory for all males between the ages of sixteen and sixty, these meetings brought together a large number of men. Particularly in time of peace, these "Training Days" furnished an opportunity for conviviality and sports.

Sometimes, after perfunctorily going through their martial exercises, the thirsty militiamen adjourned to the tavern, where the serious business of the day began. "Training Dayes," lamented Cotton Mather in 1694, "are little more than Drinking Dayes."

A Frenchman who accompanied Governor Spotswood of Virginia on an exploring expedition, described the celebration that followed upon the discovery of a pass over the Appalachians:

We had a good dinner, and after it we got the men together, and loaded all their arms, and we drank the King's health in Champagne, and fired a volley—the Princess's health in Burgundy, and fired a volley, and all the rest of the Royal Family in claret, and a volley. We drank the Governor's health and fired another volley. We had several sorts of liquors, *viz.* Virginia red wine and white wine, Irish usquebaugh, brandy, shrub, two sorts of rum, canary, cherry, punch, water, cider, etc.[3]

Miraculously, there were no casualties during the volleys.

Durand of Dauphine found that one of the unexpected hazards of traveling in Virginia was being plied with liquor by well-wishers, its being the mark of a gentleman "to force his guests to drink, and to make it an honour to send them home drunk."

Among the nonalcoholic drinks popular among the American colonists were coffee, tea and chocolate. Of these the favorite was tea; at a time when Englishmen were addicted to coffee, Americans were the greatest tea-drinkers in the world outside of China. It was not until 1767, when the British government imposed a tax upon tea and thereby made tea-drinking an unpatriotic act, that Americans turned to coffee as a substitute for the beloved tea.

[3] Reverend James Fontaine (compiler), *Memoirs of a Huguenot Family*, edited by Ann Maury (New York: G. P. Putnam's Sons, 1872), pp. 288–89.

Bibliography

Adams, James Truslow. *Provincial Society, 1690–1763.* New York: Macmillan Co., 1938.

COURTSHIP

IN colonial America, most parents considered marriage too serious a matter to be left to the young people directly concerned. Because of its financial and social consequences, the choice of a life partner was often made by parents for their offspring—a choice that the young men and women were expected to ratify dutifully. Law and custom required that a suitor make application to the parents for permission to court the young lady. If permission were not forthcoming, the young man proceeded at his peril, for the law was prepared to deal with pertinacious swain who would not take no—from the girl's father rather than from the girl herself—for an answer. Of course, when a dowry was at issue, fathers could discourage unwanted suitors by letting it be known that they intended to withhold financial assistance if their daughters married without parental consent.

As the following letter reveals, not all young ladies obeyed their father's wishes when it came to choosing a life partner. Eliza Lucas, the daughter of a British officer, was a high-spirited girl who, while still in her teens, ran her father's plantation in South Carolina:

Honoured Sir:
Your letter by way of Philadelphia which I duly received was an additional proof of that paternal tenderness which I have always Experienced from the most Indulgent of Parents from my Cradle to the present time, and the subject of it is of the utmost importance to my peace and happiness.

As you propose Mr. L. to me I am sorry I can't have Sentiments favourable enough to him to take time to think on the Subject, as your Indulgence to me will ever add weight to the duty that obliges me to consult what best pleases you, for so much Generosity on your part claims all my Obedience. But as I know 'tis my Happiness you consult, I must beg the favour of you to pay my compliments to the old Gentleman for his Generosity and favourable Sentiments of me, and let him know my thoughts on the affair in such civil terms as you know much better than any I can dictate; and beg leave to say to you that the riches of Chili and Peru put together if he had them, could not purchase a sufficient Esteem for him to make him my husband.

As to the other gentleman you mention, Mr. W., you know Sir I have so slight a knowledge of him I can form no judgement, and Case of such consiquence requires the nicest distinction of humours and Sentiments.

But give my leave to assure you my dear Sir that a single life is my only Choice—and if it were not as I am yet but Eighteen I hope you will put aside the thoughts of my marrying yet these two or three years at least.

You are so good as to say you have too great an opinion of my prudence to think I would entertain an indiscrete passion for any one, and I hope Heaven will direct me that I may never disappoint you, and what indeed could induce me to make a Secret of my Inclination to my best friend, as I am well assured you would not disaprove it to make me a Sacrifice to wealth, and I am as certain I would indulge no passion that had not your approbation, as I truely am

Dear Sir Your most dutiful & affect. Daughter

E. Lucas[1]

Miss Lucas later married Thomas Pinckney, a wealthy young South Carolinian.

To account the world well lost for love was a maxim seldom acted upon by upper-class Americans or those who aspired to enter the upper class. Rather, the principal ob-

[1] Harriott H. Ravenel, *Eliza Pinckney* (New York: Charles Scribner's Sons, 1928), pp. 55–57.

jectives of marriage were wealth, social position and love —usually in that order. Laced as they were with dowries and jointures, marriages resembled business arrangements more than plighted troths.

The manner in which negotiations were carried on is shown in the following exchange of letters between John Walker and Bernard Moore of Virginia:

May 27, 1764.

Dear Sir: My son, Mr. John Walker, having informed me of his intention of paying his addresses to your daughter Elizabeth, if he should be agreeable to yourself, lady, and daughter, it may not be amiss to inform you what I think myself able to afford for their support in case of an union. My affairs are in an uncertain state; but I will promise one thousand pounds, to be paid in the year 1765, and one thousand pounds to be paid in the year 1766; and the further sum of two thousand pounds I promise to give him, but the uncertainty of my present affairs prevents my fixing on a time of payment. The above sums are all to be in money or lands and other effects at the option of my said son, John Walker.

I am, Sir, your humble servant.
John Walker.

To: Col. Bernard Moore, Esq. in King William.

May 28, 1764.

Dear Sir: Your son, Mr. John Walker, applied to me for leave to make his addresses to my daughter Elizabeth. I gave him leave, and told him at the same time that my affairs were in such a state that it was not in my power to pay him all the money this year that I intended to give my daughter, provided he succeeded; but would give him five hundred pounds next spring, and five hundred pounds more as soon as I could raise or get the money; which sums, you may depend, I will most punctually pay to him. I am, sir, your obedient servant,
Bernard Moore[2]

[2] Arthur W. Calhoun, *A Social History of the American Family* (3 vols., Cleveland: Arthur H. Clark Co., 1917–1919), Vol. I, pp. 253–54.

No family of colonial Virginia made more advantageous marriages than did "the marrying Carters." By dint of judiciously uniting their sons and daughters in matrimony with Burwells, Harrisons, Pages, Fitzhughs, and the other First Families of Virginia, the Carters acquired wealth, social position and political influence. Moreover, they did not shirk their duty in replenishing the earth. John Carter, the lusty founder of the clan, was married five times and had twelve children. About 50,000 of his descendants are alive today—a statistiç that puts him in the same class with Pocahontas and the passengers on the *Mayflower*.

Samuel Sewall's courtship of Madam Winthrop illustrates the businesslike frame of mind with which a fortune-hunter embarked upon matrimony. In 1722, when Sewall laid seige to Madam Winthrop, the well-provided-for widow of Governor Winthrop, he had lost by death two wives, ten of his fourteen children and ten of his grandchildren. Undaunted by these repeated strokes of adversity, Sewall was eager and fresh for marriage. But Madam Winthrop drove a hard bargain: as the price for her hand, she demanded that Sewall promise to keep a coach. From a purely monetary point of view, Sewall calculated that he would lose money by consenting to Madam Winthrop's terms. He therefore broke off negotiations and later married a less exacting widow. Madam Winthrop died in 1725. Samuel Sewall, the most assiduous funeral-goer in Boston, served as pallbearer.

The long winters and the small and inadequately heated houses of New England and New York created a serious problem for unmarried young men and women. Where could the rites of courtship be performed? The family fireside, around which the entire family usually congregated, was too public for the kind of intimacy the circumstances demanded, yet to remove any distance from its benign glow was apt to chill the ardor of even the most hot-blooded lover. A solution was found in the ancient and parentally approved custom of bundling. A young man and woman, fully clothed, lay down together in bed, crawled under the blankets and exchanged confidences and, insofar as possible, endearments. Bundling was governed by a rigorous code that even the most amorous were expected to observe: "Thus far and no farther" was a motto that might appropriately have been hung at the head of a bed reserved for bundling.

Lieutenant Francis Anbury, a British officer who served in America during the War of Independence, described bundling as he knew it from personal experience:

The night before we came to this town [Williamstown, Mass.] being quartered at a small log hut, I was convinced in how innocent a view the Americans look upon that indelicate custom they call *bundling*. Though they have remarkable good feather beds, and are extremely neat and clean, still I preferred my hard mattress, as being accustomed to it; this evening, however, owing to the badness of the roads, and the weakness of my mare, my servant had not arrived with my baggage at the time for retiring to rest. There being only two beds in the house, I inquired which I was to sleep in, when the old woman replied, "Mr. Ensign," here I should observe to you, that the New England people are very inquisitive as to the rank you have in the army; "Mr. Ensign," says she, "our Jonathan and I will sleep in this, and our Jemima and you shall sleep in that." I was much astonished at such a proposal, and offered to sit up all night, when Jonathan immediately replied, "Oh la! Mr. Ensign, you won't be the first man our Jemima has bundled with, will it Jemima?" when little Jemima, who, by the bye, was a very pretty, black-eyed girl, of about sixteen or seventeen, archly replied, "No, father, not by many, but it will be with the first Britisher" (The name they give to Englishmen). In this dilemma, what could I do? The smiling invitation of pretty Jemima —the eye, the lip, the—Lord ha' mercy, where am I going to? But wherever I may be going now, I did not go to bundle with her—in the same room with her father and mother, my kind *host* and *hostess* too! I thought of that—I thought of more besides—to struggle with the passions of nature; to clasp Jemima in my arms—to—do what? you'll ask—why, to do—nothing! for if amid all these temptations, the lovely Jemima had melted into kindness, she had been outcast from the world—treated with contempt, abused by violence, and left perhaps to perish! No, Jemima; I could have endured all this to have been blest with you, but it was too vast a sacrifice, when you were to be the victim! Suppose how great the test of virtue must, or how cold the American constitution, when this unaccountable custom is in hospitable repute, and perpetual practice.[3]

Bundling began to go out of fashion about the time of the French and Indian War—perhaps because the British soldiers quartered in the colonies did not abide by the rules of the game. Clergymen began to take disapproving note of the practice in their sermons; what had once been regarded as a harmless and comfortable way of courting was stigmatized as a sin. Moreover, the construction of larger and better-heated houses in New England weakened the case for bundling. And so, after over a century of popularity, the custom was loaded with obloquy and banished from the land. Not until the advent of the automobile did young Americans recover one of the freedoms they had lost in the colonial period.

After bundling fell into disrepute, the Yankees and the Dutch each claimed that they had learned the practice from the other but the young people of both sections were more disposed to praise than to blame the originators. New Englanders also charged that the Dutch used bundling as a cover for sexual irregularities. Certainly the penalties meted out to transgressors against the code of bundling were more severe in New England than in New Netherlands. Among the Puritans, couples who had children a suspiciously short time after marriage were often compelled to confess publicly in church that they had indulged in premarital relations. More easygoing in such matters, the Dutch permitted men and women to live together after they had published the marriage bans.

[3] Francis Anbury, *Travels through the Interior Parts of America; in a Series of Letters* (2 vols., London: W. Lane, 1789), Vol. 2, pp. 37–40.

Death provided almost as much occasion for remarriage as divorce does today. It sometimes happened that a man or woman remarried so soon after the death of his or her partner that they were consoled upon the death of the late lamented and congratulated upon the choice of a successor at the same time. The first marriage celebrated in Plymouth was that between Edward Winslow, a widower of seven weeks standing, and Susanna White, who had lost her husband less than twelve weeks previously. The governor of New Hampshire married a widow ten days after she buried her husband. Before he was forty-seven years old, Samuel Washington, George's brother, had been married five times. Although colonial Americans did not quite attain the multiplicity of wives enjoyed by the patriarchs in Biblical times, they were not far behind their illustrious predecessors in that regard, even though their wives did come in sequence.

Elizabeth Hubbard, Benjamin Franklin's niece, described for the amusement of her uncle the love life of an eighty-one-year-old Massachusetts widower:

December, 1756

My Dear Papa:

Now for the Story I promised in my last; and I wish I had the nack of teling it in such a maner, as to afford you as many Hearty Laugh's, as I have had on the Occasion. You must know then, that Littel mischievous Urchin Cupid, has got a mightly odd whim in his Head, he has new strung his Bow, and let fly one of his Keenest Arrows directly aim'd, at the Heart of an Old Man (our Speaker Mr. Hubbards Father) in his Eighty first Year. He Buryed his Wife about a Month ago, and has been for many years as Blind as a Beatel, yet nothing would do but he must have another Wife. Well he immediately set about recolecting what Beauties he had formily seen; and giving my Mama the preferance, the Parson was set to work to feel her Palts [pulse] (no mischeif going forward but the Parson and the Deavel have a finger in the Pye you know) but they being very much Indisposed he was Obliged to think again, and after severiel Vain attempts, he at last thought of a Lady he had great hopes of! and as soon as Boux Phebus's Nap [morning] was out, he sent for his Granson, and told him to go to the Lady, and be sure to make a low Bow and say Madam, and give his Love to her; and tell her if She would favour him with a Visset, the Chorrote [chariot] should wate on her, but by no means to forget to make a low Bow, and say Madam, and I beleive he gave him a Copper to Quicken his Memory, for the arrent [errand] was so well done that the Lady wated on him in a few hours, when after a littel Conversation he was told she was going, he roas [rose] and by the help of a Servant, and His Hands Pawing about like a Cat drowning he found the Lady, Clasped her in his Arms; and they say almost stifeled her with Kisses, he beg'd she would retier with him to the Chamber, where we must leave them an hour or two— well the Lady is come down, and would you think it, they say her Capp, Handkercheif, and Apron, are very much Discompose'd. However the Preliminaries are all setteled, and they agreed to be Published the next day! the young Rogues say to prevent a greater discovery, but I beleive it was only to prevent his Hanging him self in his Garter, or some such Fatall accident, for he sent for his Son that Night, and desiered he might be put on the Clarks Book as early as possible the next Morning. His Son in vain indeavoured to perswade him to defer it a littel, told him every Boy in the street was talking of it, and he thought in deacencey to his Mother's Memory he might Stay a littel longer, beg'd he would Consider on it if it was but for one Week. He indeed Acknowledged it was too soon, but then he desiered him to Consider (now you must imagine him ringing up his Face, like a Child that has lost its Sugar Teat) that he should lose a World of Happiness with the Lady in that Time, and a Week was an Age, with a good deal more such stuf, and that Tomorrow must, and should be the Day. And so it was, the Minit they ware out Published the Parson Joyn'd their Hands, the Coulars [colors] were display'd, and the Gun's Fire'd, and after a Dance in the Evining, the Lambs were lade in Bed. . . .

P.S. I had forgot to tell you he has an Estate of 10000 Pounds sterling, and besides the agrement he has promised to give the Lady a thousand Pounds Old Tenor every ten Years he shall Live with her, and he is but Eighty one.[4]

---

[4] Benjamin Franklin, *Papers*, edited by L. W. Labaree and W. J. Bell (7 vols., New Haven: Yale University Press, 1963), Vol. 7, pp. 69–71.

To which Benjamin Franklin replied:

To Elizabeth Hubbart.   Jan. 13, 1757
Dear Bess

Your Story is well told and entertaining. Only let me admonish you of a small tho' common Fault of Story-tellers. You should not have introduc'd it by telling me *how comical* it was, especially a Post before you sent the Story it self: For when the Expectation is rais'd too high, 'tis a Disadvantage to the Thing expected.

But let us not be merely entertain'd by the Tale; let us draw a small Moral from it. Old Age, we see, is subject to Love and its Follies as well as Youth: All old People *have been* young; and when they were so, they laugh'd, as we do, at the Amours of Age. They imagin'd, 'tis like, that the Case would never be theirs. Let us spare 'em, then; lest the same Case should one day be ours. I see you begin to laugh already at my ranking myself among the Young! But you, my Girl, when you arrive at Fifty, will think no more of being old, than does Your affectionate Uncle

B Franklin[5]

Instead of getting on in the world by hard work, thrift and frugality, many young Americans preferred to make their fortune in an easier way—by marrying a rich widow. The high mortality rate ensured a plentiful supply of widows and, since they inherited at least one-third of their deceased husband's estate, many were accounted wealthy by the standards of the time. When a widow remarried, her property passed into the legal possession of her new husband. In consequence, an enterprising young man, provided he did not fear comparison with his predecessor, could set himself up for life by marrying a widow blessed with a sizeable jointure.

For the same reason that an unmarried woman was looked upon as a sad quirk of nature, so confirmed bachelors were thought to shirk their duty to God, the community and womankind. In some colonies, a special tax

[5] *Ibid.,* p. 95.

was levied upon bachelors in order to drive home the lesson that two could live more cheaply than one. Thus American men were presented with a hard choice, between accepting the certain penalties of the law or risking the uncertain penalties of the married state.

So brisk was the demand for widows that some Americans marveled that the maidens ever found husbands. And, indeed, the girls had reason to complain that the widows got the cream of the crop. For example, Thomas Jefferson married a wealthy widow who brought him property worth over $100,000 dollars, including 135 slaves; by this advantageous marriage, Jefferson doubled his estate. In Martha Custis, whom he married seven months after the death of Daniel Custis, Washington landed a rich prize. All of Martha's property was vested in her new husband and he was free to dispose of it as he pleased.

In the pursuit of rich widows, bachelors were given hot competition by widowers. For, by the same token that there were many widows, there were also many widowers; indeed, death, aided by excessive childbearing, tended to cut down in their prime more women than men. Particularly when they were left with the care of small children, widowers were inclined to assume that they had prior claims upon the favors, fortunes and services of widows.

Even so, few girls went unmarried, and most were wives and mothers before they were out of their teens. William Byrd observed that matrimony throve so well in Virginia that "an Old Maid or an Old Bachelor are as scarce among us and reckoned as ominous as a Blazing Star." When his eldest daughter at the age of twenty-three had not found a husband, he was inclined to write her off as an "antique Virgin." He worried lest she become "the most calamitous creature in nature"—an old maid. On the other hand, Byrd might well have rejoiced that his daughter was still alive: his sister, Ursula, married at sixteen, had died in childbirth a year later.

Bibliography

Stiles, Henry Reed. *Bundling: Its Origin, Progress and Decline in America.* New York: Book Collectors' Association, 1934.

MARRIAGE

IN seventeenth-century New England, marriage was wholly a civil matter: couples were united in wedlock by a magistrate without the sanctifying presence of a clergyman. The Pilgrims, having learned this custom in Holland, brought it with them to Plymouth but it owed its wide acceptance in New England to the fact that the Puritans found no evidence either in the Bible or in the practices of the first Christians that clergymen were authorized to perform the marriage ceremony. The secular side of marriage—the property settlements and legal obligations it entailed—reinforced the view that marriage was a function of the state rather than of the church. Marriages might be made in Heaven, but they were not valid until the fees had been paid and the entry duly made in the town records. Not until 1692 were ministers in Massachusetts authorized to perform marriages. Even so, it remained essentially a secular act: when clergymen solemnized marriages they acted as agents of the state.

By modern standards, a New England marriage ceremony was a pretty bleak affair. There was no wedding dress, no throwing of rice, no bridesmaids, music, ring, prayers or benediction. The couple simply clasped hands before a magistrate and heard themselves pronounced man and wife—a fitting introduction to life in colonial New England: plain, simple and unadorned.

In the Southern colonies, marriage was usually solemnized according to the rites of the Church of England, although, in deference to the large number of dissenters in those colonies, civil marriage was permitted. Among the

Quakers, marriage took place in the presence of the assembled meeting without benefit of clerical or secular authorities. The parties simply indicated their intention of entering the married state and this declaration sufficed to make them man and wife. Nevertheless, the Quakers, like other religious groups in colonial America, required the publication of banns to guard against the danger of a hasty and ill-considered match.

Because of their scarcity in early America, women were more highly valued than in the Old World, where they were relatively abundant. In 1619, for example, the Virginia House of Burgesses addressed itself to the weighty question: Which, in a new plantation, "be the most necessary, man or woman?" Ultimately the legislators decided that one could not get along without the other: therefore the immigration of women was encouraged by granting 50 acres of land to every married woman who came to the colony.

But scarcity alone did not produce romantic idealization of women. The fact was, women were valued, among other things, as helpmates; without them, no farm or plantation could be wholly successful. From a purely utilitarian point of view, therefore, a woman around the house was indispensable, and it was this aspect of marriage, rather than romantic love, which was emphasized in colonial America.

Childbearing and childrearing, domestic drudgery, farm duties—these were the lot of most women during the colonial period. For them, life was not enlivened by women's clubs and community activities. While servants were comparatively cheap, those who could not afford them had no recourse to labor-saving appliances. Of colonial women it has been eloquently said:

Generations of them cooked, carried water, washed and made clothes, bore children in lonely peril, and tried to bring up safely through all sorts of physical exposure without medical or surgical help, lived themselves in terror of the wilderness, and under the burden of a sad and cruel creed, sank at last into nameless graves, without any vision of the grateful days when millions of their descendants should rise up and call them blessed.

The kind and amount of labor performed by a married woman depended upon her station in life. Far more toil was exacted from a pioneer woman than from the wife of a wealthy planter or a middle-class townsman. Besides making the family clothing, soap and candles, and other duties that, in more affluent households, were left to indentured servants and slaves, the pioneer woman was expected to labor in the fields and to do work commonly assigned to draft animals. William Byrd met a frontier woman whom he described as

a very civil woman and shews nothing of ruggedness or Immodesty in her carriage, yett she will carry a gun in the woods and kill dear, turkeys, &c. shoot down wild cattle, catch and tye hoggs, knock down beeves with an ax and perform the most manfull Exercises as well as most men in those parts.

Even though the wife of a Southern planter was spared this menial labor, running a large household, even with the aid of a housekeeper and numerous slaves, was often a frustrating and nerve-wracking task. Moreover, since the planters always entertained guests at home, the main burden of providing Southern hospitality fell upon their wives.

At the same time, law and custom relegated women to an inferior status. In the eyes of the common law, a married woman had no existence apart from her husband; she was his chattel to do with very much as he pleased. She could not make a valid contract, bring suit or be sued in court, execute a deed, administer an estate or make a will. She could exercise no legal rights over her children. The most she could ask of them was reverence and respect. Women were expected to look upon their husbands with reverence, love and fear—the same emotions with which they approached their Maker. Insofar as the law and custom could make them so, husbands were as gods upon earth.

Except in New England, where a husband was not permitted to beat his wife, and, with fine impartiality, a wife was not permitted to beat her husband, the law specified how much corporal punishment a husband could inflict upon his wife. When he beat her—as, indeed, on occasion, the law recognized, he must—the stick must be no larger than a finger in diameter. When applying the rod, a husband was enjoined to bear in mind that, after all, she was his wife and that her services would again be required. It was therefore forbidden to kill or permanently incapacitate a woman, no matter how much provocation she gave her liege lord. During the colonial period, it was a fair question to ask a man if he had stopped beating his wife.

From the number of cases in colonial courts of wives' seeking protection against their spouses, it is apparent that some husbands abused their privilege of administering wholesome and character-building chastisement. In such instances, the courts compelled the husband to give bond for his future good behavior and occasionally imposed a fine to teach him better conjugal manners.

Even when buying her clothes, a woman was expected to defer to the judgment of her husband. William Byrd recorded in his diary how violently he and his wife quarreled when he learned that she had made unauthorized purchases of finery from England. George Washington avoided this kind of trouble by personally ordering his wife's and his stepdaughter's clothing. He also chose the furniture, carpets, wallpaper, and even the color of the curtains for Mount Vernon. He even directed where the furniture was to be placed. Although Martha brought him a great deal of money, she was left in no doubt as to who was running the establishment.

Even though the Puritans permitted women to become church members, they did not allow them to speak in church: if they had any questions they were advised to put them to their husbands and be guided by their superior wisdom. The fate of Anne Hutchinson, the leader of the "Antinomian Heresy" in Massachusetts, who was banished from the colony and scalped by the Indians on Long Island, was often cited as a warning to women not to meddle with theology or other matters beyond their powers of comprehension.[1]

John Winthrop put women in the place he supposed God intended them to occupy:

The woman's own choice makes such a man her husband; yet being so chosen, he is her lord and she is to be subject to him, yet in a way of liberty, not of bondage, and a true wife accounts her subjection her honour and freedom, and would not think her condition safe and free but in her subjection to her husband's authority. Such is the liberty of the church under the authority of Christ, her king and husband; his yoke is so easy and sweet to her as a bride's ornaments; and if through forwardness or wantonness, etc. she shake it off at any time, she is at no rest in her spirit until she take it up again; and whether her lord smiles upon her and embraceth her in his arms, or whether he frowns, or rebukes, or smites her, she apprehends the sweetness of his love in all and is refreshed, supported, and instructed by every such dispensation of his authority over her.[2]

It was very much a man's world but, even with law and custom on their side, some husbands were unable to exercise the authority that was their due. Masterful, domineering wives cut these would-be patriarchs down to size and they submitted to petticoat government with hardly more than a whimper of protest.

Occasionally, unhappy wives ran away from insupportable husbands. In that event, the husband usually advertised in the newspapers—the notice appeared alongside

[1] In 1635–36, Mrs. Anne Hutchinson began to criticize the Boston ministers, with the exception of the Reverend John Cotton and her brother-in-law, the Reverend John Wheelwright, for preaching a gospel of works rather than a gospel of faith. Her teachings (called "Antinomianism" by her adversaries) were based upon a more emotional and evangelical Christianity than was considered orthodox in Boston. Mrs. Hutchinson and the Reverend John Wheelwright were banished from the colony after they had been condemned by the secular and ecclesiastical authorities.

[2] J. K. Hosmer (ed.), *John Winthrop's Journal, 1630–1649 (Original Narratives of Early American History)* (2 vols., New York: Charles Scribner's Sons, 1908), Vol. II, p. 239.

advertisements for the return of fugitive servants and slaves—announcing his intention of prosecuting anyone who knowingly gave the fugitive shelter. After all, the wife, however much she might dislike her husband's bed and board, was his legal property and he had a right to her services, of which he could be deprived only by the law.

Divorce was easier in New England than in those colonies where the Church of England was established. From 1664 until the American Revolution, not a single divorce was legalized in the colony of New York. In that province and in the Southern colonies, a marriage could be dissolved only by act of the royal governor and council. As a result, many couples dragged out a loveless existence. But the courts occasionally mitigated this intolerable state of affairs by ordering legal separations and, in cases of excessive cruelty, desertion and nonsupport, required the errant husband to provide separate maintenance.

In one respect, at least, women enjoyed equality with men in colonial America: they were usually punished with equal severity for crimes and misdemeanors. Women were pilloried, ducked, whipped publicly and, for a particularly heinous offense such as the murder of a husband, burned to death. Around 1720, a woman was put to death in Philadelphia for burglary. And, as always, women who sinned against the moral code received the brunt of the punishment.

For one capital crime, witchcraft, the penalty was meted out almost exclusively to women. Only one male suffered death for selling his soul to the Devil; the rest of the victims of the witchcraft mania were women. Indeed, by definition, a "witch" was a woman; a man guilty of dealings with Satan was called a "wizard." Among the many disagreeable results of growing old, women faced the very real hazard of being taken for a witch—for old women were considered particularly susceptible to the wiles of the Evil One.

The romantic aura with which Southerners surrounded their womenfolk and the chivalry that they traditionally exhibited toward all members of the weaker sex were not always in evidence during the colonial period. In 1676, when Nathaniel Bacon and his men were under attack by Governor Berkeley's partisans in Jamestown, they made a protective shield of the wives of their enemies behind which they made good their escape. Colonel Parke, the father-in-law of William Byrd II, threatened to drag Mrs. Blair, the wife of the Commissary of the Church of England in Virginia, bodily out of her pew in full view of the congregation because she gossiped about his well-known adultery. Nevertheless the conditions of life in the Southern colonies—the threat of violence always present in the wilderness, the hostility of the Indians and the presence of large numbers of unpredictable black slaves—caused men to take an extraordinarily protective attitude toward women. In the nineteenth century, the novels of Sir Walter Scott helped prepare the way for the cult of womanhood and the elaborate courtesy and refinement of sentiment displayed by Southern males that led some travelers to conclude that, in the Southland, knighthood was again in flower.

But in colonial America it was the absolute authority enjoyed by the husband rather than the veneration accorded women that impressed European travelers. In 1780, comparing American social gatherings with the salons of Paris, Barbé-Marbois remarked that the equality of the sexes had been carried much further in France than in America:

Nothing is so rare as an unsatisfactory household; the women are sincerely and faithfully attached to their husbands; they have few pleasures outside their families, but enjoy all those which a domestic and retired life have to offer. They live in the midst of their children, feed them, and bring them up themselves. Strangers are received well here, but are rarely admitted into the intimacy of the family. Accustomed to an extreme deference for women, a European finds it hard to get used to seeing the husband the absolute master of his household. Some people believe that it is their autocratic rule which keeps the customs of this society so pure, and that the equality to which

Europeans have admitted their wives has produced first laxity and then corruption.[3]

As was to be expected in a country as desperately short of labor as was colonial America, women played an important part in activities outside the home. Women ran taverns and retail stores, operated ferries, managed plantations, and the practice of obstetrics was almost monopolized by midwives. The formidable figure of the schoolmarm began to loom over the formative years of colonial children, but custom, based on hoary prejudice, barred women's entry into such high matters as politics, church affairs, literature and the professions.

Until Aaron Burr undertook to make his daughter, Theodosia, the most erudite and accomplished woman of her generation, few Americans were prepared to agree with Mrs. John Adams when she said that "if we mean to have heroes, statesmen and philosophers, we should have learned women." Nevertheless, during the eighteenth century, the educational revolution began to catch up with women. More and more, girls were taught to write as well as to read. Increasing wealth and leisure redounded to the benefit of upper-class colonial girls, many of whom were sent to dancing schools and even to "female seminaries" where they were taught music, drawing, French and manners. The ideal of the well-brought-up young lady had undergone a drastic change since John Winthrop laid down the law as to how the "females" of Boston should conduct themselves.

Indeed, before the colonial period came to a close, some travelers were ready to pronounce American women superior to American men. Of course, American men did not always rate very high: Nicholas Creswell, for example, considered Yankees to be "the nastiest Devils in creation." Even English ladies sometimes drew invidious comparisons between American men and women. A "Lady of Quality" who came to North Carolina in 1774 observed that many

[3] Barbé-Marbois, *Our Revolutionary Forefathers. The Letters of François, Marquis de Barbé-Marbois* (New York: Duffield & Co., 1929), p. 169.

of the ladies she encountered "would make a figure in any part of the world" whereas even men of the better sort seemed no better than peasants. "To be a good marksman is the highest ambition of youth," she said, "while to those enervated by age or infirmity drinking grog remained a last consolation." When she encountered a man of breeding and manners she remarked: "tho' I believed him an American, I could not help owning he had the look of a gentleman." [4]

[4] Janet Schaw, *Journal of a Lady of Quality*, edited by Charles M. Andrews (New Haven: Yale University Press, 1922), pp. 154, 181.

Bibliography

Benson, Mary S. *Women in Eighteenth-Century America.* New York: Columbia University Press, 1935.

Dexter, Elizabeth W. *Colonial Women of Affairs.* Boston: Houghton Mifflin Co., 1931.

Spruill, Julia Cherry. *Women's Life and Work in the Southern Colonies.* Chapel Hill: University of North Carolina Press, 1938.

Winslow, Ola Elizabeth. *Samuel Sewall of Boston.* New York: Macmillan Co., 1964.

CHILDREN

THE "population explosion" that began in western Europe in the eighteenth century was most strikingly manifested in the British American colonies. Families of ten or twelve children were not unusual and the arrival of an additional member of the family was almost an annual event. Sir William Phips, governor of Massachusetts, was one of 26 children, all born of the same mother; William Rawson had 20 children by one wife; Robert "Councillor" Carter of Virginia had 17 children and Charles Carter of Shelby had 23 children by two marriages. Benjamin Franklin came from a family of 17, and John Marshall, later Chief Justice of the United States Supreme Court, was the first of 15 brothers and sisters. A South Carolina woman was credited with having brought 34 children into the world—an achievement that would certainly entitle her to be acclaimed as the All-American Mother. Yet records in this field of endeavor were made only to be broken: in 1742, a New England woman died leaving five children, 61 grandchildren, 182 great-grandchildren and 12 great-great-grandchildren.

In colonial America, large families were the rule not because there was no effective method of birth control but because the abundance of land and the scarcity of labor made children a valuable asset. Not only did Americans feel they could afford to have numerous children: they felt that they could *not* afford not to have them. Then, too, the heavy toll taken in childhood by disease necessitated a large number of offspring to ensure the survival of the family. But the main reason was economic: on

American farms, the labor of children and young adults was indispensable. Boys did field chores and learned trades while girls were occupied with the housework, milking cows and, during the harvest they helped to bring in the crops. As early as 1630, Francis Higginson of Salem pointed out that "little children here by setting of corn may earn much more than their own maintenance."

It is also true that Americans married young and had children in rapid succession because they did not fear that they would be unable to provide for them. If there was not land in the immediate neighborhood, the empty region to the west offered a seemingly inexhaustible supply of virgin soil. Thomas Jefferson said that it would take at least two centuries for Americans to fill up the country and he, of course, envisaged the people living on their own farms, not piled on top of one another in great cities. Had Thomas Robert Malthus been an American, it is hardly possible that he would have conceived the idea that population threatened to outrun the food supply.

Americans seemed to have assumed that they had been specially commissioned to replenish the earth and that no time could be lost in accomplishing this mission. The Reverend Charles Woodmason found that, on the Carolina frontier, every cabin contained ten or twelve young children and that often the children and grandchildren of the same couple were of the same age; uncles and nephews, aunts and nieces all frolicked together in the mud. The Indians could have read their doom in the census figures.

At an early age, children learned—no doubt, to their dismay—that they had been brought into the world to labor and that there was no lack of employment in America. The adage that the Devil found employment for idle hands seemed to parents to be particularly applicable to children. To guard against this danger, sport and other recreations were kept at a minimum. The Reverend John Cotton of Boston recommended that children be permitted to spend the first seven years at "lawful recreation" but thereafter, he added portentously, work must begin in earnest and the choice of a "calling" ought not be postponed beyond the twelfth year. Thus religion sanctioned a practice made necessary by the hard conditions of life in a pioneering age.

Reverence for God and parents was instilled in colonial children from an early age. In their infancy, they were taught that their parents "do bear a singular image of God, as he is the Creator, Sustainer and Governor." Their first duty was obedience; as Poor Richard said, teach your child to obey and you can teach him anything.

The Reverend Cotton Mather, who applied this theory in his own household, explained how he broke the "stubborn will" of his own children:

I first beget them a high opinion of their father's love to them, and of his being best able to judge, what shall be good for them. Then I make them sensible, tis a folly for them to pretend unto any witt and will of their own. . . . My word must be their law. . . . I would never come to give a child a blow; except in case of obstinacy or some gross enormity. To be chased for a while out of my presence I would make to be looked upon, as the sorest punishment in the family. . . . The stanch way of Education, carried on with raving and kicking and scourging (in schools as well as families) tis abominable; and a dreadful judgment of God upon the world. . . . I would put my children upon chusing their several ways of usefulness, and enkindle in them as far as I can, a mighty desire of being useful in the world, and assist them unto the uttermost.[1]

Himself a paragon of precocious godliness, Cotton Mather took emphatic exception to the saying: "A young saint and an old devil." Rather, he said, experience proved that "young Saints will make Old Angels." He found few young devils who atoned for a misspent youth by becoming pillars of rectitude. The sure way of producing an angel, he contended, was to rear a child in a God-fearing home, instill the love of God and fear of the Devil and devote many hours to family prayers and Bible-read-

[1] Arthur W. Calhoun, *A Social History of the American Family* (3 vols., Cleveland: Arthur H. Clark Co., 1917), Vol. I, pp. 113–14.

ing. Mather attributed his own conversion and salvation to the piety he learned at his mother's knee.

And yet in his own family, Cotton Mather was compelled to contend with an aggravated case of juvenile delinquency. Even though he was of the seed of the Mathers and therefore presumably assured of sainthood, Samuel ("Sammy") Mather proved to be an exceedingly wild sprout. Until he was lost at sea at the age of twenty-five, he proved to be a source of bafflement, frustration and finally despair to his anguished father.

In Sammy's inordinate fondness for play Cotton Mather detected the first signs of the child's impending fall from grace. Sammy's waywardness was soon compounded by an aversion to Bible-reading and a penchant for picking friends from along the Boston waterfront.

As Cotton Mather's diary shows, he spared no effort to rescue Sammy from his sinful ways:

[June 26, 1716:] I must think of some exquisite and obliging Wayes, to abate Sammy's inordinate Love of Play. His play wounds his Faculties. I must engage him in some nobler Entertainments. (Sammy was at this time ten years old.)

[June 1, 1717:] What shall be done, for the raising of Sammy's Mind, above the debasing Meannesses of Play!

[September 3, 1717:] Entertain Sammy betimes, with the first Rudiments of Geography and Astronomy, as well as History; and so raise his Mind above the sillier Diversions of Childhood.

[September 24, 1717:] Heap a great Library on my little Samuel.

[January 14, 1718:] Sammy is united with a Society of sober and pious lads, who meet for Exercises of Religion. I will allow them the Use of my Library, for the Place of their Meeting; and give them Directions, and Entertainments.[2]

[2] Diary of Cotton Mather (2 vols., New York: Frederick Ungar, n.d.), Vol. II, pp. 357, 457, 473, 476, 498–99.

Neither Cotton Mather nor his errant son were typical products of a New England upbringing. In general, the children who were exposed to the pervasive disciplinary influences of the home, the church and the school grew up to be hardworking, God-fearing, churchgoing men and women who strictly observed at least the outward forms of Puritanism. The moral code, buttressed by religious sanctions, remained a powerful force in New England long after the early Puritans and the zeal that they brought to the New World had vanished from the land.

For Puritan parents, the sweetness and innocence of childhood were marred by the doctrines of infant damnation and original sin. It was impressed upon every Puritan parent that they must see to the conversion of their offspring before they were taken by death—for if they died without being redeemed by religion they were the lawful prize of the Devil. Orthodox Calvinism afforded little hope to bereaved parents that infants could enter Heaven. The best that the Reverend Michael Wigglesworth could promise them was that the easiest room in hell was reserved for infants. But no Puritan was willing to accept either for himself or for his children an apartment in hell as a consolation prize for the mansions of Paradise.

The trouble was to lie in the depraved nature of children—a subject with which the Puritans, like most parents, had firsthand experience. The Reverend Benjamin Wadsworth spoke feelingly about children from the point of view of a harassed parent and a devout Calvinist:

The Hearts naturally, are a mere nest, root, fountain of Sin, and wickedness: an evil Treasure from whence proceed evil things, viz. Evil Thoughts, Murders, Adulteries &c. Indeed, as sharer in the guilt of Adam's first Sin, they're Children of Wrath by Nature, liable to Eternal Vengeance, the Unquenchable Flames of Hell. But besides this, their Hearts (as hath been said) are unspeakably wicked, estrang'd from God, full of enmity against Him, eagerly set in pursuing Vanities, on provoking God by actual Personal transgressions, whereby they merit and deserve greater measures of Wrath.[8]

[8] Edmund S. Morgan, *The Puritan Family*, (Boston: The Trustees of the Public Library, 1944), p. 51.

And the Reverend John Robinson, pastor of the Pilgrim church in Leyden, Holland, told his congregation:

Surely there is in all children (though not alike) a stubborness and stoutness of minde arising from naturall pride which must in the first place be broken and beaten down that so the foundation of their education being layd in humilitie and tractableness other virtues may in their time be built thereon. It is commendable in a horse that he be stout and stomackfull being never left to his own government, but always to have his rider on his back and his bit in his mouth, but who would have his child like his horse in his brutishness? [4]

Eradicating original sin in children required liberal use of the rod by Puritan parents. Every schoolmaster, likewise, included among the paraphernalia of his profession a switch made of birch twigs and, for obstinate cases, a walnut stick. It did no good for a child who had been whipped at school to complain to his parents; in that event, he was likely to get a whipping at home for good measure. "Better whipped than damned," said Cotton Mather; and many parents laid on the rod with right good will, persuaded that they were thereby literally beating the Devil out of the child.

But Cotton Mather did not leave parents with the stark option of sparing the rod and thereby allowing Satan to gain the upper hand: precept and example, he contended, were more effective than chastisement as a means of bringing children to glory. "When you lay them in your bosoms and dandle them on your knees," he advised his parishioners, "try by little and little to infuse good things, holy truths, into them." Anne Bradstreet, the New England poetess, treated her children with love and understanding and, perhaps partly for that reason, succeeded in bringing all seven of them to maturity. She remarked:

Diverse children have their different natures. Some are like flesh which nothing but salt will keep from putrefaction; some again like tender fruits that are best preserved with sugar: those

[4] Alice Earle, *Child Life in Colonial Days* (New York: Macmillan Co., 1899), pp. 191–92.

parents are wise that can fit their nurture according to their Nature.

To vanquish this brutishness, Puritan children at an early age—their elders were inclined to believe the earlier the better—were confronted with the terrors of Hell and their own loathsomeness in the sight of God. When his daughter Kathy reached the age of four, Cotton Mather took her upon his knee and told her what every girl ought to know about Hell. Nor did he conceal from her his opinion that unless she wholly changed her nature she was assuredly destined for that place of eternal torment. In his diary, Mather recorded:

I sett before her the sinful condition of her nature and charged her to pray in secret places every day. That God for the sake of Jesus Christ would give her a new heart.

Samuel Sewall's impressionable young daughter, Betty, treated to similar straight talk about Hell and damnation, reacted in a way that astonished her parents:

When I came in, past 7 at night, my wife met me in the Entry and told me Betty had surprised them. I was surprised with the Abruptness of the Relation. It seems Betty Sewall had given some signs of dejection and sorrow; but a little while after dinner she burst into an amazing cry which caus'd all the family to cry too. Her Mother ask'd the Reason, she gave none; at last said she was afraid she should go to Hell, her Sins were not pardon'd. She was first wounded by my reading a sermon of Mr. Norton's; Text, Ye shall seek me and shall not find me. And these words in the Sermon, Ye shall seek me and die in your Sins, ran in her Mind and terrified her greatly. And staying at home, she read out of Mr. Cotton Mather—Why hath Satan filled thy Heart? which increas'd her Fear. Her Mother asked her whether she pray'd. She answered Yes, but fear'd her prayers were not heard, because her sins were not pardoned.[5]

Puritan parents were haunted by the fear that the punishment for their transgressions—and in New England, thoughts could be fully as sinful as deeds—might fall upon their children. When Cotton Mather's child fell into the fire, he exclaimed in an agony of contrition: "Alas for my sin, the just God throws my child into the fire." In his sermons, he urged parents whose children had met with bodily harm or death, to look into their own souls—and when they saw the depravity and sin therein they would understand why God had struck down their children. Thus the sins of one generation descended to the next generation, and mankind was caught in an eternal cycle of wrongdoing and punishment in which children were the ultimate victims.

Naturally, therefore, the conviction of sin lay heavily upon children as well as upon adults. A New England conscience was usually acquired in childhood and no one pretended that it was a pleasant experience. A child's eyes were described as being "red and sore from weeping on his sins" and a two-and-half-year-old girl "as she lay in her Cradle would ask herself the Question: What is my Corrupt Nature? and would answer herself: It is empty of Grace, bent unto Sin, and only to Sin, and that Continually." Many children might well have echoed her lament:

> What pity such a pretty maid
> As I should go to hell.

The Reverend Nathaniel Mather could never forgive himself for the enormities he had committed in his youth:

When very young I went astray from God and my mind was altogether taken with vanities and follies, such as the remembrance of them doth greatly abase my soul within me. Of the manifold sins which then I was guilty of, none so sticks upon me, as that, being very young, I was whittling on the Sabbath Day, and for fear of being seen I did it behind the door. A great reproach of God! a specimen of that Atheism I brought into the world with me.[6]

---

[6] Arthur W. Calhoun, *op. cit.,* p. 110.

Anne Bradstreet was similarly afflicted:

> Stained from birth with Adam's sinful fact,
> Thence I began to sin as soon as act;
> A perverse will, a love to what's forbid,
> A serpent's sting in pleasing face lay hid:
> A lying tongue as soon as it could speak
> And fifth Commandment do daily break.[7]

Puritan New England produced prodigies of youthful piety who rebuked their parents for their laxness in conducting family prayers and their indulgence in carnal delights. One child of two years of age was credited with comprehending "the mysteries of Redemption" and another babe prattled about her love for faithful ministers and her delight in listening to sermons. These paragons were held up as examples to fun-loving striplings: for the edification of the children of New England, the Reverend Cotton Mather collected these tales of heavenly minded infants in a book entitled *Some Examples of Children in whom the Fear of God was remarkably Budding before they died.*

And yet, despite all the evidence that children were inherently depraved, Puritans believed that even these "limbs of Satan" could be saved by education and intensive religious instruction. The Reverend Thomas Hooker urged parents to bring children "as near to Heaven as we can. It is in our power to restrain them, and reform them, and that we ought to do." But admittedly, the task was not easy: childhood was conceived of as a race between death and damnation on one side and conversion and salvation on the other. Too often, epidemics gave the victory to death. Cotton Mather offered the children of New England good advice, but comparatively few of them lived long enough to act upon it:

You may die in your Childhood, but you should be ambitious, that if it should be so, you die an hundred years old; have as

[7] John H. Ellis (ed.), *The Works of Anne Bradstreet* (Charlestown, Mass.: A. E. Cutter, 1867), p. 151.

much Knowledge and Virtue, as many men of an hundred years old.

It would have been extraordinary indeed had all Puritan children submitted docilely to a code so antithetical to their normal instincts. The truth is, the behavior of the young never ceased to give anxiety to their elders; they would have been the first to admit that Puritanism had not solved the problem of how to make the manners and morals of the younger generation a carbon copy of that of their parents. The familiar lament in Puritan New England was that each generation of children was a little worse than its predecessor. The decline was uninterrupted: no one ever said that the children were better behaved, more moral and more religious than their parents. Instead, the "Lusty and Wanton Frolicks of the Young People" seemed to become progressively more lusty and wanton. Some Puritan elders arrived at the conclusion that only the Second Coming could stop this woeful deterioration.

For evidence to support this discouraging prognosis, Puritans could point to such instances as that of the young lady who pounded a constable with a Bible and the New Hampshire girl who, when accused of wearing a headdress that violated the law, told the magistrates that she "would pull off her head clothes, and come in her hair to them, like a parcel of pitifully beggarly curs as they were." Young men were guilty of similar acts of defiance: in 1700, Lord Bellamont reported that there were "a great many young men educated at the College in Cambridge, who differ much in their principles from their parents."

The Dutch in New Netherlands took a more lenient attitude toward the vagaries of children. One of the reasons the Pilgrims left Holland in 1620 was that they feared that their children were in danger of being corrupted by the example set them by the relatively emancipated Dutch boys and girls. In New Netherlands, the Dutch burghers carried on this tradition of their homeland: adolescent behavior was viewed with a philosophical resignation almost wholly lacking in Boston. The first master of the Latin School in New Amsterdam did not share this equanimity:

he complained that he was unable to keep order in school because some parents forbade him to punish their children. As a result, he said, the students "beat each other and tore the clothes from each other's back."

The brooding anxiety with which Puritan parents watched over the spiritual state of their children was not generally shared by the Southern planters. Heaven was always easier of attainment in the South than in New England; for that ascent, the Church of England afforded a more convenient and commodious launching-pad than did the Congregational churches. Baptism—granted in the Puritan colonies only to the children of church members—was freely bestowed in the Church of England, where it was held to be one of the sureties of grace.

In consequence, while Southern planters did not neglect the religious education of their children, they dwelt less upon the terrors of Hell and the innate depravity of man than did the seventeenth-century Puritans. It was not merely the more indulgent climate of the South that accounted for this comparatively relaxed frame of mind. Religion was the principal determinant: the Presbyterians of the Southern colonies shared the New England Puritans' views of original sin and they, too, looked askance upon "Pretexes for what is called innocent (tho' in Reality damnable) Recreations."

If the children of Puritan New England reflected, even though to a lesser degree, their parents' besetting concern with religion and morals, so the children of Southern planters tended to duplicate their parents' passion for sport, hunting and horse racing. While the Southern planting society produced few paragons of religious zeal, it did create boys and girls who loved an outdoor life and who excelled in the accomplishments deemed befitting young people of the upper class.

William Fitzhugh, an eighteenth-century Virginia planter, summed up the point of view of his place, time and class when he said that children had "better be never born than ill-bred." The good breeding was supplied by parental example and by etiquette books, imported translations of

French and Italian manuals. The books were designed to turn out the complete gentleman, and the perfect lady: besides teaching correct manners—how to bow or curtsey —they sought to inculcate such virtues as courage, integrity, justice, piety and chivalry in young men, and the qualities of chastity, modesty, loyalty and submissiveness to the superior wisdom of husbands in young ladies.

Bibliography

Earle, Alice Morse. *Child Life in Colonial Days*. New York: Macmillan Co., 1907.

Morgan, Edmund S. *The Puritan Family*. Boston: Trustees of the Public Library, 1941.

EDUCATION

THE Puritans came to the New World imbued with zeal for righteousness and education. They had no sooner founded their City Upon a Hill than they instituted a school system and required that all Puritan children be given at least a basic education. This emphasis upon learning proved to be one of the most enduring aspects of Puritanism: the little red schoolhouse, as much as the blue laws, remains one of the by-products of the Puritans' obsessive concern with holiness.

Originally, Puritans believed in education not because they were middle-class people who hoped to use education as a means of getting ahead in the world, but because they thought that first hand knowledge of the Scriptures was essential to salvation. It was primarily owing to their exaltation of the Bible as the holy of holies—to which the sacraments and the church itself were secondary—that the Puritans made mass education an article of their faith. If the Bible was everything they believed it to be—the Book in which God spoke directly to mankind and laid down directives for all mundane concerns—it behooved every individual to study it diligently: to read it, in short, as though his salvation depended upon it, as, in fact, the Puritans firmly believed it did.

Thus, ability to read the Bible was to the Puritans a form of insurance against perdition; if the policy was not gilt-edged, it at least greatly improved one's chances of escaping The Pit. To their way of thinking, there was a close connection between illiteracy and unregeneracy. Just as the "Old Deluder" prayed upon the idle, so he found willing recruits among the ignorant; and when idleness was combined with ignorance, the Puritans were prepared to pronounce the case hopeless.

Even though the Puritans insisted upon a religious "experience"—a mystical assurance of salvation and of oneness with God—as a prerequisite to membership in a Congregational church, they were suspicious of uneducated persons who claimed to have been vouchsafed this saving grace. Rather, conversion was envisaged as the culmination of a long and arduous process that included church going, Bible-reading and spiritual exercises—including, of course, wrestling with the Devil. To them, it was incredible that an illiterate person could pass through this ordeal: without the aid of learning, salvation was almost unattainable.

Since, in the Puritan mind, children were born ignorant as well as wicked—original sin being compounded of ignorance and depravity—obviously something had to be done about saving them from the Old Deluder. The Puritans' solution was to cram education into them as early as possible. It was a method that has made generations of schoolchildren quail, but it fulfilled the purpose of creating an educated citizenry. The Puritans' purpose, however, was concerned not only with this life but with the next: they hoped to ensure that if their children died in puberty, as they often did, they would not be denied entrance to Heaven for reasons of ignorance.

Likewise, because of the importance Puritans attached to secular government—it was the coequal of the church in furthering the work of God—they required that their public officials as well as their clergy be educated men. To satisfy the demand for educated men in both church and state, Harvard College was founded in 1636. At this time, the Bay Colony was little more than a cluster of frontier settlements:

After God had carried us safe to New England, and we had builded our houses, provided necessaries for our livelihood, rear'd convenient places for Gods worship, and settled the Civile Government: One of the next things we longed for, and looked after, was to advance Learning and perpetuate it to posterity: dreading to leave an illiterate Ministry to the Churches, when our present Ministers shall lie in the dust. And as wee were thinking and consulting how to effect this great work; it pleased God to stir up the heart of one Mr. Harvard (a godly gentleman, and a lover of learning, there living amongst us) to give the one halfe of his estate (it being in all about 1700 pounds) toward the erecting of a Colledge, and all his Library; after him another gave 300 pounds, others after them cast in more, and the publique hand of the state added the rest; the Colledge was, by common consent, appointed to be at Cambridge (a place very pleasant and accomodate), and is called (according to the name of the first founder) Harvard Colledge.[1]

Finally, there was a large number of university-trained men in New England—higher in proportion to the population than even today—who had a vested as well as a religious interest in promoting education. The "Visible Saints" who ruled both church and state were an intellectual elite, and one of the emblems of elitehood was a college degree. At no time in American history were learned men more honored, obeyed and generally revered than in seventeenth-century New England. Puritans were sure that scholars sat at the right hand of God. In this respect, New England afforded a preview of Heaven. Because of his erudition, the Reverend John Cotton was credited with knowing the mind of God more intimately than did any of his contemporaries; he was therefore asked by both the magistrates and clergy to settle difficult problems in both civil and ecclesiastical affairs.

In making war upon ignorance, the Puritans assumed that their great adversary, as in all things, was Satan or, as they sometimes said, the Wilderness. In their vocabulary, the Devil and the Wilderness were synonymous: the Wilderness was the Devil's natural habitat, the spirit of lawlessness, impiety and contempt of learning that emanated from it was his work. Not for the Puritans was the feeling of reverence and awe that comes from the contemplation of the virgin beauties of Nature: their first impulse was always to cut down the trees, dispossess the Indians and start building a church and a school.

---

[1] *New England's First Fruits* (London, 1643), p. 12.

Compact settlement by towns proved to be the Puritans' strongest weapon against these malign influences generated by the wilderness. Had the people lived in isolated homesteads scattered over the country, an educational system, and with it the New England Way, would have been impossible to maintain.

Of the three R's, the Puritans insisted only upon the first —reading. Parents or schools that taught children to read satisfied all the educational requirements of the province. As a result, in early New England, the ability to read was more common than the ability to write. In 1664, for example, when the town of Cambridge presented a petition to the General Court, out of 144 signatures, 34 consisted merely of marks. Of the nine women appointed in 1691 at Salem Village to examine the bodies of those accused of witchcraft, only one could write her name.

At first, education was left to the voluntary efforts of towns or of parents. Although some of the leading citizens of Boston hired a schoolmaster in 1635 and Charlestown followed suit in 1636, the inhabitants of the newer towns were reluctant to lay out money on a luxury like education when there was so much to be done in the way of clearing lands and building houses. In 1647, alarmed by the neglect of education, the Massachusetts General Court enacted a law establishing a school system maintained by public taxation. Each town of 50 families or more was required to provide a school open to all the children of the town.

By this law, education was made compulsory for every child, girls as well as boys, living within the jurisdiction of Massachusetts Bay. But attendance at school was not declared to be mandatory—any child who was taught at home by his or her parents or who attended a private "dame's school" was excused from attending the state-supported schools. What the Puritan leaders required was that every child be given at least a minimal education; where it was acquired was of secondary importance. But they left no loopholes for shirkers: officials were appointed by the towns to investigate households where children were not in school. After 1718, if parents neglected to instruct their children in the alphabet by the age of six, the overseers of the poor could bind out the children to families where they would be sure of receiving the rudimentary education prescribed by law.

A series of laws making more advanced education available to more children was enacted in the late seventeenth century. In 1692, every town of 50 householders was required to provide itself with a schoolmaster to teach writing as well as reading and every town of 100 or more householders had to provide a Latin grammar-school in which boys could be prepared for Harvard. Any town that neglected to obey the law was subject to a fine. Since some towns, particularly those located on the frontier, preferred to pay the fine rather than to hire a schoolmaster, the fine had to be progressively increased. Even so, the great majority of towns contained the two distinctive edifices of New England: the meetinghouse and the schoolhouse.

Education was not "free" in the sense that every boy and girl was admitted without charge to a school wholly supported by taxation. Only the children of the poor enjoyed free tuition; people of means were required to pay for their offsprings' schooling or, if they pleased, to instruct them at home. Thus, while all householders paid school taxes, the schools were not wholly supported by taxation. Moreover, the obligation of parents did not end with the payment of taxes and fees: those who could afford it were expected to supply the wood necessary to keep the schoolroom warm in winter. The unfortunate urchins whose parents neglected to send their quota of wood were banished to the coldest corner of the schoolroom—an inversion of the kind of punishment usually envisaged by the Puritans.

Despite the fact that education was one of the most ancient functions of the church, the New England Puritans placed it, together with marriage and divorce, wholly in the hands of the secular authorities. After 1700, a clergyman was not permitted to serve as a teacher in the Massachusetts town schools. Far from fearing state aid in education, the Puritans welcomed it; from the beginning they acted on the principal that "unless school and college flourish, church and state cannot live." It was in this spirit that the Massachusetts General Court established Harvard College in 1636. Over half the colony's total revenue for that year was allocated to the college at Cambridge.

The intimate conjunction between church and state existing in Puritan New England was everywhere apparent in education. One of the purposes of education, as conceived by the Puritans, was to teach the young respect for the magistrates and ministers and to bring them to "think as their leaders thought." Accordingly, the instruction given in the schools was Puritan in tone; Bible-reading was a daily assignment; students memorized the catechism and the laws on capital punishment; and the local minister often acted as tutor to boys preparing for college. The *New England Primer,* the first edition of which appeared early in the 1680's and which went through many reprintings, was designed to instruct the young in religion as well as in letters. Moral maxims were exemplified by stories from the Old Testament. Hatred of Roman Catholicism— the most deeply rooted prejudice of the American Mind— was given pictorial representation in the *New England Primer:* the frontispiece showed the Pope and the Devil pierced with arrows.

Puritan education was not "permissive" and there was no thought of encouraging the free development of personality. Instead, in the grammar schools the fundamentals of education—grammar, arithmetic and spelling—were drilled into the students. Slow learners received special treatment—often in the form of extra innings with the birch. Discipline in school was regarded as the foundation of good citizenship in later life. The Reverend Jeremiah Wise, a New England minister, summed up the Puritan philosophy when he said:

The Education of Youth is a great Benefit and Service to the Publick. This is that which civilizes them, takes down their Temper, Tames the Fierceness of their Natures, forms their minds to virtue, learns 'em to carry it with a Just Deference to

Superiors; makes them tractable or manageable; and by learning and knowing what it is to be under Government, they will know the better how to govern others when it comes their Turn.

The Reverend Cotton Mather thought that in applying the birch, New England schoolmasters and parents rather overdid it. He himself practised a very different method:

> When the Children are capable of it, I take them alone, one by one; and after my Charges unto them, to fear God, and serve Christ, and shun Sin, I pray with them in my Study and make them the Witnesses of the Agonies, with which I address the Throne of Grace on their behalf.[2]

During the colonial period, the Massachusetts school system was established in all the New England colonies with the exception of Rhode Island. As a result, New England children were the best-educated in the English-speaking world, including England itself. Oligarchic as was the system of colony-government in seventeenth-century New England, the educational system was democratic. It instituted schools in which most of the children, irrespective of wealth, were educated together and in the same manner. The American ideal of equality was most strikingly exemplified in the New England schools.

Outside New England, no colony made elementary education compulsory or established a school system comparable to the Puritans'. Some religious denominations were suspicious of or hostile to education, but even where religion supplied the motive for mass education, it found itself thwarted by the absence of compact communities such as the New England towns. The difficulties created by a dispersed population proved to be an almost insurmountable barrier to a successful assault upon the Old Deluder. True, the civil governments did not really try; instead, they abdicated their function to the churches and to individuals. In consequence, most educated colonists acquired whatever measure of learning they possessed at

[2] Elizabeth Deering Hanscom, *The Heart of the Puritan* (New York: Macmillan Co., 1917), p. 88.

church schools, charity schools, and private schools or from their parents or private tutors. Not until long after the time that Americans raised the cry of "no taxation without representation" did they insist that part of the money raised by taxation should be devoted to public education.

In New Netherlands, while education was held to be the joint concern of church and state, comparatively little was done toward implementing this responsibility. Nor, until the establishment of King's College in 1754, was colonial New York much more successful in this regard. In 1695, there was only one schoolmaster in the entire province. A free school was opened in 1702 but it lasted only eight years, and thereafter the effort to establish similar schools was halfhearted at best. By the middle of the eighteenth century, church schools were providing virtually the only education in New York City, and no schools whatever existed in the country.

Cadwallader Colden, a New York scientist and government official, described the state of education in New York circa 1750:

"Tho' the Province of New York abounds certainly more in riches than any other of the Northern Colonies, yet there has been less care to propagate Knowledge or Learning in it than anywhere else. The only principle of Life propagated among the young People is to get Money, and Men are only esteemd according to what they are worth—that is, the money they are possessed of.[8]

The attitude of a religious denomination toward education was often determined by whether it required an educated or an "inspired" clergy, or, indeed, whether it required any clergy at all. The Lutherans, Moravians and members of the Reformed Church insisted upon an educated clergy, whereas the mystical German sects, even though they did not oppose elementary education, had no use for higher education. The Church of England, with

[8] Esther Singleton, *Social New York under the Georges 1714–1776* (New York: Appleton, 1902), pp. 314–15.

its long tradition of drawing its clergy from the Universities, actively promoted education in the American colonies through the Society for the Propagation of the Gospel. The Scotch-Irish Presbyterians were equally insistent on a trained clergy; with them, churches and schools went hand in hand into the depths of the wilderness.

The early Quakers, on the other hand, were distinguished by their anti-intellectualism. George Fox, the founder of Quakerism, declared that "to be bred at Oxford or Cambridge does not fit a man to be a minister of Christ." He and his followers relied on the Inner Light and the special revelations it made possible; in their opinion, education, particularly in its higher branches, was apt to be a clog on the Spirit. Finally, having no trained ministry, the Quakers permitted a common laborer to speak as authoritatively on matters of religion as a college graduate— a proposition to which no Puritan could have assented without fear of putting his soul in jeopardy.

By the time they arrived in Pennsylvania, the Quakers, although they still depended on the Inner Light to illuminate the way to personal holiness, had lost much of their anti-intellectualism. Moreover, William Penn, himself a graduate of Oxford, was no despiser of education. The Frame of Government he drew up for Pennsylvania in 1681 required that children be given a basic education until they reached the age of twelve years, when they were to be taught "some useful trade or skill, to the end that none may be idle, but the poor may work to live, and the rich, if they become poor, may not want." Profiting from the example of New England, Penn at first refused to allot land to settlers except in townships because, he said, "in that way the children can be kept at school and much more conveniently brought up well."

But Penn's plan encountered resistance from the people, most of whom refused to give up as much of their children's time to schooling as the Founder required. While some elementary schools were established with state aid, the colony never developed a system of free public education. Friends' Schools and privately endowed schools provided virtually all of the elementary education available in Pennsylvania.

A strong utilitarian bent combined with zeal to ameliorate the condition of mankind led the Quakers to emphasize the useful side of education. Not surprisingly, therefore, it was the Friends' Schools that first gave science an important place in their curriculum. More than half the founders of the American Philosophical Society were Quakers; the first medical school in the American colonies was established by a Quaker, John Morgan; and the Pennsylvania Hospital, the leading institution of its kind in colonial America, was staffed largely by Quakers. Philadelphia likewise took the lead in prison reform and in the treatment of the insane.

Quaker humanitarianism, joined in the eighteenth century by the spirit of the Enlightenment, produced some experiments in education of far-reaching importance. Anthony Benezet, a Philadelphia Friend, established a school for Negroes and, hardly less revolutionary, a school for girls, in which the curriculum consisted of reading, writing, arithmetic and grammar. But it was two non-Quaker Pennsylvanians, Benjamin Rush and Benjamin Franklin, who, in the realm of both theory and practice, most decisively influenced the American educational process. Both men saw in free, public education the means of regenerating mankind. Before this goal could be reached, however. Rush and Franklin believed that the whole approach to education must be changed. In particular, they emphasized the beneficial effects of utilitarianism and nonsectarianism. Benjamin Rush warned that the study of Latin and Greek tended to produce juvenile delinquency. "Many sprightly boys of excellent capacities for useful knowledge," he asserted, "have been so disgusted with the dead languages, as to retreat from the drudgery of schools to low company." In his plans for the Philadelphia Academy and the College of Philadelphia (later the University of Pennsylvania), Benjamin Franklin tried to convince the businessmen of Philadelphia that such an institution would confer benefits upon them as well as upon the students:

. . . The Benefits expected from this Institution, are,

1. That the Youth of Pensilvania may have an Opportunity of receiving a good Education at home, and be under no Necessity of going abroad for it; whereby not only a considerable Expence may be saved to the Country, but a stricter Eye may be had over their Morals by their Friends and Relations.

2. That a Number of our Natives will hereby be qualified to bear Magistracies, and execute other public Offices of Trust, with Reputation to themselves and Country; there being at present great Want of Persons so qualified in the several Counties of this Province. And this is the more necessary now to be provided for by the English here, as vast Numbers of Foreigners are yearly imported among us, totally ignorant of our Laws, Customs, and Language.

3. That a Number of the poorer Sort will hereby be qualified to act as Schoolmasters in the Country, to teach children Reading, Writing, Arithmetick, and the Grammar of their Mother Tongue; and being of good Morals and known Characters, may be recommended from the Academy to Country Schools for that Purpose; The Country suffering at present very much for want of good Schoolmasters, and oblig'd frequently to employ in their Schools, vicious imported Servants, or concealed Papists, who by their bad Examples and Instructions often deprave the Morals or corrupt the Principles of the Children under their Care.

4. It is thought that a good Academy erected in Philadelphia, a healthy Place, where Provisions are plenty, situated in the Center of the Colonies, may draw Numbers of Students from the Neighbouring Provinces, who must spend considerable Sums yearly among us, in Payment for their Lodging, Diet, Apparel &c. which will be an Advantage to our Traders, Artisans, and Owners of Houses and Lands. This Advantage is so considerable, that it has been frequently observed in Europe, that the fixing a good School or College in a little inland Village, has been the Means of making it a great Town in a few Years; And therefore the Magistrates of many Places, have offer'd and given great yearly Salaries to draw learned Instructors from other Countries to their respective Towns, meerly with a View to the Interest of the Inhabitants.[4]

---

[4] Benjamin Franklin, *Papers,* edited by L. W. Labaree and W. J. Bell (7 vols., New Haven: Yale University Press, 1963), Vol. 4, pp. 34–46.

Even the wisdom and virtue gained from education by the few, Franklin believed, could be turned into a social and economic asset:

> . . . I think with you, that nothing is of more importance for the public weal, than to form and train up youth in wisdom and virtue. Wise and good men are, in my opinion, the *strength* of a state: much more so than riches or arms, which, under the management of Ignorance and Wickedness, often draw on destruction, instead of providing for the safety of a people. And though the culture bestowed on *many* should be successful only with a *few*, yet the influence of those few and the service in their power, may be very great. Even a single woman that was wise, by her wisdom saved a city.
>
> I think also, that general virtue is more probably to be expected and obtained from the *education* of youth, than from the *exhortation* of adult persons; bad habits and vices of the mind, being, like diseases of the body, more easily prevented than cured.
>
> I think moreover, that talents for the education of youth are the gift of God; and that he on whom they are bestowed, whenever a way is opened for the use of them, is as strongly *called* as if he heard a voice from heaven; nothing more surely pointing out *duty* in a public service, than *ability* and *opportunity* of performing it.[5]

It was especially in the Southern colonies that the dispersal of the population and the scarcity of towns adversely affected education. With the exception of Charleston, South Carolina, the South lacked a metropolis comparable to the Northern cities and even small towns were few and far between. As early as 1662, a clergyman of the Church of England lamented these untoward side effects of the plantation system:

> The cause of their dispers'd Seating was at first a privilege indulged by the royal Grant of having a right to 50 Acres of Land, for every person they should transport at their own charges: by which means some men transporting many Servants thither, and others purchasing the Rights of those that did, took possession of great tracts of Land at their Pleasure, and by Degrees scattered their Plantations through the Country. . . .
>
> And hence it is, that the most faithful and vigilant Pastors,

[5] *Ibid.*, pp. 40–42.

assisted by the most carefull Church-wardens, cannot possibly take notice of the Vices that reign in their Families, of the spiritual defects in their Conversations, or if they have notice of them, and provide Spiritual Remedies in their publick Ministry, it is a hazard if they that are most concerned in them. . . . spend time in visiting their remote and far distant habitations, they would have little or none left for their necessary Studies, and to provide necessary spiritual food for the rest of their Flocks.

Lastly, their almost general want of Schooles, for the education of their Children, is another consequent of their scattered planting, of most sad consideration, most of all bewailed of Parents there. . . . This want of Schooles, as it renders a very numerous Generation of Christian Children born in *Virginia* (who naturally are of beautiful and comely Persons, and generally of more ingenious Spirits than those in *England*) unserviceable for any great Employments either in Church or State, so likewise it obstructs the hopefullest way they have, for the conversion of the Heathen, which is, by winning the Heathen to bring in their Children to be taught and instructed in our Schooles, together with the Children of the Christians.[6]

In none of the Southern colonies were the educational needs of the people even remotely met. A few charity schools were established—in 1635, for example, a Virginia planter deeded by will 200 acres of land and the increase and milk of eight cows to provide funds for a charity school—and the Society for the Propagation of the Gospel sent teachers and books to the colonies, but in general, mass education was conspicuously neglected. When Governor William Berkeley of Virginia rendered thanks to Heaven in 1671 that there were no free schools or free presses in Virginia, he was almost right: there were only two free charity schools in the entire province.

With few exceptions, the wealthy planters who controlled the Chesapeake colonies were content to provide education for their own children and let those of the poorer farmers and backcountry pioneers pick up whatever learning they could by whatever means were at hand. No serious effort was made to overcome the obstacles created by the dispersal of population. As a result, illiteracy was far more wide-

[6] *Virginia's Cure*, by R. G. (London, 1662; Washington: U. S. Government Printing Office, 1844), pp. 6–8.

spread in the South than in New England; the planters were sustained in power by an electorate seriously disadvantaged in respect to education. The tendency of the educational practices of the South was to increase the disparity between rich and poor by destroying all possibility of equality of opportunity. On the part of the planters, there was more disposition to rejoice in these disparities than to try to eliminate them in the interests of equality. In 1748, a Virginia father wrote his sons:

> You cannot . . . sufficiently adore the Divine Providence who has placed your Parents above the lower class and thereby enabled them to be at the expence of giving you such an Education (which if not neglected by you) will preserve you in the same Class & Rank among mankind.[7]

If it were not the best of all possible educational systems for the children of the well-to-do, it certainly tended to set them apart as an educated elite. In almost every parish of the Chesapeake area, the local minister served as a schoolmaster for the children of those planters who were willing and able to pay tuition. These "public schools" (they were public in the sense that they admitted any child who paid tuition) were attended by the comparatively small number of children who lived near enough to the vicarage to be day scholars. Mary Ball, the mother of George Washington, in a letter written when she was fifteen years old, described such a school to a friend:

> We have not had a schoolmaster in our neighborhood till now in nearly four years. We have now a young minister living with us who was educated at Oxford, took orders and came over as assistant to Rev. Kemp. The parish is too poor to keep both, and he teaches school for his board. He teaches Sister Susie and me and Madam Carter's boy and two girls. I am now learning pretty fast.[8]

[7] Lucille Griffith (ed.), "Education for Virginia Youth. Some Eighteenth-Century Letters," *Virginia Magazine of History and Biography* (Richmond, Vol. 69, 1961), p. 15.

[8] Alice Earle, *Child Life in Colonial Days* (New York: Macmillan Co., 1899), p. 95.

Since the number of clergymen was limited, most planters were obliged to hire private tutors or to send their children to neighborhood "private schools" (they were private because the person or persons controlling the school could deny admission to applicants). The teachers were often educated indentured servants or even transported convicts. It was in such a school and from a convict whom his father bought as a private tutor that George Washington acquired most of the knowledge of reading, writing and mathematics that constituted his formal education.

Although it was not required by law, many parents took time from their labors to teach their children to read and, less commonly, to write. In this regard, Patrick Henry was particulary fortunate: he received a solid grounding in the classics from his father, who was a graduate of King's College, Aberdeen, Scotland. But college graduates were scarce in the Southern colonies and, since the ability to read and write was not a prerequisite of parenthood, most children grew up to be as innocent of book learning as were their parents.

After the establishment of the College of William and Mary in 1692, the Chesapeake planters were able to send their sons to the grammar school—for many years the only part of the College that really functioned. At first, comparatively few planters availed themselves of this opportunity; those who could afford to, preferred to have their sons go to England for their grammar-school training. Those who went abroad often remained to study at a British university or at the Inns of Court and Lincoln's Fields, the centers of legal training in the British Isles. But with the improvement of the College of William and Mary, the straitened circumstances in which many planters found themselves as a result of the decline of the price of tobacco, and the deterioration of Oxford and Cambridge as centers of learning—in 1774, Henry Laurens of South Carolina declared that he really "trembled" at the thought of exposing his son to the dissolute way of life prevalent at those universities—an ever-increasing number of Virginia and Maryland students began to attend the local college.

Bibliography

Morison, Samuel Eliot. *Three Centuries of Harvard, 1636–1936.* Cambridge, Mass.: Harvard University Press, 1936.
————. *The Intellectual Life of Colonial New England.* New York: New York University Press, 1956.
Wright, Louis B. *The Cultural Life of the American Colonies.* New York: Harper and Brothers, 1957.

THE PRACTICE
OF MEDICINE

ALTHOUGH it was never mentioned in the advertising, America was the crossroads of the diseases of three continents. A recently arrived European, however immunized to the diseases endemic in his native land, was obliged in America to withstand the onslaught of a disconcerting variety of germs, any one of which might prove fatal. Particularly if he had been debilitated by illness and malnutrition, the usual consequence of a long sea voyage, he fell an easy prey to the host of microbes lying in wait for him.

About 1790, Dr. Benjamin Rush of Philadelphia compiled statistics, based upon his long experience as a physician, that reflect the heavy mortality among all segments of the population. Of 100 persons born in one year, Dr. Rush found, at the end of

Years								Remained Alive
6	.	.	.	.	.	.	.	.	64
16	.	.	.	.	.	.	.	.	46
26	.	.	.	.	.	.	.	.	26
36	.	.	.	.	.	.	.	.	16
46	.	.	.	.	.	.	.	.	10
56	.	.	.	.	.	.	.	.	6
66	.	.	.	.	.	.	.	.	3
76	.	.	.	.	.	.	.	.	1

Among the "unruly distempers" that struck down thousands of colonists were malaria, dysentery, typhoid fever, yellow fever, consumption, cholera, diphtheria, typhus, measles, whooping cough, scarlet fever, fluxes and smallpox. Dysentery, sometimes called the "camp disease" because of its high incidence among soldiers, was a particularly virulent killer. Measles were generally more severe in America than in Great Britain: in the epidemic of 1713, the Reverend Cotton Mather lost five members of his family, including his wife, in two weeks. Even though they did not call it "influenza," the colonists were certainly familiar with its symptoms. Under the name of "malignant fever," influenza epidemics ravaged the colonies in 1732, 1760 and 1772. But diphtheria, particularly among children, was even more severe: in the so-called throat-distemper epidemic of 1735–37, five thousand people died in New England alone. John and Mercy Wilson of Andover lost eight children within one week and there were many other instances of multiple deaths in one family. Mainly in consequence of successive epidemics, of the fifteen children born to the three wives of Cotton Mather, only two survived him.

In New England, March was called "a sickly, dying, melancholy time" but summer and autumn were not far behind. During the summer and autumn "sickly season," disease-carrying mosquitoes began to feast upon the colonists: in North Carolina, William Byrd reported, the inhabitants lost as much blood in the summer "by the infinite number of mosquitoes, as all their beef and pork can recruit in the winter." After a hot summer in Maryland, Dr. Alexander Hamilton found that the people "looked like so many staring ghosts. In short," he concluded, "I was sensible I had got into Maryland, for every house was an infirmary, according to ancient custom."

The heavy mortality at Jamestown was occasioned in part by dysentery contracted by drinking polluted water. Beriberi and scurvy, both dietary-deficiency diseases, came from eating too much venison, pork and corn and too little fruit and vegetables. The incapacitating effects of these illness produced much of the apathy and langour that John Smith attributed to sheer laziness. When the sufferers from these debilitating maladies were denied rations in order to force them to work, the result was an aggravation of the very condition that made them incapable of sustained labor.

Under these circumstances, the physicians sent out by the Virginia Company could be of little help to the settlers. In one instance, however, a physician was credited with having worked a near miracle. When Captain John Smith was badly mauled by a stingray, his symptoms became so alarming that his friends, on familiar terms with sudden death, began to dig his grave a few hours after the accident. But the grave went untenanted—not for long, however, for at this point tenants were waiting in line—because "by the helpe of a precious oile Doctor Russel applyed, ere night his [Smith's] tormenting paine was so wel assuaged that he eate the fish to his supper."

But the news from America was not so much of miraculous cures as of sickness and sudden death. Every newcomer, it appeared, had to submit to the ordeal of "seasoning." To counteract this bad impression, Americans undertook to advise prospective immigrants how to cope with the manifold diseases to which they were certain to be exposed:

If People are sick there, 'tis generally in Effect of their bad Conduct, and not knowing how to regulate themselves suitably to the Country where they live: for 'tis very certain that those who observe Precautions have as good Health as they would in other Places. But the better to understand this Affair: you must know that the uncultivated Lands of *Carolina* as well as the other adjacent Provinces, which extend much further than *Canada,* being wholly covered with large Pine trees, very cold in their Nature, and when the Vapours, which they have attracted and retained come to be dispers'd by a Northerly Wind, you feel a Cold almost as sharp as in *Europe*; so that in one Day you may find considerable Change of Air: This then, together with the Debauches made by Punch, strong *Madeira* wines and the eating unripe Fruits, is the real Source of the Sicknesses there. For sensual Persons, who have not the Power to deny themselves any thing, when they find that a hot Day is succeeded by a great Coolness towards Evening, expose themselves to it with great pleasure without troubling themselves with the Consequences; and when this Pleasure is succeeded by

Rheumatisms, Fevers or other Distempers, they never fail of roaring out Curses on the Country, rather than upon their own Carelessness or Excess. And 'tis very common for those newly arrived, to say, whenever they have got any Illness, *That 'tis a tribute they must pay to the Climate.* But such as take care to keep their Breasts always warm, to shun the great Transpirations of the Air, to cover themselves well in the Night especially in Summer, and in other Respects live regularly, will certainly enjoy as good Health there as in any other Part of the World.[1]

John Jesselyn accompanied his description of the diseases endemic in New England with a few of his favorite nostrums:

The Diseases that the *English* are afflicted with, are the same that they have in *England*, with some proper to *New-England*, griping of the belly (accompanied with Feaver and Ague) which turns to the bloudy-flux, a common disease in the Country, which together with the small pox hath carried away abundance of their children, for this the common medicines amongst the poorer sort are Pills of Cotton swallowed, or Sugar and Sallet-oyl boiled thick and made into Pills, Alloes pulverized and taken in the pap of an Apple. I helped many of them with a sweating medicine only.

Also they are troubled with a disease in the mouth or throat which hath proved mortal to some in a very short time, Quinsies, and Imposthumations of the Almonds, with great distempers of cold. Some of our *New-England* writers affirm that the *English* are never or very rarely heard to sneeze or cough, as ordinarily they do in *England,* which is not true. For a cough or stitch upon cold, Wormwood, Sage, Marygolds, and Crabs-claws boiled in posset-drink and drunk off very warm, is a soveraign medicine.

Pleurisies and Empyemas are frequent there, both cured after one and the same way; but the last is a desperate disease and kills many. For the Pleurisie I have given a *Coriander*-seed I prepared, *Carduus*-seed and *Harts-horn* pulverized with good success, the dose one dram in a cup of wine.

The Stone terribly afflicts many, and the Gout, and Sciatica, for which take Onions roasted, peeled and stampt, then boil them with neats-feet oyl and Rhum to a plaister, and apply it to the hip.

<hr>

[1] *A Description of the Province of South Carolina* (London, 1731; Washington: U. S. Government Printing Office, 1837), pp. 10–11.

Head-aches are frequent, Palsies, Dropsies, Worms, Noli-me-tangeres, Cancers, pestilent Feavers. Scurvies, the body corrupted with Sea-diet, Beef and Pork tainted, Butter and Cheese corrupted, fish rotten, a long voyage, coming into the searching sharpness of a purer climate, causeth death and sickness amongst them. . . .

For falling off of the hair occasioned by the coldness of the climate, and to make it curl, take of the strong water called Rhum and wash or bathe your head therewith, it is an admirable remedie.

For kibed heels, to heal them take the yellowest part of Rozen, pulverize it and work it in the palm of your hand with the tallow of a Candle to a salve, and lay of it to the sore.

For frozen limbs, a plaister framed with Soap, Bay-salt, and Molosses is sure, or Cow-dung boiled in milk and applyed.

For Warts and Corns, bathe them with Sea-water.[2]

During the early part of the eighteenth century, Boston physicians prescribed the swallowing of a leaden bullet for "that miserable Distemper which they called the Twisting of the Guts."

The theory behind much of this pharmacopeia was that, if the concoction could be made nauseous enough, it would surely drive out the disease. But the principal effect was to make the cure seem worse than the disease itself. A more promising therapy was discovered in the herbs that abounded in America and that were used by the Indians for medicinal purposes. Two apothecaries accompanied the expedition sent to Virginia in 1608 and they collected and sent back to England an assortment of roots, woods and berries. Large quantities of sassafras, reputed to be a sovereign cure for the "French pox," were loaded aboard ships in the hope that it would make everyone, settlers and stockholders alike, rich.

Quinine, generally called the "bark," proved to be one of the most important contributions of the New World to the physical health of mankind. The success of "Peruvian bark" helped to crystalize the image of the Indian as a

[2] John Josselyn, *An Account of Two Voyages to New England* (*Collections of the Massachusetts Historical Society*, Third Series, Vol. III) (Cambridge, 1833), pp. 331–34.

healer—an image that ultimately produced the Indian medicine show. In the nineteenth century there were at least 150 Indian medicine shows, most of them billed as the "Original Kickapoo Indian Medicine Company," touring the United States. It was at least easier to take snake oil than boiled and pounded toads, or crab's eyes mixed with vinegar.

Impressed by the value attached by the Chinese to ginseng—in China it was worth almost its weight in gold—Americans began to use the plant, a native of the western hemisphere, in the treatment of disease. William Byrd pronounced it to be the "king of plants"; when he found some growing on the estate of Colonel Spotswood, he carried it back to Westover "with as much joy," he said, "as if every root had been a graft of the tree of life." If ginseng had possessed a fraction of the salubrity Byrd attributed to it, the herb would have been rightly acclaimed one of the great benefactions given mankind.

Together with ginseng, Byrd strongly recommended the use of tobacco for its health-promoting properties. In 1721, he published anonymously in London—for it would not have strengthened his argument had it been known that he was one of the principal tobacco-growers in Virginia—a pamphlet entitled *A Discourse Concerning the Plague, with Preservatives Against It*. Among the therapeutic measures he favored were fasting, repentance and above all "fresh, strong and quick-scented Tobacco," which, he declared, dissipated the "pestilential taint, beyond all the antidotes that have been yet discovered."

John Josselyn expressed the opinion commonly held in the colonial period concerning the benefits of tobacco:

The vertues of Tobacco are these, it helps digestion, the Gout, the Tooth-Ach, prevents infection by scents, it heats the cold, and cools them that sweat, feedeth the hungry, spent spirits restoreth, purgeth the stomach, killeth nits and lice; the juice of the green leaf healeth green wounds, although poysoned; the Syrup for many diseases, the smoak for the Phthisick, cough of the lungs, distillations of Rheume, and all diseases of a cold and moist cause, good for all bodies cold and moist taken upon a full stomach it precipitates digestion, immoderately taken it dryeth the body, enflameth the bloud, hurteth the brain, weakens the eyes and the sinews.[3]

Such claims, medicinal and otherwise, for tobacco were hardly necessary to promote its use in colonial America. Old and young, rich and poor smoked tobacco, usually in long clay pipes. Durand of Dauphine observed:

[In Virginia] everyone smokes both at work and at rest. When I went to church (all their churches are in the woods) I saw the parson and all the congregation smoking in the churchyard while waiting for the hour of service. When the sermon was over they did the same thing before separating. There are seats provided in the churchyards for this purpose. It was here that I saw that everyone smoked, women and girls and boys down to the age of seven years.[4]

A large amount of time and energy was expended by both laymen and physicians in the search for a "miracle herb." As might have been expected, the search, so strenuously pressed, produced claims to spectacular success. Dr. John Tennent, an English physician resident in Virginia, asserted that he had discovered an infallible cure for practically the entire spectrum of disease. What was equally remarkable was that this all-embracing nostrum was a well known plant. Having "discovered" that all diseases were produced by a poison similar to that of rattlesnake venom, Dr. Tennent announced to a waiting world that the sovereign cure for all the maladies to which mankind was subject was rattlesnake root, long used by the Seneca Indians as an antidote to rattlesnake bite. For meritorious service to mankind Dr. Tennent was awarded 100 pounds by the Virginia House of Burgesses.

Dr. Tennent brought the glad tidings to Americans in his book *Every Man his own Doctor,* published in 1734. The subject matter of Dr. Tennent's book was not what to do until the doctor arrives but how to keep the doctor away —permanently. It laid down "Plain and Easy Means for

[3] *Ibid.,* p. 262.

[4] Durand of Dauphine, *A Frenchman in Virginia* (Privately Printed, 1923), p. 111.

Persons to cure themselves of all, or most of the Distempers, incident to this Climate, and with very little Charge, the Medicine being chiefly of the Growth and Production of this Country." A dose of rattlesnake root would put everything right!

In general, physicians treated disease in terms of the pathology formulated by the ancient Greeks. Bleeding, purging and blistering were the remedies prescribed by the traditional medical knowledge of the eighteenth century. For complaints ranging from an upset stomach to yellow fever, bloodletting (effected with an unsterile instrument) was the indicated treatment. While this therapy did not bring about cures, it often succeeded in putting the patient out of his misery.

As a result of the frequently fatal consequences of calling in the doctor, many Americans lived almost as much in dread of the physician as of the disease. "Our American practitioners are so rash and officious," said Dr. William Douglass of Boston in 1721, "that the saying in Ecclesiasticus may with much propriety be applied to them: 'He that sinneth before his Maker let him fall into the hands of the physician.'" Thomas Jefferson said that whenever he saw three or more doctors gathered together he looked aloft to see if there were any buzzards waiting for the kill. On the other hand, it was said of Dr. Samuel Fuller, the Plymouth physician, that, thanks to his practice of depleting his patients of large amounts of blood, he "did a great cure for Captain Littleworth. He cured him of a disease called a wife."

The great majority of American doctors were either self-trained or had served as apprentices to practioneers who had themselves served as apprentices or were self-trained. In 1776, only five percent of American medical men held the degree of M.D. Since there were no examinations or regulations of any kind for the medical profession, virtually anyone could set himself up as a physician, apothecary or surgeon. "Quacks," lamented a New Yorker in 1757, "abound like locusts in *Egypt*." The first physician to practice in Boston was fined five pounds in 1630 "for taking upon him to cure the scurvy by a water of no worth nor value, which he solde att a very deare rate." Dr. Alexander Hamilton declared that a Maryland colleague had begun his career driving a turnip cart and trundling a wheelbarrow through the streets.

Every educated man was supposed to have absorbed enough medical knowledge at school and sufficient experience of the healing art in prescribing for their family, servants, slaves and neighbors to qualify as doctors. A Massachusetts law of 1649 directed that no person could administer medicine "without the advice and consent of such as are skillful in the same Art (if such may be had) or at least of some of the wisest and gravest then present." Since gravity and wisdom were believed to appertain particularly to the clergy, it was usually the local minister who was called in on difficult cases, thus prescribing for their parishoners' bodies as well as souls. Cotton Mather thought that there was "an angelic Conjunction" between medicine and religion. Certainly it was true that for centuries the medical schools of Europe had been staffed by ecclesiastics; the colonial parson-physician was their lineal descendant.

Similarly, there was a close conjunction between medicine and astrology. The movement of the stars was believed to exert a profound influence on the health and welfare of human beings; the word "influenza," for example, was first used in Italy by astrologers who believed that celestial bodies determined the state of health of terrestrial beings. It was partly to this circumstance that almanacs owed their popularity in the American colonies. Medical astrology was widely disseminated by these publications, many of which found their way to remote settlements beyond the reach of newspapers. "Since," as Poor Richard said, "the Family frequently sick can rarely if ever thrive," the almanacs were believed to fill an important public need.

Besides pointing out the direct influence of zodiacal signs upon the various parts of the human body, the almanacs gave their readers the traditional folk wisdom contained in "Rules for Health and Long Life," "Rules for

Temperate Living," "Rules for Preserving Health in Eating and Drinking," as well as advertisements for such patent medicines as Kitterate's Incarnative Ointment, Toothacre's Gout Balsam, Adam's Bone Ointment and The Frenchman's Cancer Salve. In addition to exhortations to hard work, thrift, frugality and chastity, *Poor Richard's Almanac* printed a cure for syphilis labeled "the poor man's medicine."

Southern planters and their wives often acted as physicians and nurses to their families and slaves. With the aid of *The British Housewife,* a popular do-it-yourself book, the wife was expected to prescribe for gout, agues, fluxes, "vapours," "hysteric fits" and "hypochondriac complaints." Washington and Jefferson prescribed for the ills of their slaves; on one occasion, Jefferson personally inoculated over 70 of his servitors at Monticello. William Byrd II so delighted in acting the doctor that few of the members of his household or his slaves were free from his ministrations. But he baulked at bloodletting: when that became necessary, as it frequently did, he called in the doctor.

During the seventeenth century, the practice of medicine was largely in the hands of barber-surgeons, old wives and clergymen. John Winthrop of Massachusetts served his constituents both as governor and as medical adviser, and his son John Winthrop, Jr., the governor of Connecticut, rode a regular medical circuit through the towns of his province—a seventeenth-century version of Medicare.

As for the regular practitioners of medicine, their fees were regulated by law. On four different occasions, the Virginia House of Burgesses, taking cognizance of "the immoderate and excessive rates and prices exacted by practitioners of physick & chyrugery" enacted laws fixing the amount of money a doctor could charge for visits, drugs and medicine. Nevertheless, complaints against "griping and avaricious" physicians were common in colonial Virginia partly for the reason that, because of the great distances between plantations, physicians insisted on being compensated for traveling time. Some patients, having happily recovered from their illness, considered the doctor's charges so unreasonable that they haled them into court to bring their fees more in accord with their former patients' present state of health. The legislation governing the practice of medicine tended to give the doctors the wrong kind of incentive: they were permitted by law to recover from the estates of deceased patients.

A woman was well advised to marry young, for when she reached the age of thirty she had usually lost not only her first bloom but her complexion, her beauty (if she ever had any) and her teeth. Even Englishmen were startled by the bad teeth of American women—a phenomenon Benjamin Franklin attributed to the custom of eating hot soup and frozen apples. John Josselyn was one of the first travelers to include losing one's teeth among the hazards of a remove to America:

> The Women are pittifully Tooth-shaken; whether through the coldness of the climate, or by sweet-meats of which they have store, I am not able to affirm, for the Toothach I have found the following medicine very available, Brimstone and Gunpowder compounded with butter, rub the mandible with it, the outside being first warm'd.[5]

Usually the pangs of toothache were assuaged by plucking out the offending tooth. For this purpose, since there were no dentists, the services of the local barber or blacksmith were enlisted. On a surveying expedition in 1733, William Byrd found himself troubled by "an impertinent tooth. 'Drawers we had none amongst us, nor any of the Instruments they make use of. However, Invention supply'd the want very happily, and I contriv'd to get rid of this troublesome Companion by cutting a Caper"—i.e., by the time-honored method of tying a string to his tooth and jerking violently.

In the seventeeth and eighteenth centuries, losing one's teeth was a deadly serious matter: there were no store teeth available and few craftsmen were capable of turning out a set of dentures. As a result, despite the vast market for false teeth, the supply was almost nonexistent. George

Washington's jaw was permanently deformed by his mal-
fitting false teeth. Under the circumstances, the only recourse was a diet of soft food and plenty of liquids.

The eighteenth century produced some notable advances
in the treatment of disease. A new kind of chemical therapy, in which drugs were compounded from chemicals,
was evolving. Self-medication was less relied on and the
parson-physician almost wholly disappeared. Even the
functions of the midwife were passing into the hands of
the doctor—not always, however, with beneficial results
to either mother or child. The standards of the American
medical fraternity were progressively being raised as an
increasing number of Americans went to the University of
Edinburgh—the leading institution of its kind in the English-speaking world. Quarantine regulations designed to
prevent the introduction of infectious diseases were established in most of the larger colonial seaports and the importance of sanitation and the isolation of those with com-
municable diseases were coming to be appreciated. The
first hospital in the American colonies was opened in Philadelphia in 1751; financed mostly by private funds, it served
both charity and paying patients. In 1765, the first medical
school, also in Philadelphia, was established as part of the
College of Philadelphia. It was followed, in 1768, by the
medical school attached to King's College (later Columbia
University) and in 1783 by the Harvard Medical School.

Nevertheless, the most significant single step in the
advance of American medicine during the eighteenth century was in large measure owing to the efforts of the Reverend Cotton Mather, his fellow Congregational ministers,
and Dr. Ezekial Boylston, a Boston physician who had been
trained by his father. In 1721, thanks to their courage and
conviction, Boston became the scene of the first mass
inoculation against smallpox in the English-speaking world
—despite the opposition of most of the medical fraternity
of the town. Before the epidemic had run its course, of the
6,000 people who had contracted the disease, 900 died,

but the proportion of fatalities was much less among those who submitted to inoculation. Even so, the last six people to be inoculated were in such danger of meeting with violence at the hands of the mob that they had to be removed to an island in the Bay for safety. There was good reason for this fear of inoculated persons. No one thought to isolate the patients who had received the disease by artificial means and, since they actually had a mild case of smallpox, they spread the disease among those who had no immunity.

The well-attested reports of successful inoculation in Boston helped establish the practice in England. But the opposition of clergymen, physicians and the people themselves was not easily overcome. In France, largely because of clerical disapproval, inoculation made little headway until the middle of the eighteenth century, when it was adopted by the philosophers of the Enlightenment as part of their crusade against obscurantism, ignorance and bigotry.

In colonial America, likewise, the idea of seeking immunity from a disease by contracting it voluntarily was a novelty that made slow headway. At one time or another, most of the provinces prohibited the practice by law. Not until inoculated patients were quarantined did many American physicians embrace the practice. Moreover, inoculation was condemned as a presumptive and even sacrilegious attempt to interfere with the designs of Providence: it was the prerogative of God, a South Carolinian pointed out in 1738, to preserve or destroy whomever He pleased and to rebuke a community for its sins by means of an epidemic.

In consequence, Americans were obliged to endure successive epidemics of smallpox. Benjamin Franklin described one such epidemic:

About 1753 or 54, the Small Pox made its appearance in Boston, New England. It had not spread in the town for many years before, so that there were a great number of the inhabitants to have it. At first endeavours were used to prevent its spreading by removing the sick or guarding the houses in which they were: and with the same view Inoculation was forbidden; but when it was found that these endeavours were fruitless, the distemper breaking out in different quarters of the town, and increasing, Inoculation was then permitted.

Upon this, all that inclined to inoculation for themselves or families, hurried into it precipitately, fearing the infection might otherwise be taken in the common way; the numbers inoculated in every neighbourhood spread the infection likewise more speedily among those who did not choose Inoculation; so that in a few months, the distemper went thro' the town, and was extinct; and the trade of the town, suffered only a short interruption, compar'd with what had been usual in former times, the country people during the seasons of that sickness fearing all intercourse with the town.

As the practice of Inoculation always divided people into parties, some contending warmly for it, and others as strongly against it: the latter asserting that the advantages pretended were imaginary; and that the Surgeons from views of interest concealed or diminished the true number of deaths occasion'd by Inoculation, and magnify'd the number of those who died of the Small Pox in the common way. . . .

Notwithstanding the now uncontroverted success of Inoculation, it does not seem to make that progress among the common people in America, which was at first expected. *Scruples of Conscience* weigh with many, concerning the *lawfulness* of the practice: And if one parent or near relation is against it, the other does not choose to inoculate a child without free consent of all parties, lest in case of a disastrous event, perpetual blame should follow. These *scruples* a *sensible Clergy* may in time remove. The *expense* of having the operation performed by a Surgeon, weighs with others, for that has been pretty high in some parts of America: and where a common tradesman or artificer has a number in his family to have the distemper, it amounts to more money than he can well spare. Many of these, rather than own the *true motive* for declining Inoculation, join with the scrupulous in the cry *against it,* and influence others. A small Pamphlet wrote in plain language by some skilful Physician, and published, directing what preparations of the body should be used before the Inoculation of children, what precautions to avoid giving the infection at the same time in the common way, and how the operation is to be performed, the incisions dressed, the patient treated, and on the appearance of what symptoms a Physician is to be called, &c. might by encouraging parents to inoculate their own children, by a means of removing that objection of the expense, render the practice much more general, and thereby save the lives of thousands.[6]

Despite Franklin's opinion that it was impious to reject "a Method discovered to Mankind by God's good Providence, whereby 99 in 100 are saved," he neglected to have his son, Francis ("Franky") Folger inoculated. In 1736, at the age of four, Franky died of smallpox. Since Franklin was known to be an advocate of inoculation, it was presumed that his son had died of the effects of inoculation. To refute these reports, Franklin published the following notice in his newspaper:

Understanding 'tis a current Report, that my Son Francis, who died lately of the Small Pox, had it by Inoculation; and being desired to satisfy the Publick in that Particular; inasmuch as some People are, by that Report (join'd with others of the like kind, and perhaps, equally groundless) deter'd from having that Operation perform'd on their Children, I do hereby sincerely declare, that he was not inoculated, but receiv'd the Distemper in the common Way of Infection: And I suppose the Report could only arise from its being my known Opinion, that Inoculation was a safe and beneficial Practice; and from my having said among my Acquaintance, that I intended to have my Child inoculated, as soon as he should have recovered sufficient Strength from a Flux with which he had been long afflicted.[7]

By the time of the American Revolution, the colonies had repealed their laws prohibiting inoculation, insisting only that safeguards be taken against the spread of the infection by inoculated persons. In 1776, General Washington ordered the inoculation of the American army. The War of Independence was the first international conflict in which armies took advantage of the techniques of preventive medicine.

[6] Benjamin Franklin, "A Collection of Letters" in *Collections of the Massachusetts Historical Society* (Second Series, Vol. VIII Boston, 1833), pp. 72–74.
[7] Benjamin Franklin, *Papers,* edited by L. W. Labaree and W. J. Bell (7 vols., New Haven: Yale University Press, 1962), Vol. 5, p. 154.

Bibliography

Blanton, Wyndham B., *Medicine in Virginia in the Seventeenth Century*. Richmond, Va.: The William Byrd Press, 1930.

Caulfield, Dr. Ernest. *Some Common Diseases of Colonial Children* ("Publications of the Colonial Society of Massachusetts," XXXV, 1942-1946). Boston, 1951.

Dunn, Richard S. *Puritans and Yankees: The Winthrop Dynasty of New England, 1630–1717*. Princeton: Princeton University Press, 1962.

Holmes, O. W. *Massachusetts and Its Early History*. Boston: J. R. Osgood & Co., 1869.

Hughes, Thomas P. *Medicine in Virginia: 1607–1699*. Williamsburg, Va.: Virginia 350th Anniversary Celebration Corp., 1957.

King, Lester S. *The Medical World of the Eighteenth Century*. Chicago: University of Chicago Press, 1958.

Shryock, Richard H. *The Development of Modern Medicine*. Philadelphia: University of Pennsylvania Press, 1942.

CRIME AND PUNISHMENT

UNFORTUNATELY for the plans of those who dreamed of founding godly communities in America, a voyage across the Atlantic and exposure to the bracing moral environment of religion-oriented societies did not eradicate crime or remove the necessity of punishment. Of course, the Puritans, viewing the majority of human beings as "wolves chained up," were prepared to cope with transgressors against the laws of God and man. Moreover, from the beginning they were obliged to contend against the criminal instincts of the "chaff" that had sifted through the winnowing when God selected the personnel of His Own Plantation in America. What did surprise them, however, was that there seemed to be more crime and sexual irregularities in Puritan New England than in the mother country, from whose abominations the Puritans had fled. As John Winthrop said, "as people increased, so sin abounded." Obviously, in trying to live without sin in a sinful world, the Puritans had their work cut out for them.

Even in Plymouth, where for several years there were so few disciplinary problems that the services of a justice of the peace were dispensed with and where the only capital crimes were treason, rebellion against the colony and "solemn compaction or conversing with the Devil," a "crime wave" occurred in 1642. William Bradford attributed this outbreak to three major causes:

Marvelous it may be to see and consider how some kind of wickedness did grow and break forth here, in a land where the same was so much witnessed against and so narrowly looked unto, and severely punished when it was known, as in no place more, or so much, that I have known or heard of; insomuch that they have been somewhat censured even by moderate and good men for their severity in punishments. And yet all this could not suppress the breaking out of sundry notorious sins (as this year, besides other, give us too many sad precedents and instances), especially drunkenness and uncleanness. Not only incontinency between persons unmarried, for which many both men and women have been punished sharply enough, but some married persons also. But that which is worse, even sodomy and buggery (things fearful to name) have broke forth in this land oftener than once.

I say it may justly be marveled at and cause us to fear and tremble at the consideration of our corrupt natures, which are so hardly bridled, subdued and mortified; nay, cannot by any other means but the powerful work and grace of God's Spirit. But (besides this) one reason may be that the Devil may carry a greater spite against the churches of Christ and the gospel here, by how much the more they endeavour to preserve holiness and purity amongst them and strictly punisheth the contrary when it ariseth either in church or commonwealth; that he might cast a blemish and stain upon them in the eyes of the world, who used to be rash in judgment. I would rather think thus, than that Satan hath more power in these heathen lands, as some have thought, than in more Christian nations, especially over God's servants in them.

2. Another reason may be, that it may be in this case it is with waters when their streams are stopped or dammed up. When they get passage they flow with more violence and make more noise and disturbance than when they are suffered to run quietly in their own channels; so wickedness being here more stopped by strict laws, and the same more nearly looked unto so as it cannot run in a common road of liberty as it would and is inclined, it searches everywhere and at last breaks out where it gets vent.

3. A third reason may be, here (as I am verily persuaded) is not more evils in this kind, nor nothing near so many by proportion as in other places; but they are here more discovered and seen and made public by due search, inquisition and due punishment; for the churches look narrowly to their members, and the magistrates over all, more strictly than in other places. Besides, here the people are but few in comparison of other places which are full and populous and lie hid, as it were, in a wood or thicket and many horrible evils by that means are

never seen nor known; whereas there they are, as it were, brought into the light and set in the plain field, or rather on a hill, made conspicuous to the view of all.[1]

If "wholesome laws" and their strict execution could have eliminated crime, the early Americans would have assuredly worked that miracle. The statute books were filled with legislation defining offenses and prescribing proper punishments. In early Virginia and Massachusetts Bay, some crimes punishable in the mother country by imprisonment were made capital. This severity was occasioned in part by the conditions of life thrust upon the settlers. Selling guns or ammunition to the Indians, for example, might well mean death to the whites—hence it was made a capital crime. Likewise, in early Virginia, where the supply of food was precarious, stealing hogs was a far more serious matter than it was in the mother country. Therefore, in Virginia, the law ordained that for the second offense of this kind the culprit should be branded with the letter "H" on the forehead; for repeaters, the punishment was death.

But, for the most part, when Americans invented new crimes or increased the severity of the punishment meted out to those guilty of infractions of the laws of the mother country, they were seeking to attain purity, for which they had come to the New World. Especially this was true of the Puritans; and no where did the Puritans conduct a more unremitting and uncompromising war upon sin in all its manifold manifestations than in New Haven.

In inflicting punishment, Americans relied mainly on the salutary effects of public humiliation. The idea was to disgrace the offender in the eyes of his fellowmen; after the realization of his infamy had sunk in, he was expected to change his erring ways and become a respectable member of the community. The punishment, in short, was expected to work its own reformation.

For this reason, the stocks and the pillory were frequently used in the colonies. Because the wrongdoer was com-

[1] William Bradford, *Of Plymouth Plantation*, edited by S. E. Morison (New York: Alfred A. Knopf, Inc., 1959), pp. 316–17.

pelled to assume a sitting position in the stocks, this form
of punishment was reserved for plebeians. A gentleman
could demand that he be sentenced to the pillory where he
stood with his head and hands protruding through aper-
tures. But in either case, he was forced to endure an ordeal
of insults and jeers—and sometimes of rotten eggs.

The most popular form of punishment—popular, that
is, from the spectators' point of view—was a whipping.
The colonists acted upon the theory that there was nothing
quite so effective in showing delinquents the errors of their
ways than a brisk session at the whipping post. These
posts were a prominent part of the colonial landscape: in
Boston, there were three well patronized posts. Together
with the stocks and the pillory, the whipping post was
usually placed in front of the meetinghouse for the convenience of the audience and as a reminder of what lay in
store for transgressors. Tying a man or woman to the tail
of a cart and whipping him or her through town or, better
still, through several towns, was specially favored by the
magistrates because it provided a maximum of both pub-
licity and pain.

The authorities at New Haven found Biblical sanction
for laying on the lash:

> Stripes, or whipping, is a correction fit and proper in some
> cases, where the offence is accompanied with childish, or brutish
> folly, with rude filthiness, or with stubborn insolency, with
> beastly cruelty, or with idle vagrancy, or for faults of like nature.
> But when stripes are due: it is ordered, That not above forty
> stripes shall be inflicted at one time; Deut 25, 3.[2]

Under this high authority, the lash was resorted to on
slight provocation. In early Virginia, even "launderers and
laundresses" who gave old, torn linen for good linen or
threw out "the water or suds of fowle clothes in the open
streets" were whipped. In New England, when repeated
corporal punishment failed to effect a reformation, the
offender was banished or sold into bondage in the West

[2] J. Hammond Trumbull, *The True-Blue Laws of Connecticut and
New Haven.* (Hartford: American Publishing Co., 1876), p. 263.

Indies, where, laboring on a sugar plantation, he had ample opportunity to reflect upon the adage that crime does not pay.

Although the reformation of the offender could hardly be said to be the end in view, hangings also took place in public. Invariably they attracted a large number of spectators; indeed, few spectacles brought out bigger crowds. In 1704, seven pirates were publicly executed in Boston. "When the scaffold was let to sink," Samuel Sewall recorded in his diary, "there was such a Screech of the Women that my wife heard it sitting in our Entry next to the Orchard, and was much surprised at it; yet the wind was Sou-west. Our house is a full mile from the place." In accord with good old English custom, the pirates' bodies were hung in chains. In 1676, when Nathanel Bacon, the leader of a revolt in Virginia, died in the hour of victory, his friends concealed the body lest Governor Berkeley dig it up and exhibit it on the gibbet.

The custom of compelling wrongdoers to wear letters sewn upon the garments—"A" for "adulterer," "B" for "blasphemer" or "burglar," "D" for "drunkard," "I" for "incestuous marriage," "T" for "thief," and so on through the alphabet to "V" for "venery"—was at least as old as the twelfth century. Americans introduced some variations on this theme: in New England, a white woman "suffering an *Indian* to have carnal knowledge of her, had an *Indian* cut in red cloth sewed upon her right arm, and enjoyed to wear it twelve months." When the offender belonged to the servant class or in cases involving repeated transgressions, the appropriate letter was branded upon the forehead; had Hester Prynne been a serving wench she would not have gotten off so lightly as she did. Although *The Scarlet Letter* has forever identified the use of such letters with New England, in actuality the practice was widespread in the colonies: in eighteenth-century Pennsylvania, persons found thrice guilty of adultery were sentenced to receive 21 lashes, serve seven years in prison and be branded with the letter "A" on their forehead.

Besides using letters to designate the nature of the crime,

a convicted person was sometimes compelled to wear a rope or halter around his neck, or, in the case of rape, an iron collar. For cursing or swearing, the offender's tongue was put in a cleft stick. Thus was the punishment made to fit the crime.

Colonial courts took cognizance of "common scolds"— women who indulged in malicious gossip, railed in public at their husbands, slandered their neighbors and otherwise disturbed the peace of the community. For such as these, the ducking stool, according to immemorial English custom, was the prescribed punishment. As Doctor Samuel Johnson said: "Madam, we have different modes of restraining evil—stocks for men, a ducking stool for women, and a pound for beasts." Instead of being given a divorce, quarrelsome couples were sometimes tied back to back and immersed in cold water. In Virginia, where, in 1662, each county was ordered to erect a ducking stool at public expense, a woman was sentenced to be ducked four times but, after one immersion, it was decided to postpone further action until the arrival of more clement weather. The taxpayers might well have felt cheated for they had constructed the apparatus especially for the occasion.

By common law, a husband was responsible not only for his wife's conduct but for what she said about the neighbors—perhaps the heaviest responsibility ever imposed on hapless males. If a woman were accused of slander, her husband was treated as an accomplice. But the law provided a saving grace: it was within the husband's option to pay the fine assessed by the court or permit his wife to be ducked. Some husbands succumbed to the temptation to pay back their ill-tempered partners: they refused to pay the fine and let justice take its course. A man who exercised this option was wise to stay well out of reach when they released his drenched and spluttering helpmate.

In cases involving robbery or burglary—capital crimes in England if the value of the property stolen exceeded a shilling—colonial courts, partly because human life was considered less expendible than in the mother country, usually confined the punishment to restitution of the goods and a whipping. If the culprit were unable to restore the stolen articles, he might be sentenced to labor as a bound servant, often to the injured party himself, until the claim was satisfied. Creditors had a preferred claim to their debtor's person as well as to his real property. As a result, comparatively few debtors were imprisoned in the colonies —in contrast to England, where they languished in prison for years on end. So infrequently was the debtor's prison in Williamsburg used that, in 1722, its accomodations were reserved for convicted criminals.

In general, the colonists favored the kind of punishment that was most speedy and least expensive to the community. In a country suffering from a chronic labor shortage, there was no point in sentencing offenders to long prison terms, thereby adding to the cost of government, rendering families destitute and depleting the labor force. Nor did the colonies possess many buildings where criminals could be kept in custody for a long period of time. The main function of the early lockups, therefore, was to serve as places of detention for those under arrest and awaiting trial. In New York City, the garret of the City Hall was used as a prison for felons. Jail breaks were common: one escape artist claimed to have broken out of 24 different jails from Maine to Virginia.

Comparatively few Americans ever saw the inside of a prison, but some of those who did had harrowing tales to tell. A South Carolinian who landed in the Charleston jail declared that the conditions he encountered were worse than anything aboard the galleys of the King of France or the slave pens of the Barbary pirates:

Persons of every class each are promiscuously confined together in a space where they have not room to lie, and no distinction made between offenders, but thieves and murderers, debtors to the king, offenders in penal laws, vagrants and idle persons are closely huddled in one mixed crowd.[3]

[3] Merrill Jensen (ed.), *American Colonial Documents to 1776* (*English Historical Documents,* Vol. 9) (New York: Oxford University Press, 1955), p. 595.

While the Quakers tried to out-Puritan the Puritans in the enforcement of their moral code—in 1702, for example, a Philadelphia butcher was indicted "for swearing three oaths in the market place, and uttering two very bad curses"—they adopted, as befitted men who believed in the innate goodness of man, a criminal code distinguished by its mildness and tender concern for erring brethren. Only one crime was made capital.

But the Quakers learned that leniency toward criminals was an invitation to crime. In 1718, after an outbreak of burglaries, highway robberies and other crimes of violence, Pennsylvania revised its criminal code along English lines. By 1767, 16 crimes were punishable by death in the colony, and during the period 1745–75, 61 executions took place. In this respect, the Quakers' experience was similar to that of the Puritans: as population increased crime kept pace.

Gottlieb Mittelberger described how the laws were enforced in Pennsylvania about the middle of the eighteenth century:

In general, however, crimes are punished severely, especially larceny. If someone steals objects of as little value as a handkerchief, a pair of stockings, shoes, or a shirt, and suit is brought against him, he is tied to a post in the public market, stripped to the waist, and lashed so terribly with a switch or even with a horse- or dog-whip in which knots have sometimes been tied that patches of skin and flesh hang down from his body. If such a one is guilty of theft once again, even if he only steals a horse or something worth twenty gulden, he receives short shrift. He is placed, bound, into a cart, transported to the gallows, and has a rope put around his neck. The cart is then driven away and he is left to hang. Many suffer miserably, and die in agony. In this country it does not matter who carries out the office of hangman; for £5, or 30 florins, anyone who wishes can do so. While I was there one of the executions had to be carried out by such a clumsy hangman (this is the name they are called). And it took him so long that finally some distinguished gentlemen who were present got impatient and called out, asking why he took so long about his business. But the hangman was a man of ready wit and answered boldly, "Gentlemen, if you can do my office better than I can, come here and perform it." At which the people laughed their fill at these gentlemen.[4]

For the victim, however, it was no laughing matter. The woman who, in 1731, was ordered to be burned alive for the murder of her husband suffered cruelly from the ineptness of the executioner:

It was designed to strangle her dead by the hangman previous hanging [her] over the fire, and before it could reach her; but the fire broke out in a stream directly on the rope round her neck, and burnt off instantly, so that she fell alive into the flames, and was seen to struggle therein.[5]

Outside New England, it was customary to attribute crime to British convicts transported to the American colonies. For, besides being a refuge for the oppressed and a haven for seekers of Utopia, America was a dumping ground for felons. At least 30,000 of these undesirables were sent to the colonies, where they were sold as laborers for terms ranging from seven to fourteen years. Particularly in Maryland they were an important part of the labor force —some also served as schoolmasters—on the plantations. After finishing their term they, like indentured servants, were given their freedom. But in many instances they gave free rein to their criminal proclivities; colonial newspapers abounded in accounts of acts of violence for which transported felons were held responsible.

[4] Gottlieb Mittelberger, *Journey to Pennsylvania*, edited by Oscar Handlin and John Clive (Cambridge, Mass.: Harvard University Press, 1960), pp. 72–73.

[5] John F. Watson, *Annals of Philadelphia and Pennsylvania* (3 vols., Philadelphia: J. M. Stoddart, 1879–81), Vol. I, p. 309.

No doubt, transported convicts were blamed for many crimes they did not commit simply because it was so difficult to believe that a native-born American of respectable parents could turn out badly. But the evidence did not always support this comforting theory: in 1644, two ministers' sons, students at Harvard, were caught red-handed in the act of burglary—for which they were soundly whipped by President Dunster. In 1704, William Penn, Jr., was indicted for inciting a riot at an inn: "Young Penn called for pistols to pistol [shoot] them." And in 1761 some of the scions of the best families in Philadelphia were found guilty of terrorizing the citizens by slashing women's gowns and petticoats with razors.

Nowhere in the colonies was crime more rampant than in the Carolina backcountry where "Gangs of Banditti" roamed the country stealing horses, cattle and slaves, and terrorizing and sometimes killing the inhabitants. The frontiers of North and South Carolina contained an unusually large proportion of the human flotsam and jetsam that tended to collect on the frontiers. This riffraff preyed upon the industrious and law-abiding settlers until, emboldened by success, they organized themselves into entire communities of horse thieves and cattle rustlers. Here they lived almost unmolested with their wives, concubines and children. Through confederates in other provinces they disposed of the property they had stolen. But they kept the girls they abducted: when 35 of these young women were recaptured they were found to be too corrupted by their life with the brigands to be reclaimed. Even the later Wild West could not boast anything quite the equal of these outlaw bands.

The principal reason that these bandits could plunder the Carolina backcountry with almost complete impunity was that law enforcement in the region had broken down. Neither the courts nor the justices of the peace were backed by sufficient authority to suppress the desperadoes. It was not until law-abiding citizens took matters into their own hands and organized vigilante or "regulating" bodies of armed men who tracked down the gangs and administered a rough and ready justice—the rougher and the readier, the better—that order was restored.

In colonial courts of law, Americans enjoyed all the traditional "rights of Englishmen" guaranteed by the common law. Despite the Puritans' veneration of the Mosaic Law and their eagerness to live by its ordinances, they usually followed English precedents in their courts of law. The Laws and Liberties of Massachusetts, adopted in 1648, show a concern for such basic civil liberties as freedom from arbitrary arrest, trial by jury, rules of due process, and exemption from cruel punishments or torture to extract confessions. These Laws and Liberties even proclaimed the right of freedom of speech and assembly, but anyone who put these particular "rights" to the test in Puritan Massachusetts was certain to regret his temerity.

During the colonial period, it was advisable to have at least a smattering of law because, in most of the provinces, the right of an accused to have the benefit of counsel was not recognized until comparatively late in the eighteenth century. Although the Pennsylvania Charter of Privileges of 1701 declared that all persons accused of having committed a crime "shall have the same Privilege of Witnesses and Council as their Prosecutors," other colonies were slow to follow Pennsylvania's example. Nowhere was legal counsel provided at public expense for those too poor to afford a lawyer. As a result, most Americans who appeared before a court on criminal charges conducted their own defense as best they could.

In the seventeenth and early eighteenth centuries, colonial judges, with few exceptions, were laymen. Almost any educated person was deemed qualified to preside over a court of law. Certainly at no time in American history has knowledge of the law been so widely disseminated among the educated class. By 1775, almost as many copies of Blackstone's *Commentaries on the Law of England*, the most important book on English law written in the eighteenth century, had been sold in America as in England. Not surprisingly, therefore, Americans used legal terminology in stating their rights against Great Britain: it was a vocabulary understood by the literate members of the community.

In England, the severity of the criminal code was mitigated by permitting first offenders charged with crimes other than murder, rape, arson, burglary or robbery to "plead their clergy." This privilege, originally granted only to clerics in order to protect them from punishment by the secular courts, was ultimately extended to include all who could read and, early in the eighteenth century, to women and, finally, to illiterates. Instead of being sentenced to death or to a long term of imprisonment, the culprit was merely branded on the thumb—a stigma that debarred him from pleading his clergy a second time and marked him for the rest of his life as a person of dubious character.

Benefit of clergy was a common plea in colonial courts. One of the British soldiers convicted of manslaughter for his part in the Boston Massacre of 1770 pleaded his clergy and was burned on the thumb. On those unable to take advantage of this legal loophole, a more severe mutilation was often inflicted. Ears were particularly vulnerable. They were cut off for a variety of offenses, including "malicious and scandalous speeches against the government" and publishing libels. One or both ears were removed, depending upon the heinousness of the offense. The usual procedure was to put the criminal in the pillory, nail his ear to the board and, after the crowd had had its fill of jeering, cut it off.

Despite Americans' lamentations that crime was on the increase and that they were being inundated with convicts, in actuality there was far less lawlessness in the colonies than in England. No matter how assiduously England disburdened itself of its criminal population, new recruits stepped into the places of those who were thrust upon the colonies. During the eighteenth century, Great Britain was the most lawless country in the civilized world —and this in spite of a criminal code that made over 200 different offenses punishable by death. In the twentieth century, the United States reversed this state of affairs by winning the unenviable distinction of being the most crime-ridden of all civilized nations.

Bibliography

Blumenthal, Walter Hart. *Brides from Bridewell*. Rutland, Vt.: C. E. Tuttle Co., 1962.

Brown, Richard Maxwell. *The South Carolina Regulators*. Cambridge, Mass.: Belknap Press, 1963.

Haskins, George Lee. *Law and Authority in Early Massachusetts*. New York: Macmillan Co., 1960.

Proceedings of the American Antiquarian Society. New Series, Vol. 53. Worcester, Mass., 1943.

Scott, A. P. *Criminal Law in Colonial Virginia*. Richmond, Va., 1930.

Watson, John F. *Annals of Philadelphia and Pennsylvania*. Philadelphia, 1885.

Woodmason, Charles. *The Carolina Backcountry on the Eve of the Revolution*. Chapel Hill, N. C.: University of North Carolina Press, 1953.

RELIGIOUS SCENE

THE religious impulse that sent thousands of Englishmen and other Europeans to the New World encountered there powerful hostiles to the realization of its Utopian ideals. Opportunities for material gain, the multiplicity of religious sects and the marked tendency among eighteenth-century Americans as well as Europeans to subordinate emotion to reason, all conspired to weaken the hold of organized religion upon large numbers of people.

Among the enemies of the life dedicated to the glorification of God and the erection of a Heavenly City upon earth, the chief was economic prosperity. In America, the churches of the poor and downtrodden became middle-class churches, and in the process they lost much of their original fervor and mystical idealism. The only thing that the other-worldly sects could not endure was economic success: they thrived upon persecution and poverty but their sense of dedication was undermined by the sense of having arrived economically and socially.

Unknowingly, these religious bodies contained within themselves the seeds of their own destruction. The Puritan doctrine that success in one's calling was presumptive evidence of Divine favor became, with the passage of time, a justification for pursuing worldly ends. So, too, the Quakers who, like the Puritans, acted on the assumption that industry, thrift and a plain way of living were acceptable ways of glorifying God, became a "God-fearing, money-making people." By the early eighteenth century, Quaker businessmen and large landowners were being denounced by less successful Americans as wealthy, privileged, purse-proud aristocrats. Thus in America did the lower- and middle-class entrepreneurs of one generation become the plutocrats of the next generation. Self-denial, labor and thrift begot the wealth that, in turn, vitiated the spiritual values upon which these sects set such high store.

William Penn expected the world to become like Philadelphia; the New England Puritans were equally confident the the world would model itself on Boston. In actuality, neither Philadelphia nor Boston provided the blueprint for the religious and social order of the future. Instead, the two cities of righteousness gradually succumbed to the stain of the worldliness they had been founded to combat.

Laws, however blue, failed to provide a substitute for private morality. Once the feeling of participating in a great spiritual adventure—the building of a City of God—began to be subordinated to the desire to get on in the world on the world's own terms, it became clear that the Puritan code of ethics, one of the most exacting codes devised by any religious sect, ran counter to some of the most powerful instincts in human nature. Moreover, it was of little avail for the clergy to inveigh against covetousness and preoccupation with moneymaking: the people could always reply that they were engaged in glorifying God by laboring in their callings and were being properly rewarded for their efforts.

By the end of the seventeenth century, so painfully evident was the decline in religious fervor that the sermons of the Puritan clergy consisted largely of Jeremiads—lamentations over the laxity of morals, the worldliness and the preoccupation with moneymaking. "Time was when in New England," said the Reverend Increase Mather in 1682, "they durst not continue whole nights in Taverns, in drinking and gaming, and misspending their precious time . . . .Time was when in this Boston men durst not be seen in Taverns after the Sabbath is begun." The Reverend Cotton Mather, Increase Mather's son, drew up a whole catalog of abominations that had sprung up in New England since the days of the Founding Fathers: mixed dancing, cockfighting, cards, dicing, smoking, reading unprofitable books, engaging in wanton conversation, Sabbath-breaking, "disobedience in Inferiors toward Superiors," sleeping in church, the "Flaming Wickedness of Children," and neglect of family prayers. Mather warned delinquents that they must give an account to Christ on the Day of Judgment for every hour they had spent in taverns.

The theme of these Jeremiads was that the glory was departing from New England because of "the Apostacy and Iniquity of the People there." As the clergy described it, it was a fall from grace almost comparable to that of the Original Pair: a general defection by the people of New England from the purity and piety of the first settlers. Instead of trying to return to apostolic times, the ministers now would have settled gladly for turning the clock back to the days of John Cotton and John Winthrop. The Reverend Increase Mather feared the worst: after the Last Judgment, he predicted, America would be the site of hell.

Conditions were not so bad—indeed, they could not possibly be—as the Puritan clergy imagined. True, with the increase in wealth, there was growing inclination among people of all ranks to seek pleasure as well as profit. By 1700, Boston had a bowling green and a large number of taverns, many of which provided entertainment for sailors and dock workers. No doubt, things went on there that were not supposed to happen in Boston, but in general the people were law-abiding, orderly and, by present-day standards if not by those of the first Puritans, religious-minded.

But this provided no consolation for the idealists who had founded colonies in the expectation that the millennium was just around the corner. Most of the Puritan leaders of the Great Migration died lamenting that their work had come to nothing and that their lives had been failures. Surveying Plymouth Plantation toward the end of his life, William Bradford concluded that the Lord had turned His back on His People: "It is a question," he said, "whether the greater part be not grown the worse." In 1665, when the Reverend John Davenport left New Haven, he declared that the place had gone to the Devil. William Penn was convinced that the "Holy Experiment" had failed. "The Lord forgive them their great ingratitude," he said of the people of Pennsylvania; ". . . . surely such a people dwell not upon the face of the earth. God, I hope, will deliver me from them."

The religion of the Age of Reason consisted largely of an unimpassioned, coldly analytical cataloguing of the attributes of the Deity as revealed to man through Nature and Nature's Laws. The philosophers of the Enlightenment approached religion in the spirit of scientists and reported the results of their investigations with scientific certitude. Deism's appeal was to those who asked of religion neither ecstasy nor contrition; for them, there were no ineffable joys or torment of soul. The religion of Nature, as Deism was sometimes called, was bland, cheerful and heartwarming. The God of the Deists was good-humored, kindly and well disposed toward mankind—in every respect the antithesis of John Calvin's Jehovah.

Even the most Bible-oriented denominations were affected by Deistic thought; sermons tended to become learned disquisitions rather than appeals to the emotions; and Heaven and Hell were on the way to becoming mere abstractions. In consequence, religion became intellectualized to the point where it ceased to have much immediate meaning for the majority of people.

Beginning with the 1730's, Deism's postulates were challenged by the revivalistic movement that broke out almost simultaneously in Great Britan, Western Europe and British America. One of its first manifestations was the "methodism" adopted by John and Charles Wesley in England. These young men and their disciples marked out for themselves a way of life distinguished by "methodical" observance of rules and regulations, frequent prayer and austere conduct and dress. No Puritan more vehemently condemned swearing, buying and selling on the Sabbath, the use of ornaments, or indulgence in spiritous liquor and tobacco than did the Wesleys; indeed, it was mainly through Methodism that these particular "thou shalt not's" were transmitted to the twentieth century. Furthermore, the

Wesleys' spiritual message was similar to that of the Puritans: each individual, John Wesley declared, must experience personally his own utter unworthiness, the infinite power of God and a sense of redemption from sin. But here the resemblance to Calvinism ended, for the Wesleys promised free, full and certain salvation to all believers.

In the American colonies, the revolt against Deism took the form, as it did in England, of an affirmation of the emotional side of religion. Brief revivals occurred among the Pietists in Pennsylvania and among the Congregationalists in Northampton, Massachusetts, where the Reverend Jonathan Edwards struck terror among his congregation by describing with almost scientific detachment the torments of Hell and the wrath of a justly offended God. Edwards admitted that he hoped to frighten people into seeking the Lord, for he was persuaded that their salvation depended upon experiencing a mystical feeling of oneness with God. On every score, he rejected the teachings of Deism. The rational faculties of man, upon which the Deists relied so heavily, seemed to Edwards to demonstrate the truths of the Old Testament creed that God was just but that He was incensed, and with reason, against mankind and that no individual could hope to escape the awful punishment in store for mankind unless he surrendered himself wholly to Christ. The facts of life, as Edwards saw them, provided no basis for the comfortably optimistic philosophy of the Deists: how, for example, could human suffering—especially the suffering of little children—be reconciled with the Deists' concept of a benevolent Creator animated by love of mankind?

The revival at Northampton in 1734 was merely a brief stirring in the long repose of the eighteenth-century religious spirit. It was not until 1739, when the Reverend George Whitefield began his evangelical tour of the American colonies to raise funds for an orphanage in Georgia, that the Great Awakening occurred. Wherever he went, Whitefield preached to large crowds—so large that in many places the meeting had to be held outdoors. In Philadelphia he addressed an audience estimated by eyewitnesses to number ten thousand people.

Whitefield launched a veritable crusade for souls. Everyone was urged to "press on into the Kingdom of Heaven," where all were sure of admittance provided that they surrendered themselves wholly to Christ. On the other hand, those who wilfully refused to come to the Lord were assured no less certainly of eternal hellfire. For Whitefield preached the depravity and damnation of natural man and he was no more inclined than was Jonathan Edwards to gloss over the pains and penalties that awaited transgressors in the hereafter.

Benjamin Franklin, rationalist that he was, was amazed that Whitefield's audiences "admir'd and respected him, notwithstanding his common abuse of them, by assuring them they were naturally *half beasts and half devils*." And yet, against his better judgment, Franklin fell under the evangelist's spell. Happening to attend one of Whitefield's sermons, Franklin described in his *Autobiography* how he melted under the fervor of Whitefield's preaching:

I perceived he intended to finish with a collection, and I silently resolved he should get nothing from me. I had in my pocket a handful of copper money, three or four silver dollars, and five pistoles in gold. As he proceeded I began to soften and concluded to give the coppers. Another stroke of his oratory made me asham'd of that and determin'd me to give the silver; and he finish'd so admirably that I empty'd my pocket wholly into the collector's dish, gold and all.

But not even Whitefield's eloquence could convert Franklin: "he [Whitefield] us'd, indeed, sometimes to pray for my conversion," Franklin said, "but never had the satisfaction of believing that his prayers were heard." For his part, Franklin found Whitefield the answer to a publisher's prayer: Whitefield's journals and sermons were published by B. Franklin of Philadelphia.

But in resisting Whitefield's appeals to come to Christ, Franklin was an exception among Americans of his generation. Far more typical was the impression made by the evangelist upon a New England farmer:

Now it pleased God to send Mr. Whitefield into this land; and my hearing of his preaching at Philadelphia, like one of the old apostles, and many thousands flocking to hear him preach the Gospel, and the great numbers were converted to Christ, I felt the Spirit of God drawing me by conviction; I longed to see and hear him and wished he would come this way. I heard he was come to New York and the Jerseys and great multitudes flocking after him under great concern for their souls which brought on my concern more and more, hoping to see him; but next I heard he was at Long Island, then at Boston, and next at Northampton. Then on a sudden, in the morning about 8 or 9 of the clock there came a messenger and said Mr. Whitefield preached at Hartford and Wethersfield yesterday and is to preach at Middletown this morning at ten of the clock. I was in my field at work. I dropped my tool that I had in my hand and ran home to my wife, telling her to make ready quickly and to go and hear Mr. Whitefield preach at Middletown, then run to my pasture for my horse with all my might, fearing that I should be too late. Having my horse, I with my wife soon mounted the horse and went forward as fast as I thought the horse could bear; and when my horse got much out of breath; I would get down and put my wife on the saddle and bid her ride as fast as she could and not stop or slack for me except I bade her, and so I would run until I was much out of breath and then mount my horse again, and so I did several times to favour my horse. We improved every moment to get along as if we were fleeing for our lives, all the while fearing we should be too late to hear the sermon; for we had twelve miles to ride double in little more than an hour and we went round by the upper house parish. And when we came within about half a mile or a mile of the road that comes down from Hartford, Wethersfield, and Stepney to Middletown, on high land I saw before me a cloud or fog rising. I first thought it came from the great river, but as I came nearer the road I heard a noise something like a low rumbling thunder and presently found it was the noise of horses' feet coming down the road, and this cloud was a cloud of dust made by the horses' feet. It arose some rods into the air over the tops of hills and trees; and when I came within about 20 rods of the road, I could see men and horses slipping along in the cloud like shadows, and as I drew nearer it seemed like a steady stream of horses and their riders, scarcely a horse more than his length behind another, all of a lather and foam with sweat, their breath rolling out of their nostrils every jump. Every horse seemed to go with all his might to carry his rider to hear news from heaven for the saving of souls. It made be tremble to see the sight, how the world was a struggle. I found a vacancy between two horses to slip in mine and my wife said "Law, our clothes will be all spoiled, see how they look," for they were so covered with dust that they looked almost all of a colour, coats, hats, shirts, and horses. We went down in the stream but heard no man speak a word all the way for 3 miles but every one pressing forward in great haste; and when we got to Middletown old meeting house, there was a great multitude, it was said to be 3 or 4000 of people, assembled together. I turned and looked towards the Great River and saw the ferry boats running swift backward and forward bringing over loads of people, and the oars rowed nimble and quick. Everything, men, horses, and boats seemed to be struggling for life. The land and banks over the river looked black with people and horses; all along the 12 miles I saw no man at work in his field, but all seemed to be gone. When I saw Mr. Whitefield come upon the scaffold, he looked almost angelical; a young, slim, slender youth before some thousands of people with a bold undaunted countenance. And my hearing how God was with him everywhere as he came along, it solemnized my mind and put me into a trembling fear before he began to preach; for he looked as if he was clothed with authority from the Great God, and a sweet solemnity sat upon his brow, and my hearing him preach gave me a heart wound. By God's blessing, my old foundation was broken up, and I saw that my righteousness would not save me.[1]

These were the first pangs of the "new birth"—a process whereby, Whitefield said, Christians were purged of sin and otherwise prepared for their advent into Heaven. In many of his auditors, his impassioned prayers, exhortations and calling down of the wrath of Heaven induced hysterical shouting, frothing, writhing and other physical manifestations, all of which were considered certain evi-

[1] Merrill Jensen (ed.), *American Colonial Documents to 1776* (*English Historical Documents*, Vol. 9) (New York: Oxford University Press, 1955), pp. 544–45.

dence that the spirit of the Lord was at work and that the "new birth" was taking its normal course.

For those who feared that the Great Awakening did more harm than good to the cause of true religion, much worse than the evangelism of George Whitefield was in store. Whitefield was succeeded by itinerant exhorters who denounced an educated clergy and urged the people to abandon "unconverted" ministers. In their zeal to produce the physical evidences of the new birth, these men went far beyond Whitefield: they were described as "perpetually roaring out *Hell-Flames, Fire and Brimestone, Incarnate Devils, Damnation* &c till some are frighten'd of their Senses and others fall into Convulsions and epileptic-like Fits; and others scream and roar with hideous Voices."

Teen-age girls were particularly susceptible to the mass hysteria created by the evangelists. One observer noted:

Most of the young Women would go about the House praying and exhorting; then they would separate themselves from the other People, and get into a Corner of the House to sing and rejoice together and then they would break forth into as great a Laughter as could be, to think, as they exprest it, that they should go hand in hand to Heaven. They would begin laughing and singing, jumping up and down, and clapping their Hands together. . . . And all this, when, at the same time, there were three score Persons lying, some on the floor, some across the Seats, while others were held up and supported in great Distress. . . . Some would stand in the Pulpit exhorting, Some in the Body of the Seats, Some in the Pews, and some up the Gallery; and oftentimes, several of them would speak together; so that some praying, some exhorting, and testifying, some singing, some screaming, some crying, some laughing, and some scolding, made the most amazing Confusion that ever was heard.[2]

Thus, in its first manifestations, the reaction to the excessive intellectualism of the Enlightenment took the form of rabid anti-intellectualism. But the Great Awakening also stimulated debate on theological questions that was anything but anti-intellectual; indeed, so heated did these dis-

[2] Charles Chauncy, *Seasonable Thoughts on the State of Religion*, (Boston, 1743), p. 93.

putes become that the Congregational, Baptist and Presbyterian churches were temporarily divided into "Old Light" and "New Light" factions. Wherever he went in New England, Dr. Alexander Hamilton encountered tavern keepers and rustics to whom abstruse points of theology were as engrossing as politics was to later generations:

> Mather and I had some talk about the opinions lately broached here in religion. He seemed a man of some solidity and sense and condemned Whitefield's conduct in these parts very much. After dinner there came in a rabble of clowns who fell to disputing upon points of divinity as learnedly as if they had been professed theologues. 'Tis strange to see how this humor prevails even among the lower class of the people here. They will talk so pointedly about justification, sanctification, adoption, regenerations, repentance, free grace, reprobation, original sin, and a thousand other such pritty, chimercal knick knacks as if they had done nothing but studied divinity all their life time and perused all the lumber of the scholastic divines, and yet the fellows look as much, or rather more, like clowns than the very riff-raff of our Maryland planters. To talk in this dialect in our parts would be like Greek, Hebrew, or Arabick.[8]

Caustic as was Dr. Hamilton in his criticism of his contemporaries, he was too perceptive an observer to fall into the error of believing that Americans were merely a practical-minded, pragmatic people devoted solely to the acquisition of material goods.

Finally, much of the "College Enthusiasm" of the latter part of the eighteenth century stemmed from the Great Awakening. It was at this time that the pattern that required that every Protestant denomination establish one or more colleges became dominant in American life. Of the six colleges founded between 1746 and 1769, only one—the College of Philadelphia (later the University of Pennsylvania)—was nonsectarian.

Despite the revival of interest in theology that accompanied the Great Awakening, the emphasis in American

[8] Carl Bridenbaugh (ed.), *Gentleman's Progress. The Itinerarium of Dr. Alexander Hamilton* (Chapel Hill: University of North Carolina Press, 1948), pp. 162–63.

religion was on emotion rather than upon the exercise of the reasoning faculties. The downgrading of emotionalism that had characterized the Enlightenment was abruptly reversed by the Great Awakening: the Deistic Divine Being was dethroned and the Jehovah of the Old Testament was restored. The supernatural, miraculous element was reestablished in religion; in effect, the Great Awakening proclaimed the insufficiency of reason and the necessity of an emotional basis for religion. "Fundamentalism," the creed of the evangelical sects, put an end to intellectual discussions and speculation; the Bible, taken in its most literal sense, was regarded as an infallible work of history and science as well as of ethics and theology. The Puritan view of the centrality of Scripture triumphed: Americans remained a Bible-reading and a Bible-worshiping people. Indeed, they could hardly escape its pervasive influence: because of the close connection between the Protestant sects and the schools, the Bible was read in almost every classroom.

After the Great Awakening, American religion was marked by a series of revivals punctuated by long intervals of spiritual lethargy. The second great revival came in 1800; thereafter, waves of religious excitement periodically swept the United States. During the breathing spells between these upheavals, religious indifference seemed to be one of the most pronounced American characteristics. The American Revolution and the framing of the Federal Constitution occurred in a preeminently secular age when only about one in five Americans was a church member. It was during this period of religious quietude that Crèvecouer described the American religious scene:

Let us suppose you and I to be travelling; we observe that in this house, to the right, lives a Catholic, who prays to God as he has been taught, and believes in transubstantiation; he works and raises wheat, he has a large family of children, all hale and robust; his belief, his prayers offend nobody. About one mile farther on the same road, his next neighbor may be a good honest plodding German Lutheran, who addresses himself to the same God, the God of all, agreeably to the modes he has been educated in, and believes in consubstantiation; by so doing he scandalises nobody; he also works in his fields, embellishes the earth, clears swamps, etc. What has the world to do with his Lutheran principles? He persecutes nobody, and nobody persecutes him, he visits his neighbors, and his neighbors visit him. Next to him lives a seceder, the most enthusiastic of all sectaries; his zeal is hot and fiery, but separated as he is from others of the same complexion, he has no congregation of his own to resort to, where he might cabal and mingle religious pride with worldly obstinacy. He likewise raises good crops, his house is handsomely painted, his orchard is one of the fairest in the neighbourhood. How does it concern the welfare of the country, or of the province at large, what this man's religious sentiments are, or really whether he has any at all? He is a good farmer, he is a sober, peaceable, good citizen: William Penn himself would not wish for more. This is the visible character, the invisible one is only guessed, and is nobody's business. Next again lives a Low Dutchman, who implicitly believes the rules laid down by the synod of Dort. He conceives no other idea of a clergyman than that of an hired man: if he does his work well he will pay him the stipulated sum, if not he will dismiss him, and do without his sermons, and let his church be shut up for years. But notwithstanding this coarse idea, you will find his house and farm to be the neatest in all the country; and you will judge by his waggon and fat horses, that he thinks more of the affairs of this world than of those of the next. He is sober and laborious, therefore he is all he ought to be as to the affairs of this life; as for those of the next, he must trust to the great Creator. Each of these people instruct their children as well as they can, but these instructions are feeble compared to those which are given to the youth of the poorest class in Europe. Their children will therefore grow up less zealous and more indifferent in matters of religion than their parents. The foolish vanity, or rather the fury of making Proselytes, is unknown here; they have no time, the seasons call for all their attention, and thus in a few years, this mixed neighbourhood will exhibit a strange religious medly, that will be neither pure Catholicism nor pure Calvinism. A very perceptible indifference even in the first generation, will become apparent; and it may happen that the daughter of the Catholic will marry the son of the seceder, and settle by themselves at a distance from their parents. What religious education will they give their children? A very imperfect one. If there happens to be in the neighbourhood any place of worship, we will suppose a Quaker's meeting; rather than not show their fine clothes, they will go to it, and some of them may perhaps attach themselves to that society. Others will remain in a perfect state of indifference; the children of these zealous parents will not be able to tell what their religious principles are, and their grandchildren still less. The neighbourhood of a place of worship generally leads them to it, and the action of going thither, is the strongest evidence they can give of their attachment to any sect. The Quakers are the only people who retain a fondness for their own mode of worship; for be they ever so far separated from each other, they hold a sort of communion with the society, and seldom depart from its rules, at least in this country. Thus all sects are mixed as well as all nations; thus religious indifference is imperceptibly disseminated from one end of the continent to the other; which is at present one of the strongest characteristics of the Americans. Where this will reach no one can tell, perhaps it may leave a vacuum fit to receive other systems. Persecution, religious pride, the love of contradiction, are the food of what the world commonly calls religion. These motives have ceased here; zeal in Europe is confined; here it evaporates in the great distance it has to travel; there it is a grain of powder inclosed, here it burns away in the open air, and consumes without effect.[4]

The future of American Protestantism belonged largely to the denominations that profited most from the Great Awakening—the Presbyterians, the Baptists and, although they were still within the Church of England, the Methodists. These were the organized religious groups that were most closely attuned to the conditions of American life and that brought Christianity in its most dynamic form to the largest number of people. By means of lay preachers who emphasized the equality of all believers and the direct communication between God and the individual, they helped to democratize religion. In the United States, religious democracy antedated political and social democ-

[4] J. Hector St. John de Crèvecoeur, *Letters from an American Farmer* (London: Dutton, 1926), pp. 49–51.

racy. Moreover, by participating in the westward advance they assured themselves of a dominant place in American religious life: the course of religion, as well as of empire, ran westward.

Bibliography

Brydon, George Maclaren. *Religious Life in Virginia in the Seventeenth Century*. Williamsburg, Va.: Virginia 350th Anniversary Celebration Corp., 1957.

Gewehr, Wesley M. *The Great Awakening in Virginia: 1740–1790*. Durham: Duke University Press, 1930.

Greene, Evarts B. *Religion and the State*. New York: New York University Press, 1941.

Savelle, Max. *Seeds of Liberty; the Genesis of the American Mind*. New York: A. A. Knopf, Inc., 1948.

Sweet, William Warren. *Religion in Colonial America*. New York: Charles Scribner's Sons, 1942.

CONCLUSION

THERE are no static periods in American history: all is change and movement, and every period is a period of transition. Not least remarkable in this record is the growth of the American colonies and the progress of a whole people—always with the exception of the black members thereof—toward affluence. Even before 1776, America was a revolutionary force in the world: by its very example it infected the older societies with discontent and gave the common people new aspirations and hopes.

If the rule of American life has been constant change, it is also true that change has taken place within the framework of a well-defined and seemingly immutable tradition. It is this tradition which gives continuity and permanence to the history of a people who, from the beginning, have been engaged in a constant search for new roads to happiness, both for the individual and for society as a whole. The ideals of equal opportunity, individual rights and religious freedom that compose the basic content of this tradition took form during the colonial period. In origin they were not distinctively American—they were the product not of the American wilderness but of the cultural heritage of Western society—but the conditions of life in America made their realization appear to lie within the grasp of men. To every generation of Americans the hope has been given that these ideals will be achieved in their fullness.

Crèvecoeur was one of the first to perceive that America was creating a new type of man that, in his opinion, was infinitely superior to its European prototype. The conviction of American superiority in all things and especially in morals, government and social organization, was most eloquently set forth by a Frenchman to whom the American colonies were an adopted home:

I could point out to you a family whose grandfather was an Englishman, whose wife was Dutch, whose son married a French woman, and whose present four sons have now four wives of different nations. *He* is an American, who, leaving behind him all his ancient prejudices and manners, receives new ones from the new mode of life he has embraced, the new government he obeys, and the new rank he holds. He becomes an American by being received in the broad lap of our great *Alma Mater*. Here individuals of all nations are melted into a new race of men, whose labours and posterity will one day cause great changes in the world. Americans are the western pilgrims, who are carrying along with them that great mass of arts, sciences, vigour, and industry which began long since in the east; they will finish the great circle. The Americans were once scattered all over Europe; here they are incorporated into one of the finest systems of population which has ever appeared and which will hereafter become distinct by the power of the different climates they inhabit. The American ought therefore to love this country much better than that wherein either he or his forefathers were born. Here rewards of his industry follow with equal steps the progress of his labour; his labour is founded on the basis of nature, *self interest;* can it want a stronger allurement? Wives and children, who before in vain demanded of him a morsel of bread, now, fat and frolicsome, gladly help their father to clear those fields whence exuberant crops are to arise to feed and to clothe them all; without any part being claimed, either by a despotic prince, a rich abbot, or a mighty lord.[1]

Thus, despite all the evidences of diversity, there was an American character before there was an American nation. This character was the product of the interaction between the American environment, with all its infinite possibilities of human betterment, and the European and English farmers, artisans and peasants who came to these shores. For the most part, these people were ambitious, restless and dis-

---

[1] J. Hector St. John de Crèvecoeur, *Letters from an American Farmer* (London: Dutton, 1926), pp. 43–44.

contented with their lot; had they been otherwise they would have remained at home and lived the lives of quiet desperation Providence had seemingly designated for them. In their eyes, America was the land of opportunity—and that was all they asked of it.

And in America they found a new world of opportunity. In this hemisphere, the good life, conceived in terms of a moral and religious regeneration as well as a plenitude of material comforts, seemed from the beginning to be an attainable goal. In consequence, the qualities of energy, ambition and optimism that had originally impelled Englishmen and other Europeans to undertake the voyage across the Atlantic were enhanced by the conditions they found in the New World. Thus Crèvecoeur's New Man, the American, came to be distinguished by his eagerness to strike out for new horizons, his dissatisfaction with things as they are, and his conviction that his country had been divinely commissioned to show the way to happiness to mankind.

The circumstances that led the majority of Americans to concentrate their energies on the accumulation of material wealth did not extinguish the idealism that many colonists, notable the Puritans, had brought to the New World. Rather, it gave this idealism a new direction and, in the end, a new vitality. For if the material needs of man could be provided for so easily, why could not a wholly new moral, social and economic order be established, in which poverty was abolished, justice for all men made the rule of life and equal opportunity given to every individual? In America, there seemed to be no limit to human capacity; the society of the future was one in which everything was possible and man himself perfectible. Thus, paradoxically, idealism and materialism were made to go hand in hand.

But for almost 20 percent of the population of the American colonies—the black slaves and freemen—America lacked the richness of promise it held for the white majority. During the colonial period, the cardinal and as yet unresolved contradiction of American life—the fact that the most dynamic and progressive society in the world existed alongside one of the most static and inert societies—

came into being. Then, as now, color constituted the great cleavage in American life. It remains the supreme challenge to American idealism.

Additional Books Dealing with Life in Colonial America

Adams, James Truslow. *Provincial Society.* New York: Macmillan Co., 1927.

Andrews, Charles M. *Colonial Folkways.* New Haven: Yale University Press, 1921.

Dow, George F. *The Arts and Crafts in New England, 1704–1775.* Topsfield, Mass.: The Wayside Press, 1927.

Earle, Alice Morse. *Home Life in Colonial Days.* New York: Macmillan Co., 1898.

Potter, David M. *People of Plenty.* Chicago: University of Chicago Press, 1954.

Smith, Helen Evertson. *Colonial Days and Ways.* New York, 1900.

Speare, Elizabeth George. *Life in Colonial America.* New York: Random House, 1963.

Tunis, Edwin. *Colonial Living.* Cleveland: World Publishing Co., 1957.

Wish, Harvey. *Society and Thought in Early America.* New York: Longmans, Green & Co., Inc., 1950.